OUT AND BACK

A FAMILY'S JOURNEY

CURTIS G. SMITH

Dedication

To my amazing family. Without them this book would not be possible.

Table of Contents

Part I

Chapter 1 – Day Dreaming

"If you can dream it, you can do it." – Walt Disney

Life is a journey, not a destination. It is an adventure to experience every day of our lives. True, some days are more exciting than others, but each day has the potential to carry us away on new exploits, meet unique people, or see old places afresh. We all have the ability to turn drab, monotonous times into days filled with excitement, wonder, and astonishment if we summon the courage to make the change. You need to tightly embrace the life of your dreams because if you do not, it will remain elusive and quietly slip past.

I was pondering this dilemma at work one dreary Seattle morning. Usually, the normal grey drizzle of Pacific Northwest winters does not faze me much. Having lived here for several years, I have grown accustomed to short days, little sunlight, and damp clothes for long weeks at a time. We are hardy folk. You know that you're from Seattle when half of your wardrobe is made from Gore-Tex and the other half flannel. This January, however, more than just the dismal weather was getting me down.

I was in a rut. I tried my standard blahs remedy, a large mocha from Starbucks, to no avail. Usually, the warm green glow and intoxicating aroma when I walk in the door of my beloved coffee purveyors help chase away the doldrums. Not even their magic coffee-chocolate potion could shake the feeling that I was just marking time in life. I felt living but not alive.

I pondered what had gone wrong. How had I gotten to this place and time? In almost every way, my life was good by society's measure. I had a good job. I was the director of a small private career college. The pay and benefits were adequate and afforded my family a stable upper-middle-class life. The position came with some level of prestige and a sense of personal accomplishment, too.

I was healthy. I exercised regularly. For being 40, I was in very good shape and even a little vain about my hard-earned physique. I wasn't as young and energetic as I used to be, but all things considered, I was happy with the reflection in the mirror.

I had, and still have, a wonderful family. My loving wife of 15 years at the time is truly my best friend, inspiration, and support. She is my soulmate, for sure. Our two boys are amazing. They are both highly successful in the four S's: school, sports, Scouts, and social activities. They have made us proud.

In every way I could think of, I was blessed. Yet, I felt unfulfilled. This feeling of emptiness gnawed at me as I sat back and drank my mocha while I stared blankly at the computer screen in my office, pretending to work. I knew I shouldn't feel this way, which made me feel guilty for not appreciating what I had. What was wrong with me?

I reflected on my situation. I remember, as a young man being enthralled with National Geographic, which showcased exotic locations and people. I wanted to visit every place they presented in the pages of their magazine. Their centerfolds were truly awe-inspiring. Playboy couldn't have excited me as much. I was addicted to travel. Little did I realize that it would be a life-long psychological condition.

After graduating high school, I went off to college in another state by myself. While most of my classmates opted for the local in-state university, I yearned for something different. Leaving old faces and places behind for new sights and fresh experiences stimulated me like nothing else could. I jumped at the chance when I got accepted to a faraway university and didn't look back even once.

After school, I joined the United States Navy. Their old recruiting slogan resonated with me, *"It's not just a job, it's an adventure."* The Navy must have written that just for me. They were selling adventure, and I was buying. Sold! I craved adventure. I dreamed of faraway exotic destinations with strange food, languages, and customs. I shipped out and didn't look back again.

While in the Navy, I met the love of my life, who became my wife. She shared my obsession with travel. Indeed, she had been to more places than me. Her father was in the Navy, so her family lived in Spain, Cuba, and Mississippi.

Ok, maybe the last one is not that exotic, but the first two would be really cool places to grow up. She has many fond memories of traveling in Europe with her family and going to school on Guantanamo Bay Naval Base. I wish I had that childhood.

I left the Navy after seven years to pursue a new career in education. One door closed, and another opened. I entered a whole new world very different from the military. Teaching middle school science was maybe not the most glamorous job, but it was the start of a very rewarding and successful career. I jumped up to high school and eventually higher education. Now, here I was, the head honcho on campus.

Despite my success, both personal and professional, I was not feeling very successful spiritually. I do not mean spiritually in the religious sense but in the sense of my inner free spirit, which felt caged.

Little did I know that higher powers were scheming to teach me some badly needed lessons. I was allowing self-doubt, anxiety, complacency, and a sense of duty to prevent me from realizing my dreams. I wanted to live a purposeful life, but I was totally clueless about how to do it.

My days were always busy with the mundane chores of modern existence. I didn't allow myself the chance to explore the infinite possibilities that were out there.

Life was too simple and easy. Get up, go to work and be the boss, come home and be the husband and father, sleep, and repeat. Never be me.

Today was more of the same. I had much to do, as usual, at work, but I wasn't getting any of it done. One of the advantages of being the boss is that I don't have to report to anyone, at least not directly. So, as my mind strayed to faraway places, my fingers strayed to the computer keyboard. I googled education jobs abroad. Be careful what you wish for and of Google searches.

Almost straight away, I found a company that specialized in recruiting teachers for the United Kingdom. Intrigued, I clicked on the site. As I read the recruiter's sales pitch, I became more and more enthralled. Here was an extraordinary opportunity to do something I had always dreamed of Eureka!

Something resonated inside me about the chance to teach in England. The British Isles have long held a fascination for me. I had a romantic infatuation with the area. Maybe I've read J.R.R. Tolkien's books too many times and have delusions of Middle Earth. Maybe I harbor a deep desire to connect with my ancestral roots. Maybe I'm looking for a simpler pastoral life in the English countryside. Whatever my reasoning, I was ecstatic about the prospect of moving across the pond.

Anxiously, I filled out the online application and attached my resume and cover letter for the recruiter. Admittedly, I had a little trepidation as I went to send my information across the internet. I couldn't just quit my job, pack up the house, and move my family to another country on a whim. Could I? What about the boys' schooling? Our home? My wife's job? Friends? Our medical care? The cars? The list of worries suddenly rolled out before me. I convinced myself that there was no harm in inquiring. After all, I wasn't committing to anything. Innocently, I hovered the mouse icon over the send button. I'm not sure if I consciously or unconsciously clicked the mouse. Either way, the deed was done. At the speed of flowing electrons, my profile was off. I breathed a sigh, closed the website, and finally got back to my real job.

I decided to keep my little daydream indulgence to myself. I didn't want to stir up any unnecessary contention with my wife. All I did was send some teacher recruiter in England my information. I probably wouldn't even hear from them, I thought. I reasoned that my wife did not need to know that her husband was having extramarital fantasies; at least they weren't about other women. Honestly, I did feel a little unfaithful keeping secrets from my wife. I don't think that Rupert Holmes had foreign travel in mind when he wrote the Pina Colada song, though.

Two weeks passed. I had almost forgotten and abandoned the whole incident until I got an email reply. Nervously, I opened it. I was torn between being disappointed that it might be a rejection letter and frightened that they might be interested in me after all. To my utter amazement, the first line hit me like a ton of bricks falling on my head, "We have a school interested in interviewing you over the phone for a position." *What?! Seriously?*

This was my first lesson in learning to live a purposeful life: You'll never know unless you ask. I assumed, wrongfully, that I was stuck in my situation. I would never have known that I had options if I hadn't replied to that recruiter.

I don't know if fate lent a hand or if it was just dumb luck, but I would have taken the opportunity either way. That one simple decision

7

to send some information to a stranger on the other side of the world if they had a need for me changed our lives forever. Why hadn't I done that much earlier?

My advice to everyone is to seek out opportunities all the time, no matter how far-fetched they may seem. All someone can do is say no. For that matter, they can say no a hundred times or more. You only need one yes to change your life.

I think back painfully to all of the missed opportunities in my life. "What ifs" are hard to deal with later in life, I am finding. Do not get me wrong, I think I turned out ok. I would not change my family and friends for anything in the world, honestly. I can't help but wonder, however, what alternative timelines could have been if I only had bothered to explore them. Unfortunately, alternate timelines only exist in science fiction; in our world, we are stuck with just one forever.

My favorite poet, Robert Frost, was as literarily gifted as he was wise. I wish I had paid him more heed in school. The road not taken will always be unknown. We can only choose one path. "Two roads diverged in a wood, and I—I took the one less traveled by, and that has made all the difference." I made another road for myself through my modern urban wood. In doing so, I potentially solved my current predicament.

My next dilemma, however, was a bit more complicated. I needed to come clean with my wife. Luckily for me, my wife has grown very tolerant of my crazy ideas. She realizes that I am a perpetual dreamer. Some days, I'm not sure if she finds it charming or annoying. I was really hoping that she would find this time charming. More importantly, I wanted her to say yes.

Chapter 2 – Reckoning

"For the past 33 years, I have looked in the mirror every morning and asked myself: 'If today were the last day of my life, would I want to do what I am about to do today?' And whenever the answer has been 'No' for too many days in a row, I know I need to change something." – Steve Jobs

I really do love my wife, and I know she really loves me. If it wasn't for our mutual love, I would probably be in serious trouble. She has weathered many storms in our marriage. Asking her to move across the world might finally capsize our ship.

As I said earlier, we met while I was on active duty in the Navy stationed in Pensacola, Florida. Naval life can be extremely hard on relationships. Fortunately, being a Navy brat, she knew this. So, when the Navy decided to send me to San Diego, she happily followed. We started a new life in a new state without regret. Albeit, we were young and without kids, so moving was much easier.

A year after we were married, I decided that my time in the Navy was at an end. I am a very proud veteran and extremely happy I served. I would do it all over again without hesitation. A twenty-year Navy career, however, was not for me. Like most sailors, we sense when our time to go has come. Good and bad, nautical life was not what I envisioned. I realized I needed to keep my ship in port and be home for my family. The transition from sailor back to civilian was not smooth sailing, though.

I started a new career as a teacher. I left active duty in June and entered the classroom in August of the same year. I had just over two months to acclimate to a new normal.

The last time I was a civilian, I couldn't even legally drink. I had never had a true career outside the military before. The rules of the game were all different.

I needed to quickly learn a new culture with a different language and strange customs. I felt bombarded by questions and decisions which I didn't have the answers for. Medical insurance? What is that?! PPO versus HMO? Why can't I just go to the doctor and get examined? I need to put money in a 401K? Huh? Union dues! What is a union? You mean I don't need to fill out a form to do this? How do I take leave? I no longer have to salute and stand at attention when my boss walks in? Cool! Every day for a long while, I learned something new.

The barrage of new ways of doing practically everything took its toll. I became irritable and detached, which led to depression. This, in turn, led me to having regrets about my decision to leave the Navy. I remember wanting desperately to go back during a particularly low period. Patiently, my wife helped me through this dark time. I emerged stronger and happier into the light of a new life, but I know it was difficult for her, too.

We moved again when we decided to have children. Our jobs were good, but the location was not. San Bernardino is not exactly the quintessential small-town America where we wanted to raise our boys. Even though we were settled in southern California, we knew that we wanted to live in a different environment to raise our family. "Cali" was not how I grew up. I selfishly wanted our boys to have a similar childhood to mine so I could, hopefully, relate to them better. To have that, we needed to move north, way north.

My darling wife, from the warm climates of the world, obliged me, and we moved to where it gets cold. We found our little small-town paradise in western Washington. At 47 degrees north latitude, Port Ludlow is just over halfway from the equator to the North Pole. We fell in love with it immediately. The town's tagline is "A village in the woods by the bay." That says it all.

There was one small problem with our newly discovered Mayberry, jobs were difficult there. Historically, the Olympic Peninsula has been a logging and fishing industry area with support services sprinkled in. Unfortunately, logging has scaled way back in recent years, and fishing is almost dead. The communities on the peninsula have gone through difficult economic times. Some have adjusted, some are still figuring out what to do.

To worsen things for us, educators do not make much in Washington, and many schools in our area are facing declining enrollment. We really love the area but needed to find a way to make it financially work for us. So, that led me to my current position doing the long and hectic commute to Bellevue, where I could make the big bucks that would keep my family settled, such is the burden of being a responsible husband and father.

For three years, I kept up the pretense of being happy with the situation. So, now I am back full circle to how I got to my self-inflicted melancholy state. The logical part of my brain knew I had a great life, but the emotional part knew this wasn't for me. I really did feel torn. The indecisiveness only amplified the stress inside me.

The one person who I always turned to in difficult situations like this, is my best friend, who happens also to be my wife. The problem, however, was she was the one I was most nervous about talking to about my feelings. After all, how could I ask her to leave our home that had taken us a long time to find through more than a few trials and tribulations? I knew that it was not going to be an easy conversation, but I obviously needed her to buy in if my plan was to be at all possible.

She loved Port Ludlow just as much as me. One difference between our situations, however, was that she worked from home. She didn't do the hour-and-a-half commute in traffic via motorcycle and a ferry ride across Puget Sound throughout the year. I went many days during the winter months without seeing our house in the daylight; I'd leave in the dark and come home in the dark. I also gave up my coveted summer vacation when I moved into administration. So, she got to enjoy much more of our home than I did.

Still, she sacrificed for the family by moving north in the first place. She enjoyed teaching online, gardening in the yard, decorating the house, and, most importantly, being there for our boys while I was at work. How could I ask her to leave? We had settled into a comfortable routine. We were living the American dream. Sadly, it was not my dream though.

I finally mustered the courage to talk to her about the prospects of taking a job in England. As we sat on the couch drinking some wine one evening, I told her about the overseas recruiter and the interview with a school in England. She listened patiently until I finished my best sales pitch. I felt I did a pretty good job, too. I should be a television pitch man I thought. For this low, low cost, you'll get an exciting all-inclusive trip to Europe! Wait, that's not all! With this move, you'll also get a new set of luggage! If you say yes in the next five minutes, you'll receive a set of travel accessories, too!

I tried to read her face as I relayed my bold plan to her, but she stayed steadfast and did not betray any evidence of what she was thinking. Which way would this go, I anxiously wondered. She took a deep breath, and I got my answer. Calmly and thoughtfully, she said, "No."

Before I could counter-argue, she carefully explained why we could not make such a move at that time. Her reasoning was sound and accurate. The boys were in school with friends and Scouts. We had a house to pay for and keep up. She had a good job. We had established roots. If I was unhappy in my job, the simpler solution was to find another one within commuting distance, she argued. England definitely was not commutable.

My wife and I have been together a while. I know when she has made up her mind and how determined she can be. I also know that she loves me very much and wants to make me happy, within reason. I want her to be happy, too. So, we were now locked in a battle of wills. Each of us, deep down, wants to support and help the other while keeping our own sanity at the same time.

The problem for us is that we look at issues from completely different angles. Mishele is very logical and practical. I, on the other hand, tend to be over-emotional and impractical. She is the doer, and I am the dreamer. Together, we make a potent duo who, most times, complement each other extremely well. Sometimes, we can frustrate the hell out of each other too. This was shaping up to be the later time.

Clearly, we were in opposite camps on this issue. I was not interested in hearing why we couldn't make this plan work; I wanted to talk about how we could make it work. She was approaching it from a strictly pragmatic view of how unfeasible the plan was. To hear her talk, moving to another continent in six months was a big deal. I was thinking we could pack a few clothes, maybe take some toys for the boys, and ship the dog in a crate. Somehow, we needed to see each other's viewpoint and reach a solution. At least for that night, we were at a stalemate.

The next morning dawned without any solution miraculously appearing. We agreed to disagree and that there was no harm in just doing the interview. After all, I might not even get the job, so getting into a debate now was pointless. Besides, we were both very busy, and the daydream of yesterday seemed to vanish with the hustle and bustle of the present.

The two weeks before the interview passed quickly. I almost missed it, actually. I had become so involved in life that I realized it just in time to rush home and settle in. My mind started to race with all the possible questions that the school interview panel could ask me. This was not my first interview for a teaching position, but I was unsure of the British take on things. I wondered what they would want to know. Should I tell them that I was having a mid-life crisis and was desperately seeking an escape from reality? Probably not, I guessed.

I looked at my watch, and it read two minutes until the school was to call. I took a deep breath and checked my appearance. I felt a little foolish as I was running my fingers through my hair because I realized that they wouldn't be able to see me. Nervously, I glanced back at my watch. It was now two minutes after zero hour. I anxiously got up from the dining room table and paced around the kitchen. I looked again at my watch, and it read six minutes after the call time. It was getting very late. Had they forgotten? Did they figure out I was just a perpetual unrealistic dreamer?

More time passed. I was getting a little impatient when the phone finally rang. My heart raced as I looked at the international phone number on the screen. I waited for the obligatory second ring and then answered. A very polite woman with a thick English accent asked for me. I responded that this was Curtis Smith. I almost told her to wait and I would go fetch him, but thought better of it. The woman identified herself as the Vice-Head of the school and apologized profusely for being late. Apparently, they had gotten to school early just for my

16

interview. Then it dawned on me that the time difference was nine hours ahead, so 7:00 am London time.

The interview panel asked fairly standard questions, to which I gave fairly acceptable answers. They wanted to know typical teacher things, like how do I engage all students, what was my experience in the classroom, how do I develop lessons, etc. The question of why do I want to move to England, however, caused me to pause. I knew that they would ask this, but I really hadn't formulated a decent answer. I strongly believe that honesty is the best policy, so I told the truth; I was looking for an adventure.

The call concluded after only 30 minutes. We both thanked each other and went back to our own time zones. Immediately, my wife came out of the bedroom and asked how it went. I honestly had no idea. Did my American sense of humor collide with their British formality? I could only wait and see.

Two days passed, and I received another international call. It was from the Vice-Head again. To my utter astonishment, she congratulated me on a job well done and offered me a position with the school. As the English say, I was over the moon thrilled! I enthusiastically thanked her and assured her, prematurely, that I would accept.

My day of reckoning was here. I had successfully turned a daydream into a reality. Unbelievably, I had secured a job in England. The rest were just details, at least in my simple-mindedness. The only obstacle now was to convince my reluctant wife to move.

This was my second lesson in living a purposeful life. Change is difficult. Some change is easier than others, but all change causes some degree of stress.

Allowing the stress, fears, and doubts to govern you will prevent you from living your daydream. If I had never persevered through the changes in my life, I would not have ever left home. Remember, life is a journey, not a destination, so be prepared to move on when the time comes.

My transition from civilian to sailor was hard. Luckily, the U.S. Navy has a well-established indoctrination program to help you adjust. Transitioning back to civilian life was even harder. Luckily, again, I had someone to help me. Transitioning to another country probably would be the toughest change so far in our lives.

I do not think that I could manage such changes by myself. Having someone to help you is a crucial key to successfully managing transition periods in our lives. Family and friends can help you, so don't be ashamed to lean on them when you are stumbling. After all, misery loves company.

Chapter 3 – Hard Decisions

"We are not living in a world where all roads are radii of a circle and where all, if followed long enough, will therefore draw gradually nearer and finally meet at the center: rather in a world where every road, after a few miles, forks into two, and each of those into two again, and at each fork, you must make a decision." – C. S. Lewis.

Ok, now came the tough decision, to stay or go. My wife and I needed to have a very serious conversation about which road in the woods we would take. The one more traveled kept us on the familiar, well-worn road of home, which was safe and predictable. The one less traveled took us on a new road to a faraway country, which was strange and unfamiliar. Which one should we take?

My wife and I are both science teachers so we tend to be pretty analytical about most things, albeit we sometimes may go overboard analyzing decisions. When we were deciding if and where to move, we even prepared detailed spreadsheets with various categories to rank different merits and drawbacks of possible places to live. We rationalized that if we assigned numerical values to the attributes that were important to us of different candidate cities, like walkability, affordability, crime, and things to do, we could avoid subjectivity and make a completely objective decision, which would be the most proper course of action. It was purely logical.

Major life decisions are not purely logical, we learned, however. I look back at pivotal moments in my life that changed me for all time and realize that they were primarily emotionally driven. I made decisions based almost solely on my heart's desire, not on my brain's reasoning. I may have tried to rationalize them post-decision after I made up my mind, but the decisions were really made beforehand. All I really did was get my heart and brain in sync. So far, so good.

Joining the Navy was emotional. Yes, serving my country was honorable and patriotic, but honor and patriotism are deep-rooted emotions. From a practical consideration, I benefitted financially from my service through money for college, a loan for our house, a steady paycheck, and marketable training.

To be honest, the real reason I joined was for the adventure, to live a life less ordinary. I jumped aboard without too much thought and didn't worry about the details. I made it work.

Getting married was definitely emotional. To be honest, I also made a lousy bachelor. I don't drink, I'm painfully shy, I don't watch sports, and I'm pretty much a geek. My idea of a fun night is a batch of warm chocolate cookies and Star Trek re-runs. The fact that I found a cute, successful redhead to fall for me was amazing. I was completely in love and didn't care about practicality when I proposed. Amazingly, she said yes and the rest has been history. We have made it work.

Having kids is in no way logical or practical. Trust me on that if you're not a parent. Yet, we did it twice. I would not change being a father for anything, despite the challenges, frustrations, and worries. The emotional reward has been enormous in ways that I don't think I could ever truly explain to anyone who has not been a proud father. We have had our ups and downs, but through it all, we have stayed together. Our family has made it work.

Time and time again, my wife and I have made emotionally based decisions that have turned out fine. The decisions themselves were not really the issues. Following through with them by working through difficulties and problem-solving once we chose a path was the key to success. As Christian educator Charles Swindoll said, "Life is 10% what happens to you and 90% how you react to it." Looking back with regrets every time a rough patch hits, which they have a habit of doing, will trip you up. We learned to lean on each other and capitalize on each other's strengths. We just simply persevered.

Now, my heart was yelling at me to take the job in England while my brain was trying to calm me down. I was ready to make the leap, but I knew my loving wife did not have the same emotional motivation to take the jump across the ocean as I did. I desperately needed her to feel my passion for going, and she needed me to see her rationale for staying. So, we were at an impasse. Since the school needed a decision, and I said I would take the job, my wife and I needed to break our deadlock soon.

We scheduled a time when the boys were asleep, and the house was quiet to talk it through. A little wine always helps ease conversation, so we opened another bottle. We each gave the other time to explain their thoughts and reasoning while the other sipped their wine. She went first as I sipped. I patiently listened to my wife as she laid out her argument.

As expected, her rationale was spot-on and persuasive. I, however, was not to be persuaded.

My turn came, she drank. My argument was built on the adventure of it all. I tend to get animated and excited when I talk about things that I am passionate about, sort of like an over-caffeinated marionette puppet. That night, I was really trying to convey how this was a once-in-a-lifetime opportunity. I excitedly rambled on about the thrill of going, the romance of traveling Europe, the amazing learning opportunities, the unique cultural experiences, the incredible enrichment of our boys, and more. She drank more. I tried to read my wife's face, but I wasn't sure if she was softening or the wine was working. Slowly, I could see by the brightening twinkle in her eyes that the adventurous side of her was awakening as I talked. There was hope!

I knew I had won her over when she started to list all of the things we needed to do to get ready. Her mind had switched from coming up with reasons why we could not go to coming up with answers of how we could go. Once she switched over, I knew we were going. My wife is an amazing strategic planner and doer who can accomplish more in a single day than most people can in a week. Her superpower is organization. With her on board, we were already halfway to Europe!

This was my third lesson in living a purposeful life. Go after your dreams. I know that sounds very cliché like, but it's true. Life is too short, so live it while you can. One of many quotes that have inspired me comes from American author and professor John A. Shedd, "A ship in harbor is safe, but that is not what ships are built for." Set sail!

If I had always made rational, logical, and practical decisions my entire life, I would never have had all of these incredible experiences. True, I would not be as stressed, and we would have less tension in the marriage at times, too. However, one stress would have just been replaced by another, and something else would have caused tension eventually. Life happens, and we would have dealt with things as they came. Playing life safely doesn't ensure that nothing bad or unexpected will ever happen.

Since no one has a crystal ball to see into the future, no one knows what life has in store for them. Some people tend to retreat in the face of the unknown. You can stay at home where you have an illusion of safety or venture out into the world and experience it. The choice is yours. Also, a little wine helps make the decision easier.

Chapter 4 – Preparations

"Before anything else, preparation is the key to success." -
Alexander Graham Bell

Now that the big decision was made, we needed to start preparing.
There were a hundred things that needed to be done in order to pull off
this epic move to England. Despite the daunting task ahead of us, we
were energized to set the grand plan into motion. I even felt much more
alive and less depressed. We were actually going to do this!

Straight away, my wife, Wonder Woman, used her superpowers to
plan our move. She made a lengthy to-do list. She even categorized the
items by family members responsible for completing them. To my utter
amazement, I was on the list! I naively thought that, being the idea man,
I already did my part. Not a chance, I wasn't getting out of my fair share
of the work. I was merely her sidekick. I like the sobriquet "Dreamer
Boy" to her "Wonder Woman" personally.

First up on my list was the dog. Our dog, Albie, can only be
technically referred to as a member of the canine species. He is 40
pounds of furry, affectionate Wheaten Terrier. Mish lovingly refers to
him as our four-legged third son. Accordingly, he has been given the full
privileges and rights as his adopted human family members. Whether he
appreciates them has been a matter of debate. What was not in doubt
was that he was going with us.

I had absolutely no idea of how to get a spoiled pooch into the
United Kingdom or if it was even possible. Mish made it clear that Albie

was part of the deal; therefore, I had to make it happen. So, I researched bringing a dog into the U.K. What I found out was that the British like to make things difficult by being as thorough as possible and then adding some extra superfluous steps for good measure.

Here is the whole ridiculous process in ten short steps:

Step 1: Have your dog vaccinated for rabies within six months, but not less than two months of flying to England, even if he has already had his rabies shot. The Brits like to be up-to-date on things.

Step 2: While waiting for the rabies vaccine to establish itself in your dog's blood, have a European Union pet microchip inserted in your dog. Sorry, pooch, the E.U. chip is different, of course, from the American chip, so you can't use the made-in-the-good old USA one if your pet has it. The chip ensures that your dog can be scanned at the airport for authenticity and at your local grocery store for a price check.

Step 3: Apply for a European Union Pet Passport. Yes, there is such a thing; I am not making this up.

Step 4: Within four months of flying, but not less than two months, take your poor poked pooch back to the vet to have not one but two vials of blood drawn. The Brits really love redundancy, too.

Step 5: Rush the vials to the nearest overnight delivery place and have them sent in a small cooler packed with dry ice to the Kansas State Veterinary Diagnostic Laboratory. Why? The Brits only trust that particular hallowed lab to authenticate that your dog does indeed have the rabies antibodies in his blood. I'm not kidding again. The KSVDL will send you a certificate of authenticity that you will need to ship with your now-legitimized pup to England.

Step 6: Ensure that the date on the certification is not less than two months old, or the Brits will consider your dog a foreign spy and not permit him entry into the U.K. and possibly interrogate Fido to learn what secret canine intelligence he knows. In the case of our dog, however, they would find that his intelligence is rather lacking.

Step 7: Your pet is now considered to be in quarantine and may not leave the country. He may even appear on the FAA no-fly list, so be careful. While in quarantine status, apply for an International Health Certificate with your state's Department of Agriculture. Your vet may have this paperwork. If not, you must request it from the USDA. I didn't even know we had a state-level Department of Agriculture.

Step 8: If you miss any of these steps, proceed to counterfeit the certification and hope for the best.

Ok, I may or may not have, depending on whose reading this proceeded to step eight. All I will say on record is that my dog will never tell anyone what really transpired. I'll admit, I was a little nervous as the dog officials reviewed our pet's paperwork, though.

Step 9: If you make it through the first eight steps, your dog is ready to fly, almost, and you and your dog probably need a stiff drink. Now, you will need to purchase an airline-approved pet carrier. The carrier must be big enough for your dog to stand up in and turn around. On the top of the carrier, tape your pet's paperwork.

Be advised your dog may only fly into the U.K. by air cargo. So, you cannot purchase a seat in coach for him, no first-class upgrades either. Since air cargo is a different service provider than airline passenger service, your pet will most likely fly on a different plane at a different time and maybe even from a different airport. This complicates flying significantly. We had to ship our poor mutt the day after we flew out. We paid a kennel near SeaTac airport that does this regularly to handle it. We honestly had no guarantee poor Albie would arrive once we did in England. My wife had momentary thoughts of Albie winding up in some South American country dazed and confused, wondering how he got there and where we went.

Step 10: The last step! Within 48 hours, you must have your vet stamp the International Health Certificate, called a Federal Endorsement, for the airlines. Without the stamp, the airlines will not allow the dog to fly. Furthermore, your vet must give and certify that the dog was administered the tape-worm treatment 1 to 5 days before departure.

Also, you cannot give your dog any type of tranquilizer prior to flying. He is also not permitted in air bar service either, even if he is over 21 in dog or human years. He also cannot have food or water within twelve hours of the flight. Apparently, at 50,000 feet, the pilot does not allow dog walking, so he must relieve himself completely beforehand. Remember to wish him a good trip and let him know that airplanes are still the safest way to travel, so don't worry about turbulence or funny noises.

By the way, if the temperature at either the departure airport or the arrival airport is over 84°F, pets cannot fly. Go back to Step 10, pray to whatever weather god you may or may not worship, and have another drink. We kept a constant vigil on the temperature at SeaTac and Heathrow airports. When it went over 80°F we started to sweat, and not because of the heat.

If your dog makes his flight, you are as neurotic a pet owner as us and should seek counseling. Several times during this process, I wondered if Albie really wanted to go to England and would even miss us if we left him behind.

At times, I would look down at him disapprovingly, and he would look up at me with those big brown eyes that only a loving and devoted dog has, and I would fill out some more ludicrous pet paperwork and mutter under my breath the whole time about being too soft. In the end, he made it to England. We enjoyed having him with us, and he had no clue where he was except with his family.

While I was working on Albie's stuff, there were a myriad of other tasks that needed to be tackled. One of the biggest was preparing our home for an extended vacancy. We decided that renting it out was not a good option because we didn't know how long we would be gone. Plus, we wanted to take a minimal amount of stuff with us and leave the rest at home. There are pros and cons to this approach.

On the pro side, we didn't have to put a bunch of stuff in storage. We also didn't have to worry about some strangers being in our home making a mess of it while we were out of the country. We had put a bunch of money and work into making our house our home. The thought of someone else in it did not sit too well with us. Plus, we could come back over the holidays whenever we wanted. We really wanted the boys to have a sense of a home base, too. By leaving the house with their bedrooms intact, we were not really moving but going on an extended vacation.

On the con side, we would be floating our mortgage and rent in England at the same time. Ouch on the wallet. Also, the house would be vacant so nobody would be in it to ensure that it was safe and secure. We debated the pros and cons over and over and thought that leaving it empty was the best option. This may not work for everyone, but it is a serious consideration for homeowners looking at going abroad.

Getting the house ready to leave meant that all of those repairs I was slowly getting around to became priorities. My honey-do-list instantly grew. Mish and I went room by room and around the outside of the house making a list and checking it twice of everything that needed to be finished before we could leave. Procrastination was kicking me in the rear. I had a hard deadline to meet now.

While I started on my chores, Mish started on hers. She began tackling the paperwork mountain. We all needed passports. We all needed our health and shot records updated. Mish and I needed our will and trust brought up to date. We all needed luggage. The boys needed school records ordered. Our mail needed to be stopped. The list went on and on. Somehow, she steadily climbed the mountain and conquered it.

Getting our passports somehow made it seem real. I never had a passport. When I traveled overseas with the Navy, my U.S. Department of Defense ID card sufficed. Mish had one as a child, but it was now long expired. She was excited to get a new one and rack up even more international stamps from different countries. If you're going to collect something, passport stamps are pretty cool.

Since you are still reading, you have made it to the next lesson we learned on living a purposeful life: preparation is the key to success in any venture. As one of America's Founding Fathers, Benjamin Franklin, proclaimed, "By failing to prepare, you are preparing to fail." How true!

Neither my wife nor I were international travel experts. We didn't know the first thing about relocating to another country. In fact, we had never, as a family, been out of the country before, except for Canada, which doesn't count. Sorry, Canadians, we love you though. However, we know how to do research and plan accordingly.

You do not need to know everything first; you just need to know how to find the answers when you need them. Thanks to the internet, Google has made this very easy. We learned as we went. Yes, we made some mistakes, but that was part of the process and part of the thrill. Our most memorable stories come from our mistakes. Trust me, we made plenty! Keep positive and focused on the goal. Remember, a good bottle, or even a not-so-good bottle, of wine makes swallowing screw-ups easier. Marrying someone smarter than you is helpful, too, and it keeps you from drinking alone.

Chapter 5 – Committed (In More Ways than One)

"You always have two choices: your commitment versus your fear."
– Sammy Davis, Jr.

Six months went by quickly. We were so busy with getting everything ready that we almost forgot the date was fast approaching. There was still one very important thing that I needed to do. I had to resign my position with the college. That was going to be the point of no return for me, my personal Rubicon, to cross.

Admittedly, I was more than a little nervous about giving my resignation letter to my boss. He was a good person to work for, and we had a pleasant, professional relationship. I felt that I should talk to him in person before sending him my letter. Since his office was across the country, I waited until he visited my campus to talk to him. I wanted him to understand that my decision was not about him or my position but about a long, thought-out personal realization that I needed a change. Never slam the door behind you when you leave if you can help it I have learned.

When my boss arrived, I got it over with immediately. I didn't want to miss the opportunity to talk to him in person. Not surprisingly, he completely understood and wished us the best. Surprisingly, with a slight look of wanderlust in his eyes, he told me he was jealous. He wished he could do the same and travel the world, too. His honest remark caught me a little off guard. He was very successful and well-established. I realized then and there that I was not alone in desiring an escape from the drudgery of a professional career life. I was, however, the only one I knew taking action to do something about it.

I wondered briefly if I was a pioneering spirit who dared to depart from the crowd or if everyone else knew something I didn't, and I was headed for rough waters. I could only push the question out of my mind and hope for the best at this point. Denial is a perfectly acceptable state of mind.

Since I jumped off the career cliff, committing us to at least some type of change, my wife and I thought now would be a good time to inform our boys, Aaron and Elijah. That night, we sat down on the living room couch and asked them if they were interested in going on an adventure. I had read Aaron J. R. R. Tolkien's The Hobbit, so I think he envisioned us taking off like Bilbo Baggins and the dwarves to fight dragons and reclaim some treasure. His eyes became wide and sparkled at the prospect.

I hated to disappoint Aaron, but I needed him to understand that slaying dragons was not in my new job description, I hoped. He glumly accepted that we were not going to Middle Earth but was still up for the plan because old castle ruins were somehow involved. I assured him we would visit as many castles as we could and try to find a pub called the Green Dragon, which we did.

Elijah was only eight at the time. I don't think he really understood where we were moving. England was too far away and strange for such a young boy to truly grasp. He was ok with leaving our home as long as he could take some of his stuffed animals with him. Castles sounded cool, too, but he was more worried about keeping some familiar friends around him for company. When we told him he could pick some of his stuffed critter buddies to go with him, he was on board, too.

Mish went out and bought us all new bright red luggage. For her, that was the signature moment when she internally embraced the move. By having some physical manifestation of the plan, it helped her to accept that it was really happening.

With the whole family now committed, we were actually going to do it! Things were now put into motion that could not be undone. Good or bad, we were going down a new path, all together. The five of us were hand-in-hand and paw on an epic family adventure. We decided we needed a family travel name to commemorate the occasion. We didn't need to think long before we thought of one. Borrowing from one of the boys' favorite cartoons, we dubbed ourselves The Wild Smithberrys!

Life is too short. Staying safe in the comforts of home can be enticing, but there is a whole huge world outside your door waiting to be explored. When I formally resigned from my job, I overcame whatever fears were left that held me in place and set into motion an amazing journey for me and my family.

I knew, at some level, we were all a little scared. Aaron and Elijah were both little troopers who completely trusted their parents, which is a huge and serious responsibility to have as a parent. We knew that they were a little nervous about leaving the secure confines of their home, so we kept them in the loop during the entire process, which helped ease their fears of the unknown. We also knew that embracing change was going to serve them well as they grew older. We wanted their sense of safety and security to come from their own abilities, skills, and knowledge rather than from some physical location. Places come and go, but the experience stays with you for life.

Mish was nervous about the finances and boys' schooling. As I said, she is very pragmatic and logical, which balances my capriciousness and daydreaming. Her way of alleviating fear is to quantify and analyze it until she understands all aspects of the situation and then can attempt to control things as they happen, basically mitigating the collateral damage I tend to cause. It works for her and keeps the family on track and me out of too much trouble.

Chapter 6 – England or Bust!

"What other country...could possibly have come up with place names like Tooting Bec and Farleigh Wallop, or a game like cricket that goes on for three days and never seems to start?" – Bill Bryson

After months of planning, preparation, and anticipation, the fateful day arrived! We took one last long look around, locked our house, loaded our stuff into the airport shuttle, and headed out. As we pulled away from our home in the dark early hours of the morning, the full impact of what we were doing suddenly hit me. I had a queasy feeling in my gut that was not the coffee hitting my empty stomach. I squeezed my wife's hand, took a deep breath, and said a silent prayer. We were really doing this! What had I done?

I asked Mish if we were actually going to go through with this. Not at this late hour, it mattered anyway. She reminded me that since Albie was already headed to England ahead of us, we had to go at least to retrieve him. He probably was wondering where in the world we were shipping him. I'm sure he wouldn't be happy when he finally got off the plane. He's been known to give us the silent treatment when we've left him at the dog sitter before. I hoped he didn't get airsick because I don't think he could open one of those paper airsick bags if he needed to.

We looked at the boys and asked them how they felt. I think they were more excited about the airplane ride than the destination. They had fond memories of airplane snacks, free movies, and all-you-can-drink ginger ale. It's the simple things in life that make kids happy. With their little legs, they didn't need to worry about legroom either. I, on the other hand, was dreading the fourteen-hour flight cramped in a tiny seat.

Mish seemed to be so engrossed in checking our schedule and last-minute details that I couldn't get a good read on her emotions. I hoped she was doing better than me because one of us needed to be calm and collected. I certainly wasn't. I was starting to hyperventilate. She smiled at me and squeezed my hand back. Off we went!

Let me be completely honest. I do not like to fly. I have flown thousands of miles in those aluminum cans with wings but have never gotten used to the idea of hurtling over 600 miles per hour at 50,000 feet with some stranger at the controls. I have been lectured over and over about the safety and practicality of modern airplane travel. None the less, I still would have preferred to take a ship across the Atlantic in style and comfort. My logic is simple: if an accident does happen, I can swim much better than I can fly.

Unfortunately, I could not get my family to agree to the ship option, so once again, I was forced against my better judgment to board another heavier-than-air, non-gliding, out-of-my-control, nausea-inducing, who knows who fixed it, cramped, no-legroom, bad food, germ circulating modern mechanical marvel. I chased down two motion sickness pills with another coffee, buckled in, said another silent prayer, and started counting down to the end of the fourteen-hour flight. Meanwhile, Mish, Aaron, and Elijah ordered drinks, watched movies, and tried vainly to offer me words of comfort every time the plane hit some turbulence. Unlike poor Albie, I could at least open the barf bags.

Luckily, the long flight passed without incident, thank God. When the wheels touched the runway, I gave an audible sigh of relief that apparently was louder than I intended by my wife's smirk. After months of planning, preparing, dreaming, worrying, and toiling, we made it to England. We were rewarded for our efforts upon landing with the cheerful flight stewardess announcing in crisp British across the plane's address system, "Welcome to Heathrow International Airport, England!" The four of us looked at each other in almost disbelief that we were really in jolly old England. As we disembarked the plane, I proudly proclaimed, "We did it!" We were all tired with jet lag, but here at long last and ready to go.

I knew that once we arrived in England, we would need a car. Thinking ahead, I had purchased one and had it waiting for us at the airport, I hoped. I found the car on eBay and did the whole transaction through emails. It was a blue Nissan Pathfinder diesel. The bloke assured me it was in good running condition and that he would meet me at the airport to pass over the keys and paperwork. I paid a whole $400 for it, so I was confident it was a quality automobile. After all, who would falsely advertise on the internet?

I left Mish and the boys at baggage claim and went off in search of our new ride. Out in the parking lot, I spotted it right away, where the seller said he would be. That was a good sign. Our adventure was starting off grand. Then I looked at the car.

It was not exactly like the pictures. I walked around it, making sure it was going to work for us despite its initial rough appearance. I could deal with a few minor cosmetic defects. After all, it was used, but the duct-taped mirrors made me wince a little. The broken taillight could be fixed I figured. I wondered if that was a ticket-able offense in England. I noticed that the gas cap door was missing, too. I'm sure that would be fine also. Maybe Mish could sew the rips in the upholstery, I wondered.

The gentleman started up the car for me. To my relief, it ran smoothly and quietly. He offered to let me sit in it and rev the engine. That is when I suddenly realized the one flaw in my planning: the steering wheel was on the right side. I kind of knew this about England but didn't bother to think about it until now. I needed to drive on the opposite side of the road, starting now. To make matters worse, it was a stick shift. How hard could it be for the first time on little sleep and in traffic grid-locked London?

I had no choice. I thanked the gentleman and took possession of the automobile. He shook my hand, wished me cheerio, which I think is British for good luck, or offered me some breakfast cereal, and drove off, leaving me there alone with no idea how to drive our new car back to pick up my family. The roundabouts alone had me scared. I had a terrifying thought that I would get stuck on one and never see my family again. They would be waiting at the airport, wondering what had become of me. Ok, maybe a little over-dramatic, but driving in England for the first time is a daunting feat.

Somehow, I managed to navigate my way back to baggage claim and find my family. The three of them looked at my purchase with less than approving eyes. Mish tried to be optimistic and congratulate me on not getting stood up. "At least we have transportation," she comforted me. So much for eBay Auto. Maybe I should have spent $500.

We piled ourselves and our luggage into the car and went in search of air cargo to rescue Albie. Sure enough, he was not a happy pooch. Although he seemed relieved to see us again and not be abandoned in a foreign country, he looked at us as if to say, "Do you know how long I've had to hold my bladder? I didn't get free snacks or all-you-can-drink ginger ale. I didn't even get a window seat. What type of airline did you put me on?"

The airport officials reviewed his paperwork and scanned his implanted chip. Albie still looked indignant but tolerated being treated like a fury UPS parcel. For some odd reason, I was a little nervous as the very polite animal inspector took an extra-long look at his paperwork. Maybe I was being paranoid, but I'm sure she squinted at the official signature on the form.

We finally were all together and headed north to the city of Corby, our new home. Mish navigated while I desperately tried to keep up with traffic and not get us into an accident. Driving on the wrong side of the road is unnatural and nerve-wracking at first. It takes a little bit to get comfortable with everything being on the opposite side. Intolerant and impatient English drivers riding my tale and giving me very indignant looks that only the English can give didn't help either. The only saving grace is that I am a lefty, so shifting with my left hand felt proper. I always thought cars were designed for righties, this proved it.

Another unforeseen challenge was these odd circular intersections that Europeans fancy called roundabouts. Roundabout is a proper name for them, too, because we went about as around and around as you could on them. Entering one is nerve-racking enough. I had to remember that you need to go clockwise around them, not counter-clockwise as you would expect in the United States. You're not supposed to stop either, just merge right into the fray.

Once in one, we would go around looking for our exit, sort of like window shopping for the right road. My navigator, Mish, would exclaim, "That was our turn back there!" I would go around again, hoping to get off the next time. Sometimes, we went around three or four times until we finally agreed on a turn.

When ours came up, I drove for it like a Formula One race car driver to the finish line. As we played merry-go-round on the motorway, more skilled drivers would whisk in and out like pros. I'm not sure if they thought we enjoyed driving in circles or were just daft.

Once we finally got through the last city roundabout, the motorway straightened out and headed north into the heart of England. Soon, the London urban area gave way to rolling green countryside with quaint villages and farms. We marveled at the beautiful scenery as it passed by. Even though we looked at hundreds of pictures of England, they all didn't stand up to the real thing. This was the real deal. We were driving through England! What made it even more exciting was that we weren't here on a time limited vacation like some tourists; we moved here. We were officially residents of the United Kingdom.

Hard work has a tendency to pay off. This was not an easy task. Moving took months of planning, preparation, and execution, along with a few bottles of wine. In the end, we did it. There is a certain satisfaction of completing a difficult task that makes the reward so much sweeter.

Chapter 7 – Our New Home

"A place is just that, a place. But a home. A home is where your heart is." – Tessa Marie

A relatively easy two-hour drive north of London on the A1 motorway is the little village of Middleton. It lies in the Midlands of England, so called because it's the middle of the country. How clever of the English. The recruiting agency who helped get me hired had arranged for us to stay our first two nights at a quaint bed-and-breakfast in the village since it was near the school. We were coming in a day late, but figured that would not be a problem. Little did we know that we were about to get our first lesson on British punctuality.

We found the village easily enough and then located our accommodations. Mish rang the bell at the front door to announce our arrival. The elderly lady who answered looked slightly suspicious of us and asked cautiously what we needed. Mish replied in her thick American accent that arrangements had been made through an agency for us to stay here for a few days, and we would like to get settled. She was very taken aback that we had come a day late without informing her. Mish politely tried to inform her that we were traveling and did not have phone service in the U.K. to contact her, but were very sorry for being rude Americans and would still like our rooms if that was possible, seeing as how they were paid for in advance.

After a brief lecture on the courtesies of informing your host of travel changes and the civilities of being punctual, she showed us to our rooms. Feeling very uncouth and barbaric, we again apologized, grabbed our luggage, and obediently followed her.

The cottage was very beautiful and everything we had hoped for, so we quickly got over any misgivings with our host. Middleton is a picturesque stone village complete with three pubs, a county park, horses, and plenty of rolling farmland surrounding it. Tired as we were, we really wanted to take it all in. The air smelt different even. There is nothing quite like the smell of the English countryside in spring. I was already starting to feel very British.

We quickly unpacked and decided to go out and explore the village and maybe get a pint or two at one of the local pubs. We walked a short distance to a pub called the Red Lion. Since we didn't know one pub from another, it seemed like a good place to start. Plus, the boys really liked the bright red lion on a gold shield emblem hanging out in front. As long as they had cold Guinness on tap, it was good enough for me.

As soon as we walked through the doors, we were transported to another world. There is nothing in the United States that can compare to an authentic British pub. They are definitely not bars or full-service restaurants. They are, as the name states, a public house meant for the whole village to gather and drink, eat, drink some more, socialize while drinking, and exchange news over a drink. In essence, pubs are the central hub of British life.

Traditionally, only beer, wine, and cider could be served in pubs. If you wanted hard alcohol, then you needed to find a bar. By British law, all food must be made fresh on the premises too. Pub fare is considered poor man's dining, but it is wholesome and delicious. The whole family is welcome to visit and stay for a while to eat, drink, and be merry. The atmosphere is very friendly and social, complete with traditional pub games, like darts, skittles, and trivia contests. At your village pub, you truly feel like you belong.

We felt welcome straight off. The owner, or publican, Kevin, welcomed us with a warm handshake and big smile and gave us a brief schooling on pub etiquette. The unwritten rules of pub culture are daunting and complex but a necessity to master if you want to blend in with the natives. We were eager to learn, and Kevin was happy to teach us. Over some pints, he explained the history and role of pubs in British society. We found it all very fascinating and listened intently. I think Kevin really enjoyed having two Americans genuinely interested and eagerly listening as he rambled on about his establishment, too.

As we were listening to Kevin, his father-in-law strolled over. Jimmy was an old Irishman who loved to tell stories over some pints of beer, especially if you were buying. We soon learned that there is some truth to the Irish, both drinking and talking a lot. Jimmy was no exception. I think he zeroed in on us as willing listeners to his tales of Irish history and legends. Somewhere in the conversation, Kevin was phased out, and Jimmy phased himself in.

Jimmy was a real treat, though. He must have actually kissed the legendary Blarney Stone and got the gift of gab. He wove tales of Ireland like a master storyteller. We had no idea which were real and which were fabricated on the spot, but we didn't care. We were entertained and made new friends.

"I don't suppose you believe in banshees, do you?" Jimmy inquired.

"I'm not even sure what one is," I replied.

"Aye, then let me tell you about them," Jimmy offered.

The boys were all ears. He knew how to bait us in and keep us enthralled. The evening wore on and between the stories and the pints, my head was starting to spin. We decided to meander back to our cottage and call it a night. Day one in England had been amazing.

Home is where you hang your hat, as the saying goes. We left what we thought was security and comfort but soon adapted to a new normal and found good friends. Home is not a physical place but a state of mind. Wherever you are together as a family is home.

Chapter 8 – Day Two in England

"The ideal man bears the accidents of life with dignity and grace, making the best of circumstances." – Aristotle

We woke up rested and relaxed, ready to start another day in our new home. I washed up and headed to breakfast with Mish behind me. The sun was shining, and the birds outside were chirping. It was a truly splendid morning in the English countryside. As I walked down the hallway, I heard Mish exclaim, "Watch out!" and then I hit my head and everything went dark for a few seconds.

A word of caution for anyone over five feet tall visiting England: watch your head. Apparently, during the dark ages of Europe people did not grow as tall as today. I'm not sure if that was from lack of sunlight or not. Whatever the reason, they must have been very short by today's standards because all of the door frames were built for midgets. My wife, being vertically challenged, had no problems. Me, topping out at a respectable five feet eleven inches, ran into issues, literally.

Despite my wife's attempted warning, I head-butted a large, thick door beam. My thick American skull took on sturdy English oak. The oak won. As soon as I hit it, I heard a loud crack, and everything went black. My wife helped me stumble back to my feet as little English lambs danced around my head. I was dazed and confused but standing.

Mish was obviously very worried and wanted me to get checked by a doctor. It is during emergencies like this that you realize that maybe you're not as prepared for every contingency as you thought. She had no idea where the nearest emergency room was or how to use the British National Health Care System. I was of no use in my condition. I was too busy trying to count the sheep circling my head.

Bless her, she went into overdrive and took action. She ran back to the Red Lion Pub and desperately asked Kevin, who we only knew from the night before if he could assist us. Being a great bloke, he straight away got his father-in-law, none other than the story-telling Irishman Jimmy, to drive her and me to the hospital. Meanwhile, his wife, Fiona, looked after our two boys. If you think ever leaving your kids with perfect strangers is scary, try doing it in a strange country. I'm glad the boys were young, and really don't remember when mom and dad abandoned them at a pub in England.

The kindness of strangers never ceases to amaze me. These kind people dropped what they were doing to help foreigners in an emergency. We are forever in their debt. Let it not be said that the British never helped bail out an American in need.

Luckily, my concussion was mild. Some pain medication and rest were all I needed for a speedy recovery. Mish, on the other hand, needed a big hug and a stiff drink at the pub.

After recuperating from my head bashing, we needed to look in earnest for a place to live. The bed-and-breakfast cottage was nice, except for the low door frames, but it was only temporary. School was starting for all of us and we needed to be settled. So, we needed a lesson in another English practice, the art of finding a place to let, that's rent for us Americans.

We asked for advice from our now go-to experts on all things English, Kevin and Fiona. Since they knew how to find us an emergency room on the spot, we figured helping us find a flat, that's apartment for those of you keeping up with the English vernacular, would be easy. Sure enough, they did not let us down, excuse the bad pun there.

Fiona offered us a small room above the pub with a queen bed for Mish and me and bunk beds for the boys, along with a small bathroom. It was a very generous offer. Since we were in a tight spot, and the room was easy access to the pub for nightcaps, we gratefully accepted. Although it was a temporary solution, it gave us time to find a more permanent home.

We moved into the rather tight quarters and unpacked a little. Elijah straight away rescued his furry animal friends from the bottom of his luggage and placed them neatly on the bottom bunk. He staked his claim and was comfortable and secure now that he was reunited with his buddies. Aaron resigned himself that he was getting the top bunk and climbed the ladder to his bed. He has learned there are times when arguing with his little and very stubborn brother is pointless. I mouthed him a silent "Thank You" and laid down in my respective little territory for a much-needed nap. Day two in England had been a little stressful.

Chapter 9 – The First Day of School

"Education is what remains after one has forgotten what one has learned in school." – Albert Einstein

The next morning was the first day of school. Coincidently, Aaron would be attending the same school where I was teaching, so this would be a new experience for both of us together. We wanted to get to school early so we could acclimate to a new environment. All of us getting ready with one tiny bathroom was a bit of a challenge, but we made it out the door on time and excited to go.

English educational code lays out some pretty specific requirements for students and teachers that are a little abnormal for us Americans. For example, students wear uniforms to school. The exact uniform is prescribed by each school. Our school, Brooke Weston Academy, required students to wear black pants, a white collared button down the front shirt, and the official school tie. Black blazers or sweaters were optional. For male teachers, a suit and tie are definitely required. The jacket may come off in the classroom but must be worn everywhere else. Female teachers are required to wear a dress or skirt, knee length or lower. Nothing may come off. Fortunately, we knew this and had prepared accordingly. Aaron and I admired ourselves in the mirror. We looked sharp, I thought. After hugs and kisses and the obligatory first day of school picture by mom, Aaron and I headed out in our duct-taped jalopy feeling pretty sophisticated.

While Aaron and I were off to our school, Mish was left to get Elijah off to his. Luckily, his school was in the center of the village and only a short walk down the road. For Elijah, this would be not only his first day of school in England but his first day ever. He was entering second grade, but he had been homeschooled for kindergarten and first grade. Since kindergarten is a German word, naturally the English refuse to use it. Instead, they call the first year of school sensibly "first year," so technically, he was entering third grade in England.

Whatever it is called, it would be a new experience for Elijah. Needless to say, Mish and I were more than a little nervous about this big change in his little life. We love Elijah dearly. However, we know Elijah, too. How so much obstinacy can fit into that small package is beyond us.

We have learned that Elijah has two very distinct and opposing personas. When he does not want to do something, he can be very stubborn. I admire his spirit, but some days, I swore that I was going to break it. When he does want to do something, however, there is no stopping him. I call him our little unstoppable tank. Mish and I were wondering which Elijah would be attending school today.

Even first years have a school uniform. For Elijah, his uniform was black pants, a white shirt, and a red sweater. He did look pretty spiffy. I like the school uniform policy. It lends a certain professionalism to education. Plus, it makes shopping for school clothes much simpler. Neither boy seemed to mind it. In fact, I think they actually liked it.

Mish walked Elijah hand-in-hand through the village to his new school. I can't think of a more idyllic picture than that. Along the way, he got to feed and pet the local horses and sheep in their corrals. For Elijah, a devout animal lover, this was an incredible daily ritual. He made sure to bring carrots and apples with him every day. For mom, this was a win-win. Elijah was eager to go to school, or at least walk to it, and the animals got daily treats. The local livestock quickly got to know the little American kid in the red sweater. They excitedly came trotting over every time he passed by.

While my wife was dealing with Elijah, I was getting settled into a new school and helping Aaron make the transition to British education. Luckily, I was going to be his science teacher this year, so I could check in with him at least once a day. Being your child's teacher is the perfect cover for spying on them in school.

In reality, he honestly was glad that I was there. He was the only American in the entire 800-student school, which was a little intimidating. Even though the language was the same, sort of, he was a little uneasy because he knew he stood out. Having dad around gave him someone familiar to go to. I also like having him around too.

I am profoundly thankful for the simple things in life. A good cup of coffee, some quality chocolate, and a warm hug from my wife keep me going. Animal friends, imaginary or real, make Elijah very happy. As long as he can pet, feed, and talk to them he is content. He definitely gets this urge from his mother. The simple act of watching his big brown eyes light up when he is around animals makes my wife and I smile. We love watching him watch his menagerie.

Friends to socialize with make Aaron quite happy. He loves to talk to people. Unfortunately, I think he gets that from me. Maybe he'll be a teacher someday, too. Even if he doesn't, he will do well in crowds. Watching him make new friends makes me happy and relieved.

Having children definitely changes your perspective on life. Neither my wife nor I need much more than to watch our boys grow up and explore their world to be content. Children can be a great source of entertainment. I would say cheap entertainment, but children are anything but cheap.

Chapter 10 – Language Barriers

"Always try to use the language so as to make quite clear what you mean and make sure your sentence couldn't mean anything else." – C. S. Lewis

Acclaimed Irish playwright George Bernard Shaw once quipped, "Britain and America are two nations divided by a common language." How true! We knew that the British have an accent, or we have the accent, or maybe it's the Australians, but we were not prepared for just how different our languages really are.

Luckily, my British colleagues were more than happy to correct my errors. The British sense of humor can be very vexing at times, actually most of the time. They let you know that you are not doing or saying things differently, just incorrectly. I never knew how poor my vocabulary and enunciation were until they pointed them out to me.

"Sir, did you mean aluminum?" one student patronizingly asked.

Another student looked at me like I was an idiot because I couldn't find my classroom even though I insisted I was told it was on the first floor. "You need to go to the first floor," he condescendingly informed me.

"We are on the first floor," I irritably retorted.

"No," he countered, "we're on the ground floor."

How was I supposed to know that they don't count the first floor as the first floor in England?

After a hectic morning, I was ready for lunch. A colleague asked me if I was peckish. By my puzzled look, he surmised that I did not understand.

"No worries, mate. You'll learn soon enough," he assured me.

I just sighed and pretended I knew what I was doing. Once we hit the loo, we headed to the café.

I was having a rather nice lunch with some of my new colleagues at the school when as we were finishing eating, a male teacher surprisingly asked, "Hey mate, would you like to step outside and share a fag." Needless to say, I didn't know what to say.

"Uh, no thanks, but thanks for offering. I think," I managed to stammer.

"OK, suit yourself," he shrugged and walked out the door.

I was left speechless and a little red in the face. Another colleague saw my shocked look and chuckled.

"A fag," she explained to me, "is what we call a cigarette."

"Oh, thank God," I exclaimed, feeling much relieved.

For a moment, I had been completely baffled. I really needed a book on British vocabulary and customs. No one in America would ever have asked me that question in quite the same way, at least not in my social circles, I hope.

Luckily, the day went by with no more embarrassing language mix-ups, almost. When I finally met up with my son, Aaron, for class, I asked him how his day was going. Smiling broadly, he told me that another student asked him if he could borrow a rubber. My eyes widened.

"That's an eraser in America," he informed me with a sly smile.

That was another "thank God" moment. Two in one day was enough.

Aaron and I also learned some other language nuances of the Queen's English. Chips are called crisps, and fries are called chips. So, we had chips and a burger at lunch with a fizzy drink, or soda. For dessert, Aaron had a biscuit, not the KFC type, but one with chocolate chips, not to be confused with potato chips, which are actually crisps. When Aaron was cold, he put on his jumper, which I thought he had outgrown when he was a toddler. Apparently, the English have ugly jumper contests at Christmas, too.

Other British vocabulary words we learned along the way included: A "boot" is a car trunk. Hence, they have boot sales, where everyone drives to a field or parking lot on Saturday morning and sells wares from the boot of their cars. So, if you see a boot sale sign, they do not mean shoes.

A "bonnet" is the hood of the car, not something a woman wears on her head on Easter.

Traffic lights are red, green, and amber (not yellow). You stop on red, as in America, but wait for it to turn amber and then green.

Apparently, judging by their driving, this is so the Brits can count down like a dragstrip car racer and peel off the start.

A "banger" is a sausage. A typical British meal is bangers and mash (sausage and mashed potatoes). Do not cut your banger with your fork less you suffer indignant stares from any Brits looking your way. They are very offended by the incorrect selection of cutlery. God forbid you pick up pizza with your fingers, too. Be warned, that is a high crime in England. Slurping the last of the milk directly from your cereal bowl is grounds for immediate deportation.

To grow a "beaver" is to grow a beard. You thought we were talking about large aquatic rodents. Telling another man, "Hey mate, nice beaver!" is awkward sounding at best.

When something is "duff," it is of poor quality. I wonder if that is why Homer Simpson drinks Duff Beer?

"Jelly" is jello. Jello does not exist in England. I think the trademark didn't get approved in Europe.

A "knob" is a penis. Do not ask to turn someone's knob for them. You can also be called a knob. I'm just not sure if it applies to only males.

"Pecker" is to keep your spirits or courage up, not to be confused with your knob or a small annoying bird. If you look unhappy, people might tell you to "pecker up."

Someone who is "pissed" is drunk, not angry.

To stand in "queue" is to wait in line. In England, standing in long queues is considered a national pass time. I also found out that silly superficial chit-chat while in a queue is frowned upon. Brits like to be miserable in silence.

If you are called a "sod," this is not a compliment. You are an unpleasant person. So, if you start an unwanted conversation in a queue, you might be a sod. I think this may have applied to me on occasion.

"Sort" means to figure things out, not put things in alphabetical or color groups. I was constantly trying to sort out this new and strange language.

If someone asks for a "spanner, then give them a wrench. Don't question it; just pass them a 7/16.

To gain a "stone" means you gained 14 pounds. Over the holiday season, I gained half a stone (i.e. 7 pounds)! Just when you thought converting from ounces to pounds was confusing enough.

A "torch" is a flashlight. I guess when humans replaced fire with electricity, the British forgot the come up with a new word for this magical portable light device.

A "trolley" is a cart with wheels. Believe it or not, there are no actual American-type trolleys in England, so I can understand that they used the word for something else.

The "trunk" is the primary road in the area. This should not be confused with a boot, which is our trunk. So, a car with a boot can travel on a trunk.

The "underground" is the famous London subway, which literally is underground. Not very imaginative, but descriptive and accurate.

The "wing" of a car is the fender, so cars have boots and wings but no trunks because you drive on those.

"Zed" is the letter Z. I have no idea why. It just is.

The number zero (0) is called "naught," as in 200 is 'two-naught-naught." Sure.

Don't forget, at a "zebra crossing," do not wait and look for African-striped horses. It is where you cross the street on the painted white and black striped lines. Again, very descriptive and clever of them.

Lastly, a "full-stop" is the period at the end of a sentence.

There are many more terms we needed to learn on the fly. Pronunciation and spelling of British versus American English words differ sometimes, too. In general, everything that ends in "or" in American English ends in "our" in British English. For example, color is spelled colour in England. American words ending in "er," like center, are reversed in England to centre. I have no idea how these changes came about, but they kept me confused. I really needed a translation dictionary.

I was glad that Aaron had a good first day and dealt with the English language ok. Surprisingly, he was pretty chipper and excited about being the only American at the school. He seemed to be a novelty with his fellow students. They wanted to hear his American accent.

They were amazed that all of us "Yanks" don't speak like we're from Texas. He had to disappoint them with his bland Washington parlance. I told him he should throw in a "y'all" every once in a while to give them something to keep it real.

I was anxious to get home to see how Mish and Elijah got along. Since we didn't have cell phones yet, I had not heard from Mish all day. At least I didn't think an emergency had happened because she didn't contact the office looking for me, so that was a good sign. I hoped she had a good day by herself, too. She was teaching online for a public charter school back in Washington, but her school year hadn't started yet. She didn't have a car either, so I'm not sure what she was doing all day at the village pub, but hopefully not downing pints.

Aaron and I got back in our family jalopy and headed the short distance to home at the pub, which doesn't exactly sound like responsible parenting. Oh well. Luckily, the school was only about five miles away. I was really hoping we would find a permanent and more wholesome place as close. I didn't want to go back to long commutes, especially driving on the wrong side of the road and navigating roundabouts.

I still was wondering how Elijah got on at school as we pulled up. We walked into the pub, and straight away, I got an answer as Elijah greeted us wearing a huge grin with his big brown eyes beaming brightly. Mishele, smiling behind him, confirmed that Elijah had a good time. I was very relieved.

"Daddy!" Elijah exclaimed as he gave me a big hug.

59

Before I could say anything, he launched into a detailed account of his day.

"Everyone is soooooo nice. They made me the special student for the day, like I was some kind of star. The principal told everyone who I was, and I got to tell the class all about me. All the other students wanted to hear me talk American and asked about my home," he blurted out in one breath.

I listened with amusement as he went on and on without letting anyone get in a word. Mish took Aaron aside to hear about his day as I continued listening to Elijah's minute-by-minute account. Aaron was almost as exuberant as his little brother, so Mish got an earful, too.

Finally, Mish and I got our chance to catch up. I told her about my new job and some of the amusing anecdotes from the day. She had spent the day online at the pub, getting her virtual classrooms ready. She also took some breaks to look for housing but with no luck. Not finding a permanent home was the only downer to an otherwise great start to life here. I told her that something would come up eventually. We just hoped eventually meant sooner than later.

That evening, we decided to take a walk through the village to stretch our legs and become acquainted with our new surroundings. We were not sure if Middleton would be the right place for us. We just happened to be here because this is where the recruiting agency booked us a bed and breakfast. The school was actually in the city of Corby, which was not as nice as being in the outlying villages.

We learned that villages were historically part of English country life. Back in the Middle Ages, villages would form every four miles or so as a social hub for the surrounding farms. Each village came with a pub, two churches, one Catholic and one Protestant, and sometimes a small store. The villages encircled a central market town where farmers, herders, weavers, and the like would bring their goods to sell and trade. The market town usually had more skilled craftsmen, like blacksmiths and woodworkers, along with the local government offices and medical help. Market towns, by law, had to be more than a day's travel away from each other to prevent competition. So, the countryside evolved into a spoke-and-wheel type arrangement over the centuries with distinct boundaries around villages and market towns. Between villages and towns was only beautiful countryside without any suburban sprawl, not even ugly giant billboards or gas stations to mar the view.

Our village, Middleton, was attached to Market Harborough. Today, Market Harborough offers a wide range of goods and services, including Costa Coffee, England's answer to Starbucks. For convenience, we thought that it would probably be the best place to live. Our hearts, however, were already enamored with village life. It is something very unique and quite special to England. Luckily, there were several villages to pick from.

As we walked, we talked about finding the best place to live. I could tell Mish was already smitten with Middleton. I'll admit, by sheer luck, we landed in a gem. Our guardian angel was once again looking out for us. I just was not so sure that we could find a place here though.

We went down the main road heading out of the village. Almost at the edge of the village we wandered by a cute stone house with a for sale sign out front. A gentleman was in the yard pruning the tall hedges. I stopped and asked him if he would consider renting if he couldn't sell it. To our astonishment, he informed us that is exactly what he was looking at doing since the housing market was in a slump.

Right away, we told him our story. He was just as amazed as we were at the coincidence. He really wanted to get some renters because he was headed back soon to southern France, where he now lived and wanted to get his house here sorted first. He would be glad to rent to us. He told us he would get the necessary paperwork drawn up tomorrow so we could move in right away. Our guardian angel was working overtime for us.

Things were really going well. Not even a week in England and we had made friends, located the nearest hospital, started school, and found a place to live.

I told Mish, "I'm chuffed to bits!"

That's British for very pleased. I'm even learning the language!

Naturally, we knew we were going to make silly mistakes and embarrass ourselves. We didn't know the language or customs, so of course, we put our foot in our mouths for a while. It was ok. We lightened up and laughed at ourselves a lot.

Chapter 11 – Our First Castle

"Life itself is the most wonderful fairy tale." – Hans Christian Andersen

For me, England was like living in a real fairytale. Everywhere you go, there are quaint Tudor homes, old stone water mills, magnificent Gothic churches, and, of course, castles. We were all anxiously awaiting our first castle visit.

One fine Saturday morning dawned, and we decided to satisfy our castle craving. With all of the castles to choose from, we had trouble deciding which one to see first. Mish did a little research and found that there was going to be a medieval festival complete with the world's largest trebuchet at Warwick Castle this weekend. Sold! She had the boys and me at the world's largest trebuchet.

Warwick Castle is one of England's best-preserved castles. It was built by the legendary William the Conqueror in 1068 AD on the River Avon to defend the Midlands. Coincidentally, we lived in the Midlands, so the castle was very close. We piled into the family wagon, adjusted the duct tape on the mirrors, and headed off to see a castle!

When we arrived, we were in for a real treat. Unbeknownst to us, the castle was not only hosting a medieval fair, but they would be firing the trebuchet! Seeing a giant siege weapon is one thing. Watching it in action is a whole other level of cool. The boys and I were totally thrilled. Mish just rolled her eyes and hoped we would stay out of trouble.

We arrived at Warwick Castle almost giddy with excitement. We could see the castle coming into the area. It was immense! This was a proper castle, for sure. Aaron's eyes were wide with wonder and excitement. This was a young boy's dream come true. All the stories he read of knights and wizards were actually real. I couldn't help but smile at his expression.

Warwick Castle is the genuine article. To be honest, however, it has been spiced up a little to add to the entertainment value. So, it's sort of like a historical site meets Disneyland. They have regular shows and festivals along with jousting, swordsmanship, blacksmithing, and, of course, the launching of the trebuchet. If you can overlook the blatant commercialization of the medieval time period and immerse yourself in the fun of it, then you should have a very splendid time. We certainly did.

Walking around the castle, you really get a sense of how enormous it really is. The outer walls are over 20 feet thick. Everything about it is imposing. What truly amazed us was that the entire castle was built by hand, no power tools or heavy equipment. I guess when you have an unlimited peasant labor force at your disposal twenty-four-seven, you can get a lot done.

We ran around the whole place, trying to take it all in. The castle had something for each of us. Mish loves the rich history. She immerses herself in the stories behind the characters that played their part in the castle over the centuries. For her, the castle is the ultimate three-dimensional novel. Aaron loves the design and architecture. He has always been fascinated with buildings and engineering practices. For him, the castle is an interactive tutorial on medieval design. Elijah loves the fantasy. He let his imagination run freely over the castle grounds. For him, this was a living storybook complete with swords, shields, and armor. I'm not sure what I love about it. I just enjoy walking in a new and different place, I guess. For me, this was an entirely new experience. All my senses were overloaded.

I guess this is why we travel the world. There is more to see in this world than is possible in one short lifetime, not that we aren't trying. Seeing pictures of far-off places is one thing but experiencing them in real life is a whole other thing. The sights, sounds, feel, and smell of the castle, combined with knowing it's a real piece of history, is euphoric. I could tell the boys were hyper-stimulated, too. Mish and I were desperately trying to keep tabs on them as they scurried all around.

Eventually, we found our way down into the dungeon. I have heard of dungeons of course, but I never really considered them truly real before. Like many things in England, I had read about them in history and storybooks but never actually saw them. So, they remained in this quasi-real state in my inexperienced mind, somewhere between "I saw it with my own eyes" and "I saw it in a movie once."

Thinking this dungeon would be kind of like the Pirates of the Caribbean ride at Disneyland, we merrily descended the rough, uneven stairs down into the dark subterranean passages under the castle. When we reached the bottommost level, we entered a small, dimly lit room with rusted metal devices hanging on the walls and from the ceiling. I recognized one of them as an iron maiden. These terrifying contraptions were designed to torture victims in the most hideous way. Hapless prisoners were placed in an iron sarcophagus and suspended from the ceiling. Lining the inside of the device were strategically placed spikes that would impale the unfortunate victim just enough to pierce vital organs but not instantly kill them when the two halves closed. They would have a slow lingering death as they bleed out over several hours or even days. To add to the horror of it, two spikes were positioned specifically to penetrate the eyes. Whoever invented the Iron Maiden was truly sick and twisted. I shuddered to imagine what it must have been like for the poor souls who were condemned to this particularly gruesome torture. What could they have done to deserve it?

As I was explaining the iron maiden to Aaron and Elijah, I could see their faces turn white with fear. Great, I thought; I traumatized them for life again. Aaron asked me if this particular one was real. I assured him it was just a prop to show what might have been used here. That set his young mind at ease. As I walked up to it, however, the placard clearly stated that this one was the real deal. It had been actually used to torture people. I had a chilly shudder go down my spine. I kept that information to myself.

We looked around the small chamber and noticed a hole in the floor with a trap door. Apparently, this was used when the lord of the castle wanted someone to disappear and never be heard from again. They were simply thrown down into the abyss and forgotten about. What was the matter with these people?

We decided to get out of the dark and dank dungeon back into the refreshing light. The rest of the castle was not as macabre. We saw the throne room, armory, kitchen, toilets, or what they called toilets back then, and sleeping rooms. It was a magnificent example of medieval life in a fortress designed to keep an enemy at bay.

The icing on the cake was finding out that there was a sword in a stone on the far side of the keep. A congenial castle docent informed us with a wink in his eye that legend has it that whoever can pull the sword out will be king of the castle. That was all the boys needed to hear. They practically dragged us across the castle grounds in search of this mythical sword.

We found it. Perched on the remains of the old outer wall was a large dark grey stone impaled by a shiny black hilted sword. The boys approached it with awe and reverence as if it was a holy relic from ancient times. Mom and I knew, however, that a possible conflict was brewing because behind those sparkling child eyes were two very competitive brothers quickly calculating who would get the chance to first pull on the sword.

Luckily, we know our boys all too well. Before they could get into an argument with each other, our parent brains instinctively strategized a plan. That means we lied to them. We told them that according to ancient tradition the sword could only be pulled by two brothers in their birth order. Ok, maybe not true or overly clever, but it worked, and no fighting ensued.

Aaron immediately asserted himself as the older brother and stepped up to the legendary stone. He squarely planted his feet on the ground and firmly grasped the pommel of the sword. He took a deep breath, closed his eyes, and pulled. Noting happened. He took another breath and tried again harder. Still, nothing happened. He knew the sword had won. Disappointed, he stepped away from the stone in defeat to let his younger brother have a shot at the crown.

Elijah had a very different style. He ran up to the stone, grabbed the sword with both hands and pulled with all his little body could manage. His face scrunched up as he just continued pulling and pulling, but the sword did not budge. Undeterred, he kept pulling. We finally had to stop him before his head exploded.

Neither boy would be king, but that was ok. We didn't want to live in the castle anyway, too drafty and cold. Besides, I'm not sure I could sleep well knowing about the dungeon below me.

Our first castle was everything, and more we hope for. It had a mix of history, engineering, adventure, and fantasy blended into one amazing family experience. We were starting to really enjoy our time in England.

"Imagination is just as important as knowledge," proclaimed Albert Einstein. How true! We were living a fantastical life. Castles, swords, and knights were part of our reality now. Mish and I could see the boys enthralled with it all as they mixed history and legend. They were playing but learning in more ways than one.

Chapter 12 – Cambridge

"Education is not the filling of a pail, but the lighting of a fire." –
William Butler Yeats

We finally were settled in our new home in Middleton and really enjoying the pastoral village life of England. School was going well for all of us, and we seemed to be adapting to our new environment. Admittedly, there were some adjustments we needed to make to convert our Americanized habits to fit British living.

Mish taught online for her school back in Washington State, which enabled us to have her income and gave her the ability to continue her career. One slight snag, however, was the time difference. Middleton is nine hours ahead of Port Ludlow. Since she needed to teach when her students back home were awake, or at least supposed to be awake, she needed to set her clock to Pacific Standard Time. That meant that her workday began at 5:00 pm and ended at 2:00 am local time.

We lapsed into a workable, if not unusual, routine. I woke up early and got myself and Aaron ready for school. Mish slept in since Elijah didn't go to school until a bit later. When she awoke, she got Elijah ready and walked him across the village to his school, with a quick stop to feed the sheep and ponies. By the time we returned, she had worked out, done some household chores, fetched Elijah, and started dinner. Once again, she earned the nickname Wonder Woman.

When Aaron and I got home, we took off our ties and went our separate ways to relax. He went to his room to read, and I went for a run through the village. Elijah tried to stay out of trouble and not too successfully annoy his older brother. Mish promptly got on her laptop and started school with her students back in Washington State. Around 7:00 pm, we would all meet back up for dinner and talk about our day. After dinner, I did the dishes and got ready for the next school day. The system worked for the most part. Unfortunately, however, I usually had to go to bed alone while Mish stayed up to teach. Occasionally, she could sneak coming to bed with me but still would need to get up in the middle of the night to attend meetings or tutor students. We all did our parts to make the system work.

As we were getting comfortable with our schedules, we realized that we needed to get our backsides comfortable, too. Our home did not come with furniture, and sitting and sleeping on the floor was getting old. We needed to get some chairs and beds quickly. On our very tight budget, that was not going to be easy.

We asked around the village how to secure some much-needed comfortable furnishings to no avail. Apparently, having yard or garage sales in England is illegal, or might as well be. Since you cannot place signs on private or public property to advertise your sale, thanks to British laws keeping the country prim and proper at all times, attracting customers is very difficult. Most villages prohibit yard sales anyway as a matter of tidiness and decorum. To make them even less appealing, the British government enforces taxes on items sold at these sales. Bugger! I was planning on these American weekend traditions in the hope of picking up some cheap second-hand items, so much for that. I needed a plan B.

Plan B was eBay. It worked for the car, mostly, so why not for furniture. I fired up my laptop and logged into eBay UK. Straight away I started to find some appealing stuff. I really had no idea what a fair price for used furniture was in England, so I just had to stay with what we could afford, which wasn't top-of-the-line goods. When I found a chair or sofa within our meager price range, I submitted it to the boss for approval. If she liked it, I bought it. Simple. Then began the scavenger hunt.

Aaron and I would plot the address on a map and off we would go. We picked up much-needed furniture and learned our way around the area at the same time. This became our weekend ritual. On Saturday morning, we would head out, with an obligatory stop at Costa Coffee, England's answer to Starbucks, in search of a couch here or a bed there. I drove, and Aaron navigated as we sipped our coffees and savored the thrill of the hunt. After we found our quarry, we loaded all of them into our trust-worthy SUV, which was proving to be of great worth now despite its obvious lack of aesthetics. It was unconventional father-son bonding, maybe, but still fun.

We also learned about some obscure British laws while driving around England in search of used furniture. For example, you can scavenge for more than just used appliances as you drive around England. If you come across some tasty-looking roadkill, you may stop and scoop it up as legal hunting. So, you could come home with a bargain basement deal microwave and some choice venison steak. Who knew England was so versatile? We always thought that going hunting with your Chevy was only an Alabama thing.

Unfortunately, you cannot ever eat white swans. All unmarked swans belong to the Queen, and any attempt to eat them is considered illegal. Furthermore, under the royal decree of King Edward II, all beached whales, and sturgeons must be offered to the reigning monarch. We never found out why. We did get some great deals on used furniture and other stuff, but we passed on pavement pizza.

All this driving around on eBay scavenger hunts got me thinking that we needed to see some more of England's fabulous historical places. One place in particular that I always wanted to visit was the University of Cambridge. Those hallowed halls of higher education have seen such notable alumni as Stephen Hawking, Isaac Newton, Ernest Rutherford, John Milton, David Attenborough, Jane Goodall, Charles Darwin, and Florence Nightingale, to name just a few. Being a science teacher, Cambridge is like holy ground to me. I really wanted to walk where those titans of academia once walked.

The University of Cambridge was founded in 1209. It is the fourth oldest university in the world. The fact that students were studying and learning there well before Christopher Columbus was even born, let alone set sail across the ocean, astounds me. America's oldest university, Harvard, wasn't founded until 1636. We really are a young country.

One beautiful fall Saturday morning, we piled into the family wagon and headed to Cambridge. I would have loved to attend there as a student, but I would have to settle for just visiting. Maybe I could just pretend I was a student while we walked around. If they let me sit in on a class, that would be over-the-top amazing! Yes, I am a total geek, I know. But after all, it is Cambridge.

We didn't have to drive far. The university is only an hour from Middleton. Driving there, I realized that I could commute every day if they offered evening classes for adult learners. Cool! You can only imagine my incredible disappointment when I learned Cambridge doesn't do that sort of undignified type of non-traditional education. Oh well, I already had a college degree anyway. Maybe I could convince either Aaron or Elijah to apply to be a Cantabrigian.

I wasn't about to let my dream of being a Cambridge student ruin my experience visiting the school. Mish was excited, too. She read that Cambridge is also famous for its many unique bridges. The Bridge of Sighs over the River Cam is named after its more well-known counterpart in Venice, although they are architecturally very different. A popular school myth is that the bridge was named by the students for all the sighing of overworked students passing across it on their way to classes. Slackers! They should cheer up. After all, they are at Cambridge.

We reached the university in good spirits and straight off went exploring. We did find several very beautiful bridges. The boys, however, were more excited to be on the water than over it. They convinced us to take them punting on the river. A punt is a flat-bottomed boat with a square-cut bow that you propel with a long stick pushed against the river bottom. If it looks easy, it's not. It takes some serious arm and shoulder muscles, along with a strong back and proper footing, to go any appreciable distance in one. Luckily, strapping young college lads looking to make a few bucks will happily punt you around the university.

We opted to be chauffeured around campus along its many canals. Floating by gives you a unique perspective on the campus with its magnificent architectural buildings situated in beautifully landscaped gardens and greenways. It was sort of like It's a Small World at Disneyland, except without the annoying music. There even were people from around the globe to watch.

I am always at a loss for words when trying to describe certain powerful emotions that flood over me at times like this. Maybe the combination of feeling the warmth of a sunny summer day, floating quietly and smoothly on the water, looking at the picturesque scenery, and soaking in the ambience of it all created a potent elixir. I was somewhere between euphoria and contentment. This was the England I had always dreamed about. How could the English be so uptight and somber all the time?

After our outing on the river, we went in search of some much-needed sustenance. Watching that poor university student work up a sweat punting us along the river worked up our appetites. We all agreed that a pub fair was in order. With so many pubs to choose from, we debated which one would be the best to round out a wonderful day. Luckily, Mish found the perfect one. Across a bridge from the university was The Green Dragon.

For those of you who do not know that fabled pub, it was once found in a quiet corner of The Shire called Hobbiton in Middle Earth. It was frequented by Frodo Baggins and friends and the meeting place of all Shire-folk to eat, drink, and discuss the day's events and local politics, like the quality of the season's pipe-weed or grumblings of dwarves traipsing through the area. Even though this was not the same place, it was fun to pretend with the boys and get caught up in their excitement. I didn't have the heart to tell them Tolkien's Green Dragon only existed in the pages of his books. I guess that's the great thing about imagination: reality is flexible.

We walked over and found the pub in short order. It was nestled on the river, just like Tolkien's, and it even had the same thatched roof. The publican was used to people coming in and asking about hobbits and if he had seen the wizard Gandalf. He politely smiled and told us that he had not seen any hobbits or wizards lately but would keep an eye out.

We had a nice traditional pub lunch. Pub grub, as some affectionately call it, had become a favorite of ours when we went on outings. We each had our favorite dish; Mish usually ordered a Plowman, which is basically a club sandwich; Aaron preferred Shepard's Pie; Elijah liked Hunter's Chicken; and I was a Fish and Chips person. Mish usually ordered Strongbow cider, but because I was usually driving, I abstained from my favorite pub libation, a tall, cold

Guinness. We ate and drank like hungry hobbits off on a grand adventure.

We finally headed back home to Middleton, full and content. Cambridge is truly an amazing town and university. I was glad that we lived closed by so we could visit often. We just don't have colleges like that in the United States. I know it's a product of our young age, but I still wish we did. Maybe in a couple centuries, ours will gain the same stature.

Contentment sometimes comes from unexpected sources. You don't need to have brand-new designer-label stuff to be happy. You also don't always need to go to extravagant restaurants or lavish resorts to feel content. In the immortal words of Bilbo Baggins, "'It is no bad thing celebrating a simple life."

Chapter 13 – Robin Hood

"He who jumps for the moon and gets it not leaps higher than he who stoops for a penny in the mud." — Howard Pyle, The Merry Adventures of Robin Hood

I had read stories of the legendary hero Robin Hood as a boy, but I had always assumed that they were just made up. I didn't believe that Nottingham and Sherwood Forest were real places. So, you can imagine my chagrin when I learned that they were genuine locations in England. Even more surprising, they were close by! We knew where our next family adventure would be.

Nottingham is only a short trip north from Middleton, so we got up early on another Saturday morning, got in the family vehicle, and headed out on the country roads of England once more. We were going to see the actual place where the legendary bandit Robin Hood and his Merry Men robbed from the rich and gave to the poor while fighting the traitorous Sheriff. Sometimes living in England is like being in a fairy tale.

When we arrived in Nottingham, we were all giddy with excitement and anticipation. I was telling the story of Robin Hood to Aaron and Elijah, who were listening intently despite having heard it many times before. Both boys really loved adventure stories with larger-than-life heroes and pretty damsels in distress, and I loved telling them. Being a dad sometimes gives you an eager audience.

The city of Nottingham, however, was a bit of a disappointment, to be honest. It is a fair-sized city with all the hustle and bustle of modern urban life. It's not a particularly attractive city either. I was hoping for the Nottingham of the old Robin Hood movies. I loved the classic black and white ones with a dashing swashbuckler like Errol Flynn riding around in an improbably perfect costume, easily thwarting the predictable villain and winning the heart of a fair maiden. I like my movies simple, where the good guy beats the bad guy and gets the girl, end of story.

Undeterred by the initial impression of Nottingham, we set out to find the famous castle. It really does exist, sort of. The original castle sat on a promontory of rock 130 feet above the River Trent where it had a commanding position of the surrounding area. It once was a very important site due to its proximity to a strategic river crossing and the royal hunting grounds in nearby Sherwood Forest. Like many once prominent places in England, the changing winds of time eventually overtook it and left it behind. Today, it is a shadowy reminder of a once nobler past.

The historical validity of Robin Hood has been debated by scholars for centuries. I have read some research that suggests he was a real person and others that he was a fictitious character taken from old medieval ballads. To be quite honest, I don't care. I chose to believe that he once lived here in Nottingham. Maybe that is my stubborn bit of romanticism clinging on to a fanciful story, but so what?

We climbed the steep pathway up to the keep. When we got there, we noticed straight away that the castle wasn't very castle-ish looking. It looked more like a large estate house. The boys and I, now castle experts, carefully scrutinized the design of the house. It had large windows on the ground floor with tall front doors. There wasn't even a moat. How could it be defended? We were very concerned that this castle was not very well planned out. No wonder Robin Hood was able to sneak into it and defeat the sheriff.

We went inside and voiced our concerns with the tour guide. He patiently explained to us that this was not the original Nottingham Castle; it was officially Ducal Mansion. The original castle was left to disrepair and decay and eventually abandoned. In 1674, the new mansion was built on the foundations of the old castle. That mansion, however, also fell into ruin in the 1800s and was abandoned, too. Apparently, during the Industrial Revolution, Nottingham had the worst slums in the British Empire, so none of the aristocracy wanted to live there. When the poor citizens rioted, they burned down the mansion. Talk about a bad location.

The mansion shell sat as a derelict on the hill until it was restored in 1875 and re-opened as a museum. Continuing its bad luck streak, in 1996, a major landslide almost destroyed part of the outer wall and court, which had to be extensively redesigned and repaired. So, what we were seeing now was the most recent reincarnation of the original castle. Once we learned all of the history, the boys and I felt much better about the layout of the place and in our castle design prowess.

We were a little bit disappointed in not getting to see a true castle. Our tour guide, however, was not done showing all that the site had to offer. Before we lost interest, he mentioned that there were secret underground tunnels running from inside the mansion to a hidden gate at the bottom of the cliff below called Mortimer's Hole. The tunnel was used by smugglers to sneak goods from boats on the river up into the castle. Our interests peaked again.

As we descended the long tunnel, the guide further informed us that the tunnel got its name when loyalists to the king of England used it to sneak into the castle and arrest Mortimer, the lover of Queen Isabella. The unfortunate Mortimer was taken from his bed and dragged to prison in the infamous Tower of London. Some say that you can still hear Mortimer's chained footsteps haunting the tunnel. The boys intently listened but didn't hear anything, which I think was a relief for them.

When we reached the bottom of the tunnel, we had learned more about English history than I ever learned in high school. Why couldn't we take field trips to England during Social Studies? It would have made learning about all those kings and queens and beheadings much easier.

We learned another interesting thing about English culture, too. Lined up on the river by the tunnel exit were brightly colored canal boats. Back in the day, these long, narrow boats were used to transport all types of supplies throughout England on an elaborate network of man-made waterways. Today, these once-obsolete boats have been repurposed as floating RVs. Talk about cool!

I had to have a look inside one of these nautical beauties. Some of the interiors were amazing. Proud owners had lovingly decorated the interior of their boats with custom woodwork and plush furnishings. One boat even had a roof-top garden complete with a patio and barbeque. These canal yachters traveled in style.

Today, the UK has over 2,200 miles of navigable canals that recreational boaters use to travel the country. I think that this would be an absolutely incredible way to explore the villages and cities while enjoying the scenery. You wouldn't have to fight traffic or reserve lodging, just motor along at a maximum break-neck speed of four miles per hour. Efficient, relaxing, and unique. What a splendid holiday!

After marveling at the boats leisurely motoring up and down the canal, we headed back to our car. Upon finding it, we learned about another efficient British custom, parking tickets. The Brits love issuing parking tickets and seem to have the practice down to a science. We were only five minutes past the expiration time, too. Bollocks! I was feeling miffed as I grabbed the ticket off the windshield and got back in the car.

I slowly learned to not get miffed when the British parking police rob from you and give to the government. They are no Robin Hoods, but they're just doing their jobs. We later found out that they are even more methodical about collecting on tickets than they are giving them. Blast British efficiency.

We learned to embrace new and different ways of doing things, even when they were painful lessons at first. Learning to adapt saved us huge amounts of frustration, which would have turned into stress, which eventually would have turned into unhappiness. Instead, we chose to be happy by reinventing ourselves to suit our new surroundings instead of trying to change the surroundings to suit us.

Chapter 14 – Going to Take a Bath

"When I'm in England, I know I'm a visitor, but being a white man in England with ancestry that's German and Italian, I have a history with the Romans and the Saxons. I feel some connection and ancestry here, as weird as that sounds." – Nicolas Cage

We decided that our next adventure in England would be to Bath. Bath is actually a small city on the southwestern side of the country on the River Avon in Somerset near Whales. It is famous for its Roman baths, from which the city gets its name. The baths are fed by natural hot springs and were used by the Romans as far back as 60 A.D. and the Celts long before them.

The Romans aren't the only ones who loved a good soak, apparently. Actor Nicolas Cage moved to Bath from Hollywood. We were told that he is regularly seen in town. When asked previously what he loved so much about the area, Cage said, "In Somerset, I enjoy the peace of the oak trees and the rolling green hills, and I like going into Glastonbury." I can completely empathize with him.

Jane Austen, Charles Dickens, Mary Shelley, Nicholas Cage, Johnny Depp, Van Morrison, Hugh Grant, and more also have all called this old Roman spa town home. The Royal Crescent apartments overlooking the town were once a haven for up-and-coming artists, writers, poets, and thinkers.

The city stands out as an architectural anomaly in a very uniform country. As much as I love driving around England, after a while, I noticed that all the cities and villages have a similar look. The British have a very strong sense of consistency. I'm not mentioning anything that the Brits don't know about themselves already. There's the proper British way to build a house and everyone else's way. Bath, however, is different.

Since the Romans founded the city of Bath before British sensibleness standardized the country, it has a distinctively non-British feel. Technically, the dominant architectural style of the city is Georgian. I only know that from reading about it in a pamphlet I picked up at the visitor's center, not because of my vast knowledge of historical design. I also read that the city was purposefully designed by a father-son team, John Wood, the Elder, and John Wood, the Younger. The two Woods' creation is now the only entire city in England to be designated a UNESCO World Heritage site. Impressive.

We strolled around Bath taking in the ambience of it all. It truly is a beautiful city. Mish wanted to see the crown jewel of it, the ancient Roman baths. After almost two millennia, they are still there and still hot. Although you cannot swim in the original pools, the natural spa next door uses the same water, but treated for safety, as the Celts and Romans skinny-dipped in. You can, however, drink the water, which is purported to have mystical health and wellness properties. Hmmm, sipping the same water that a bunch of sweaty Romans sat in is not my thing. I told Mish I would gladly sit this one out with Albie. Dogs weren't allowed in, anyway.

Albie and I decided to go in search of a hot mocha latte with something sweet while Mish and the boys waited in line to take a shot of hot bath water with some sweat. As we walked, however, I felt numerous eyes on us and cameras pointed in our direction. I began to feel slightly uneasy. Maybe people were mistaking me for a celebrity? I thought I looked rather dashing with my new haircut and jacket. I have been working out, too. I was starting to blush a little.

I sat down on a bench across from the baths, enjoying my mocha, when two Japanese young ladies approached me. I thought they must want an autograph or selfie with me. What was I going to tell them? I'm really not Hugh Jackman, but thank you for asking. I was getting a little flustered as they walked up. Before I could speak, one of them politely asked if they could get a picture with my dog.

Wonderful! I was upstaged by a furry mutt. I had no idea that Albie, our Ewok-looking Soft Coated Wheaten Terrier, would be such a hit with Japanese tourists. In the hour I sat there waiting on my family, I had no less than two dozen strangers ask me if they could have a picture with him. I politely obliged and let the dog have his day as he smugly posed with each of them. Had I known how popular he would be, I would have put down my hat and charged two pounds a photo.

By the time Mish and the boys returned, I was ready to get out of the limelight and head home. I asked them how the water tasted. Aaron and Elijah both wrinkled up their noses and stuck out their tongues. Mish made a look like she was going to vomit. I took that as not good. Oh well, I tried to warn them.

When we arrived back home in Middleton, we were all ready for a real hot bath or at least a shower. Modern luxuries like indoor heated plumbing are a godsend. I cannot imagine bathing in a communal pool with other naked strangers, call me prudish.

There are many other modern marvels that we love and are accustomed to in the developed world. Naively, we thought that England, as a fellow member of the industrialized club, would have the same amenities. Surprisingly, it doesn't, or maybe we are just extremely spoiled in America.

In the United States, we love hot showers, the longer and hotter, the better. Finding a decent shower in England is about as difficult as finding a needle in a haystack (or a sober Brit in a pub). The English seem to make do with lukewarm trickles or baths. My wife prefers being pressure-washed with a scorching firehose instead. She probably would have preferred jumping into the Roman baths over our shower at home.

Mish also didn't approve of our combo washer-dryer unit. Admittedly, back in Washington, she had a full-size all-American separate washer and dryer. She could do a week's worth of soiled laundry in one load, which, with two growing boys, was a real time-saver. Here, she had a small combination unit that took twice as long and did half as much. Worse yet, when it went into its spin cycle, it sounded like a jumbo jet revving up its engines. The whole unit comically wobbled back and forth like an excited R2-D2 from Star Wars. We eventually banished it to the garage so we could have some quiet while the laundry was getting done.

For me, the most egregious appliance issue was the lack of an icemaker in the refrigerator door. How am I supposed to make my iced mocha? I asked a colleague if he had one in his refrigerator. He condescendingly informed me that was an American thing. I asked what he did if he wanted a glass of cold water. This time, he was shocked. "The tap water is sufficiently cool for us," he retorted. You've got to love British stoicism.

Setting up internet and phone service was a nightmare. This became a huge dilemma for Mish because she was teaching online, which kind of requires the internet. Repeated calls to British Telecom were met with vague promises of any day now. One week turned into two, then four, and then six with no end in sight. Mish was getting frantic and trying her best to cope. Although, hanging out in our car in the parking lot of an all-night McDonalds to borrow their free Wi-Fi quickly got extremely tedious. When the serviceman finally showed up at our house, I think she was ready to hug him.

To add to our domestic challenges, our refrigerator was half the size of a typical American one. Fat jokes about obese Americans aside, this made for many more trips to the market than normal for us. Bringing back a five-gallon mayonnaise jar or ten-pound block of cheese from Costco definitely would not work. I hated telling the boys that Costco didn't even have a store in the UK. Therefore, we had to adapt to a new grocery system.

Traditionally, in England, like most of Europe, people shop once a week at specialty stores in the market town. On Saturday, because nothing is open in Europe on Sunday, we would drive the short distance into Market Harborough to peruse the bakery, butcher, cheese shop, produce stands, fishmonger, and other merchants. The boys loved that they usually got free samples, just like at Costco, but better. Being young and adorable has its advantages. I found this old-world provincial style of shopping quaint and enjoyable. My wife, being more about efficiency and less about process, wasn't as enamored with market shopping.

Luckily, Mish discovered a more expedient way to shop. A neighbor clued her into home delivery. The British have home delivery for almost everything. She could order online and have the groceries delivered the same day at no charge. The friendly Asda man became a regular figure in our lives in England. I think the boys started to look at him as a distant uncle.

Although Asda was very good at delivering, I still preferred to walk around the markets with my mocha and sample the wares, and chat with the locals. So, we reached a compromise. Since Asda did not have some specialty items, the boys and I would go to the market on Saturday and bring back some surprise treats. Albeit, sending three perpetually hungry boys unsupervised shopping got a little dangerous. We found all sorts of scrumptious delicacies.

So, some things in England are definitely an inconvenience compared to our ultra-customer-oriented culture in America. Other things, however, turned out to be just fine once we adapted. We all agreed that maybe in the United States, we are a little too efficiency-focused and don't slow down enough to enjoy simple activities like shopping for food. Large one-stop shopping mega-stores open twenty-four-seven are very convenient. On the other hand, carefully selecting fresh local food stuff is enjoyable. Both are a means to an end, putting food on the table. The nuances between the two, however, make a huge difference. I'm actually beginning to like this slower-paced lifestyle.

Like the old adage recommends, take time out to smell the flowers from time to time. We were realizing that efficiency isn't the most important factor in many, if not most, circumstances. After years of running the infamous rat race, we looked for ways to actually slow down and enjoy the moment. The change was very welcome.

Chapter 15 – Halloween in England

"October, baptize me with leaves! Swaddle me in corduroy and nurse me with split pea soup. October, tuck tiny candy bars in my pockets and carve my smile into a thousand pumpkins. O autumn! O teakettle! O grace!" — Rainbow Rowell

Life in England was going well. Every week we were having new adventures, learning more history, and meeting interesting people. School had its ups and downs for all of us, though. Elijah seemed the most well-adjusted to his new school, of course, he is also the youngest, which makes him very adaptable. He was still a huge hit with his teacher and classmates and was basking in the limelight. Aaron was making friends and learning a lot. I also noticed that a couple of girls seemed to follow him around everywhere. Apparently, they loved his American accent, I was told.

Every day, I was learning how to teach in a foreign educational system. Some days were easier than others. The UK uses the General Certificate of Secondary Education (GCSE) as an academic qualification by the end of their eleventh year in public school. In short, the GCSE is a series of exams in different subject areas that earn students numbered scores, which they will use to get a job or go on to A Levels and then, from there, possibly continue to university. They are high-stakes exams, to say the least. The scores follow them through life and determine their future career offerings.

Since the UK only has compulsory education to age sixteen, students must prove their ability to continue until age eighteen. If they do, then they will spend the final two years of public school preparing for university study in their chosen field. If they do not, they may go to a trade school or apprenticeship program or get an unskilled job. It is a harsh system by our American standards for sure.

What perplexed me most was that students basically spend their entire school years preparing for the GCSE, yet they are not assessed to monitor their progress towards this critical milestone and remediated if necessary. They are given tests called Key Stage Exams every other year to document their aptitude over time, but nothing more. Students don't even repeat a grade if they are falling behind, they just keep going and falling more behind each year. They do not use weekly quizzes, tests, finals, or any other form of formative or summative assessment to give students feedback on learning either. Therefore, they do not have grades! If you ask a UK student about their GPA, they will give you a confused look and not understand.

The students with appropriately high enough scores come back the next term while the rest of the rift-raft leave for parts unknown. The elite ones that return eventually take the A Level Exams to see if they qualify for the next tier, university. Those of that select group that do qualify go off to Oxford or Cambridge or some other nice school; those that don't are told, "Oh well, better luck next life." Admittedly, they can re-sit the exams at their own expense and time. As you can probably imagine, there is a thriving exam tutoring business in the UK. And people wonder why the British drink heavily.

In the UK, they also do not have high school graduation ceremonies. Students take the GCSE, and then nothing. It's very anticlimactic in a way. So, homecoming, prom, senior skip day, the SAT, transcripts, and many more time-honored American high school traditions do not convert to counterparts in England. It's a little stuffy in British schools, to be honest.

I was finding that motivating my students was difficult for me. My normal teacher tricks and tools were of little use here. Teaching was not going as I expected. I felt like I was a first-year teacher again. This conundrum caused me to have many deep pedagogical discussions with my colleagues and wife.

On the good side, in many ways, teaching was much easier in the UK, with no mountains of papers to grade, projects to create, or tests to make up. On the bad side, it was extremely hard to motivate students. Most of my students had long ago decided what road in life they were going to take. The ones that wanted to go to university dutifully prepared for the battery of exams, the ones that only wanted a job after getting their GCSE screwed around. Unfortunately, the ones that wanted to go to university knew how to play the system and focused on intense cramming for the exams and not truly learning.

Even more dismaying was that my fellow teachers were complacent with this arrangement. This was all they knew, and were used to it. So, asking them for advice was useless. I was really struggling with the old saying, "When in Rome, do as the Romans."

More than as a teacher, as a parent I was struggling with adapting to a completely foreign educational system. I had no idea how to monitor Aaron's academic progress even though he was in the same school as me. I'd ask him how things were going, and he would respond with a shrug.

The weeks went by, and I admittedly was feeling a little depressed. The days were getting shorter and darker, which added to the dreary feeling. Autumn was creeping into the air. Then, on cue, Mother Nature worked her magic and the leaves started to turn beautiful fall colors. My grey mood lifted with the burst of reds, oranges, and yellows everywhere. This is my favorite time of the year. Any bout of homesickness was cured by the sight of the brilliant English countryside in all its colorful glory. Also, a treasured holiday was coming up at the end of October to lift my spirits. What kid, or kid at heart, doesn't like Halloween?

Our boys definitely love to dress up and go trick-or-treating. They have been superheroes, animals (both real and imaginary), a hobbit, a yard gnome (don't ask), an astronaut, Buzz Light-year, and a werewolf, to name a few. This year, we were going to go all out.

One day I asked my students what traditional costumes were in England for Halloween. Much to my chagrin, they had no idea what I was talking about.

"Is that the weird American holiday where all of you go bloody bonkers and get dressed up as scary things and nick candy from your neighbors?" one of my students timidly asked.

Not exactly how I would describe it, but accurate enough, I suppose.

I knew that the English don't celebrate American-created holidays, like the Fourth of July and Thanksgiving, but Halloween is Irish. Actually, its origins are rooted in ancient Celtic harvest festivals. Irish immigrants brought the tradition across the ocean to America, where it really flourished. While Americans embraced the chance to dress up and party, the English let the holiday slowly fade away even though it was still popular in Ireland and Scotland.

I was not sure how to tell the boys that Halloween was canceled this year. They were already talking about their costumes and how many Mars bars they might get. Mars bars were their new favorite candy bar in England. They are the English equivalent of the vaunted Milky Way bar in America. They never gave Milky Way's much consideration, but Mars bars were a different story. I guess branding is everything.

When we all got home from school, I broke the bad news to the boys. Aaron had already heard at school that Halloween did not happen in England. He was bummed but understanding. Elijah, on the other hand, was defiant. He was stubbornly determined to dress up and go out in search of free candy. I love his unquenchable little spirit.

Luckily for Elijah, Mish heard that some village folk knew about Halloween and had been giving it a try for the last few years. She wasn't sure how many homes participated in it, but we could go out and see. Mish needed to sew some costumes quickly. She is very good at improvising, and before the boys could say "trick-or-treat," she had created two adorable costumes. Free chocolate was back on the menu!

Admittedly, European chocolates are far superior to anything in America. We learned Europe has some pretty strict and time-honored laws governing chocolate. Being a discerning connoisseur of the confection, I am all for quality control of my chocolates. I do relish fine chocolate in any form now and again, and again and again.

OK, I am a not-recovering chocoholic. I'm completely accepting of my addiction. Now that our boys were trick-or-treating in England, I was really hoping they would score some of the good stuff. Usually, I have to buy my own instead of stealing theirs because they keep it under strict security hidden from dad. I was more motivated to see what they do this time.

On Halloween, we set out with a Harry Potter look-alike, a dwarf werewolf, and Albie in tow after dark to case the neighborhood. I was surprised that we did indeed run into a few other revelers out and about. Like in the United States, we found houses giving out candy with the traditional porch light left on. Probably one in every five houses was lit, so not too bad. At least Elijah was content. He merrily went scampering ahead like a moth drawn to fire.

By the time we got back home, the boys were tired and had enough candy to soothe their sweet tooth. Of course, after they went to bed, I found their stash and rummaged in the bags to take my cut for chaperoning and providing ghost security. I was not disappointed. The chocolate really is better here.

From then on, we prepared to celebrate or not celebrate traditional things when living abroad. Just visiting a foreign country is one thing, but living in one is a whole different ball game. We were in their culture. I had to remember this is one of the many reasons I wanted to move across the pond, to truly experience what it is like to be British. Some things were easy to adapt to, and others took time. We needed to stop saying, "In America..." As soon as we did, we started to fit in and enjoy ourselves more.

After Halloween, we got another cultural lesson. We decided we needed an animal fix. We love zoos, especially Elijah. Everywhere we go we find time to visit the local zoo to watch the animals. I asked around the school and discovered that there was a decent one relatively close called Woburn Safari Park. I told the family we would try it out this weekend. Elijah clapped for joy.

In America, we are very safety conscious, probably because we are sue-happy also. We love litigation, I guess. Europeans have a more "comme ci comme ça" attitude. Meaning if you're dumb enough to ignore posted warnings or lack plain common sense, then it's your own fault, deal with it.

This refreshing approach to human behavior applies to zoos, too. We were used to the animals being kept behind triple laser beam-guarded steel cages with motes in front. Our zoo designers make sure the animals cannot get out, and we cannot get in. At Woburn, a single flimsy barrier suffices. This was good and bad. Good that we got really up close and personal with the critters and bad that we had to keep Elijah from getting too close, too.

Keeping Elijah away turned out to be futile. We walked by the lemur cage and noticed that the lemurs were out sunning themselves on the railing in front of their enclosure. Immediately, Elijah's animal radar homed in on them. They had nowhere to hide. He was thrilled that he got to pet the soft lemurs. Surprisingly, the lemurs didn't seem to mind either. Before we knew it, a half-dozen miniature primates were climbing on us, seeking attention.

Eventually, their keeper came over and started to collect them so she could put them back in their cage. No big deal, just another jailbreak at the zoo. Looking for more escapees, Elijah shot off with us chasing behind. We only hoped that the tigers were more securely caged. You have to watch yourself at English zoos.

Chapter 16 – Stonehenge at Last

"I know this goes without saying, but Stonehenge really was the most incredible accomplishment. It took five hundred men just to pull each sarsen, plus a hundred more to dash around positioning the rollers. Just think about it for a minute. Can you imagine trying to talk six hundred people into helping you drag a fifty-ton stone eighteen miles across the countryside and muscle it into an upright position, and then saying, 'Right, lads! Another twenty like that, plus some lintels and maybe a couple of dozen nice bluestones from Wales, and we can party!" – Bill Bryson, Notes from a Small Island

Fall was waning quickly, and I really wanted to see one particular historical site at this specific time of year, Stonehenge. Practically everyone has seen pictures of the sacred stone circle, but not many of us have actually walked around it. The ancient Druid circle was on my long bucket list. Seeing it during the fall equinox would just add to the ethereal experience.

We had a two-week fall break coming up and decided that this would be the perfect opportunity to check it out. Since I didn't know anything about Stonehenge other than it is a very old pile of really big rocks, I decided to ask my British colleagues at school for some advice. Straight away, another science teacher offered his two pence.

"Oi, why would you want to waste your time seeing that pile of rubbish? It's just a roadside attraction some dodgy Victorian bloke dug up to take the tourists' money. Now, if you want to see genuine stone circles, then you best make for Avebury," he advised.

"Avebury? I've never heard of it," I quizzically replied.

Eager to show off his knowledge to a willing listener, my colleague then proceeded to present to me a dissertation on ancient stone circles and their monumental influence on the world. I was genuinely happy to learn but soon got lost in the dates, places, and names of history. Despite my glassy-eyed look, he lectured on and on. Luckily, the bell rang, and I politely excused myself and hurried off to class. It doesn't look good if the teacher is late, plus it gave me a quick escape. Now I know how my students feel, I thought as I scampered off to my classroom.

Around the dinner table that night, we planned our trip. We agreed to make it first for Stonehenge. Even though I was urged to pass it by, how could we come all the way to England and not see one of the most iconic structures ever built? I think that anyone in the world would recognize it straightaway. I had seen so many pictures of it in history books myself that I practically had its layout memorized. We were determined to go see it even if it truly was an old Victorian scam.

After we inspected Stonehenge to see if it lived up to the hype, we would carry on to Avebury for comparison. As usual, anything we found along the way was fair game to stop at, too. This is why we came here, to explore new things together as a family. I knew the boys would remember seeing Stonehenge for the rest of their lives, and Mish and I would remember them seeing it for the rest of our lives.

With that settled, we dug into our shepherd's pie. Mish was really getting the hang of British cooking. I know that the Brits are not world-renowned for their cuisine, but we rather liked the wholesome traditional recipes. Relatively simple to make, fairly healthy, and usually quite filling, made them a family favorite. With two growing boys and a hungry husband, there were seldom leftovers at our house.

The last week before the big break went slowly but finally ended. We packed the car, which surprisingly was still running great, and once more headed out on the motorway. Even though England is a relatively small island, it seems to take a long time to go anywhere. I think this is because I am used to American interstates where you can crisscross the country at raceway speeds. Most English motorways follow old horse-and-cart routes, so they are not very direct or straight. They make for great scenic driving but can be tedious if you are in a rush. This time, I really just wanted to get to our destination. I was very anxious to see the eighth wonder of the ancient world.

Stonehenge sits on Salisbury Plain, a huge expanse of open land about 100 miles west of London. Most of the plain consists of a large chalk plateau that is sparsely inhabited. As we drove across it, we could barely detect any signs of civilization. This only added to the suspense and mystery. You could easily imagine some mystical Druids solemnly marching across the plain on their way to rendezvous at their most sacred site for some astronomical event.

While I was fantasizing, we drove up and over a small hill, and suddenly there it was before us, Stonehenge. We simultaneously let out an audible gasp of astonishment. I truly was taken aback. I could scarcely believe my eyes as I looked at it. I don't care what my colleague said, it is an impressive sight.

To add to the dramatic effect, Stonehenge sits on a small grassy hill about one hundred meters from the road. There is nothing at all near it, not even a tree, bush, or rock. It stands like it has for over three thousand years, alone and unaccompanied by anything. It looks godforsaken as if nothing or no one is supposed to even be near it. The stark contrast of solid dark rock against bright blue sky gives it a surreal presence. It feels otherworldly, as if it was placed here by supernatural powers for some unknown purpose. To look at it is to look at one of the oldest things made by humans. It was standing tall on this plain centuries before the Great Pyramids of Egypt or the Greek Parthenon.

We parked the car on the opposite side of the motorway at the visitor center. Stonehenge is a World Heritage Site, so the visitor center is very comprehensive. We were genuinely interested in the history of the area, so we dove right in. Once again, my knowledge of European history expanded far beyond what I learned in school. I swear I can sometimes feel my brain actually grow.

I have seen several documentaries on building Stonehenge. Seeing the massive size of the standing sarsen stones, however, I quickly realized the sheer magnitude of work that went into moving them into place. Each stone is approximately a staggering twenty-five tons! How prehistoric people accomplished such a feat is bewildering. Dragging the megalithic stones from over twenty miles away and setting them upright must have been daunting enough, but capping them with more large stones defies belief. The lintel stones are thirteen feet off the ground! It is incredible, to say the least.

Looking at the site, you can see why there are many myths and legends surrounding Stonehenge. One story tells how the sorcerer Merlin moved the stones using magic from Ireland to Salisbury for Uther Pendragon, King Arthur's father. Unfortunately, the people who built Stonehenge did not leave any written record. Whatever its purpose or how it was constructed is lost to time. We can only look at it and be both amazed and puzzled.

I looked at the stones and wondered what they could have been used for. What drove prehistoric people with no modern tools, not even a wheel, to undertake such an arduous task? We do know many prehistoric people were buried here. I am not an archeologist, but I think that simple, small gravestones are sufficient for a cemetery. "Here lies Ugh, R.I.P.," with some flowers would have done nicely instead.

We left Stonehenge in awe and headed for Avebury for comparison. Avebury, according to my colleague, is reputed to be even more impressive. It is officially the largest Neolithic stone circle in all of Europe. We had trouble believing that anything could top Stonehenge now that we had seen it, but we were willing to give it a look. So, we headed across Salisbury Plain in search of more stones.

The town of Amesbury near the site of Avebury is officially credited with being the oldest continually occupied settlement in the entire UK. People have lived there from at least 8,820 BC. It must have some appeal. Even the Beatles stayed there for a few days to film a movie. Another Arthurian legend tells how Guinevere, King Arthur's bride, fled to the convent in Amesbury after leaving Arthur to repent for her sin of cheating on him with Sir Lancelot.

We found the small hamlet easily and right away saw the stones. Unlike Stonehenge, where the stones are enormous, Avebury stones are much smaller, but there are many, many more of them. There are so many stones that they encompass the whole village and a large part of the surrounding area. The entire small village is actually inside the central stone circle. You can only truly get the magnitude of the site from the air.

What makes Avebury unique is that you can walk right up to a stone and touch it. I'm sure if you crossed the rope at Stonehenge, you would be tackled by the police before you could come within arm's reach of the nearest stone. Here, we timidly placed our palms on the cold stones. Touching the ancient stones was somehow a magical experience. I know that they are just ordinary rocks, but the fact that they were carved over three millennia ago is wondrous.

We walked around touching the stones as if to make sure that they were real. I would say that we stood out as strange tourists, but looking around, we were not the only ones mesmerized by the stones. The entire area was strewn with people walking around in a trance, gawking at and touching old rocks. My colleague was right; it is more impressive.

We finally broke the spell that the ancient stones had on us and headed for a slightly more modern stonework, Salisbury Cathedral. The cathedral is very young compared to Stonehenge and Amesbury at a mere eight-centuries old. Still, it was standing tall well before Christopher Columbus set sail.

Salisbury Cathedral is impressive, if not for its age, its size. It has the tallest church spire in the United Kingdom, towering at an impressive 404 feet. Since it sits on a large, flat cathedral rose of green grass, it really stands out, and you can take in its entirety from a distance. Up close, it is even more spectacular.

I wanted to meander around the cathedral to study its architecture and walk Albie a bit. The poor dog kept being told "No!" all day for trying to relieve himself on protected stones. He and I strolled around the structure. As I looked up at the cathedral, he looked down for a place to pee. We both got satisfaction.

Mish and the boys wandered into the naïve. They found an unexpected treasure. Inside the cathedral is housed the best surviving copy of the four original Magna Carta. Latin for Great Charter, it was written in 1215 AD by the Archbishop of Canterbury as a deal between the unpopular King John and his unhappy barons. It assured the barons certain rights under law and protection from the king. This iconic document is often referenced in history books and credited with inspiring my country's Constitution. I remember reading about it in World History class in high school. Just another piece of history came to life for us.

After the cathedral, we decided to drive through Salisbury Plain and look for the famous chalk drawings. Most of the plain is covered with bright green grass. Underneath, however, it is made of white chalky limestone. Various ancient and modern people have created giant figures in the hills by cutting away the turf to reveal the white underneath, making a geoglyph.

The oldest of these artworks is the Uffington White Horse. It is an estimated three thousand years old and is 360 feet long. For centuries, local villagers have held a festival every seven years to re-scour the horse, which is why it remains today. Other giant drawings, like the Cerne Abbas Giant and the Long Man of Willmington, have been rediscovered and restored. As we drove around, we kept our eyes out for the hill figures.

Playing eye-spy was hungry work so we pulled into a pub for lunch. While we were eating a local told us about the burial mound of Merlin. Aaron and Elijah straight away locked on to the possibility that the mythical magician from King Arthur might be entombed nearby.

Finding his tomb became their quest for the Holy Grail. The gentleman informed us that legend has it that Merlin is in a grotto located on the campus of a state college in a town nearby. We knew where we were heading after lunch.

The problem was the gentleman didn't know exactly where on the campus Merlin was located. Undeterred, we headed off in search of the magician's last resting place anyway. We found Marlborough College easily enough, parked the car, and headed off on foot, ignoring the "Students and Faculty Only" signs. The boys eagerly offered suggestions as to where to look, being magician-finding experts, of course. We walked around and around but could not find anything that looked like a burial site for a legendary sorcerer.

Finally, we gave in, and I asked someone on campus where the site was. OK, I thought that this was a very simple and straightforward question. Obviously, by the look on the man's face, it wasn't. He raised an eyebrow and asked us to repeat what we were looking for, apparently to make sure he heard us correctly. He had.

I repeated the questions, trying to clarify that we had learned of Merlin's tomb from a man at a pub down the road. Once I repeated it, I realized how silly I sounded. I bit my lip and mumbled a "Never mind," and turned away. I didn't have the heart to tell the boys that we might have been the brunt of a practical joke. They looked up at me with anticipation as I came back. "Did he know where it is?" they simultaneously asked.

"He wasn't sure," I fibbed to them.

They urged me to ask someone else. What could I do? This time, I sought out a student. Maybe he could offer something that would get me out of this jam or at least find some humor in it. To my utter astonishment, he knew what I was talking about! He directed us to a large grass and shrub-covered hill called Marlborough Mound on the other side of the campus. A school myth had it that Merlin was indeed buried in a grotto at the base of the mound. Holy Grail, really?

The boys practically ran in search of the mound, with us trying to follow. Unbelievably, we found it! On the north side of the mound, we found an old stone portico inset with a tall iron gate. Behind the gate was a dark passage that led back into the mound. We peered into the darkness to see any signs of Merlin. The boys were bursting with excitement. Admittedly, so was I. Unfortunately, the gate was locked. We continued to strain our eyes in a vain attempt to spy some sign of the fabled magician.

Aaron authoritatively declared that this was the place.

"He's here alright. This is definitely a wizard's burial chamber," he proclaimed.

Elijah quickly seconded his brother's conclusion.

"Oh yeah, this is it," he confirmed.

They were completely in the moment savoring their victory at finding the site.

Whether or not Merlin is indeed buried there or if he even existed is an unimportant academic debate. Scholars can weigh in on the subject. The boys were true believers, however. No matter the authenticity of the place, they were captivated by it. It was a terrific surprise ending to a wonderful family adventure.

You never know what you will find when you're on a true adventure. Sometimes, not having an agenda or schedule can be the best thing you can do. Being flexible and making it up as you go along often yields the best memories.

Chapter 17 – Thanksgiving in England

"I am grateful for what I am and have. My thanksgiving is perpetual." – Henry David Thoreau

The school year was passing amazingly quickly. We were so busy with work and travel that some things fell off our radar. We have always been a Scouting family. Both boys started in Cub Scouts and have worked hard to earn badges and rank. We really wanted them to continue and hopefully make Eagle Scouts someday. Now that we were living in England, they were no longer in a troop.

I went to the Boy Scouts Website and found out that there was an American troop that met on the Royal Airbase at Alconbury, where there are a bunch of U.S. military personnel stationed with NATO. The base was only about forty-five minutes away, but I did not know if I could get on the military base or not. I used the contact email from the website and inquired. Within a day, someone got back to me and explained that I would be issued a guest pass for being in the troop and welcomed us onboard. What luck!

I enthusiastically informed the boys that we were back in Scouting. We were now in a new troop and could continue doing Scout stuff. This was a relief off my mind because I do full-heartedly support Boy Scouts and wanted the boys in it ever since they were born, literally. Scouting is familiar to them so going would hopefully give them a sense of home and consistency. Plus, meeting and interacting with other American boys once a week would be good for them, Mish and I thought.

Mish and I were very happy that the boys were getting to socialize and have friends. Those are important things as we grow up. We were so focused on them, however, that we forgot to take time for ourselves.

Mish and I have always, we feel, had a very special relationship. We are best friends, soul mates, and partners in life. There is no one I would rather spend time with. Having other friends and people to interact with is good, too. I spend the workweek at school with other adults to talk to, but Mish works from home and doesn't have the chance to meet people. She wanted to have friends like we did in the States.

One day, a lady from the village stopped Mish while she was walking Albie and asked her if she would like to attend Sweets in the village. Sweets is an old English village tradition where the ladies get together once a week at someone's house for a social with wine and treats and, of course, local gossip. She gratefully accepted. Once again, we lucked into things.

She also learned that the men of the village have a similar event called Ramblers. Men drink beer and eat meat and discuss politics, sports, and other manly stuff. I was game, it sounded fun. The events are purposefully scheduled on different nights so at least one parent is home to watch the kids, Sweets is on Wednesdays, and Ramblers on Thursdays. The British take their drinking very seriously and make sure it is scheduled in every week.

Mish got to go first. When Wednesday evening came around, she was very excited to meet the other village ladies. The ladies all must dress nicely so they can complement each other and show off their

109

wardrobes. Mish spent the week trying to figure out the perfect outfit. I was planning on showing up at Ramblers in my usual home lounging attire. We men do not dress to impress each other.

Wednesday evening finally came. I told Mish multiple times that she looked splendid and would fit right in. I kissed her goodbye and assured her that I had the boys under control. She always thinks that I need to be chaperoned with the boys. I had this. To the pub it was!

Since Sweets is in the village, Mish could easily walk to it. I was glad that she was going to get out. It was also some good father-and-son time. I wasn't sure how long she would be, but since it was a school night, I figured she would be home at a reasonable hour or not.

As I said, the Brits take their drinking very seriously. They grow up drinking whiskey in their baby bottles. Not quite, but darn close. In the UK, you can have wine, beer, or cider with a meal in a public place accompanied by your parents at age sixteen. At eighteen, you can drink whatever and with whomever you want. Traditionally, they actually start younger than what we learned.

We Pilgrim descendants in America look at alcohol as an evil brew that corrupts minds and leads to other debaucheries. Therefore, we sensibly raised the drinking age to twenty-one. Ironically, in America, you can drive a car and fly an airplane at sixteen. You can buy a gun, smoke, serve in the military to kill or be killed for your country, own property, get married, have a child, and vote at eighteen. But God forbid you should have a beer until twenty-one. We must keep the young ones safe. I have a hard time explaining some of our laws to people here.

The boys and I had a fine meal at the pub and played a few rounds of skittles. Looking at my watch I figured I would be a responsible father and head home to get the boys cleaned up and tucked in bed. I was expecting Mish home before the boys fell asleep and wanted to proudly show her that I was capable of being a single parent for an evening.

I got the boys in bed, but still no sign of Mish. I allowed the boys to stay up a little longer so they could see mom before bedtime. Plus, Elijah wanted another story. The evening wore on and I ran out of books, but no wife in sight yet. I started to get a little worried, but rationalized that the social was in the village so she wasn't driving anywhere. It wasn't a very big village to get lost in either. The clock hands moved closer to midnight.

I was just starting to nod off when finally I heard keys going into the front door. I waited but kept hearing the keys clanging about. Puzzled, I got up from the couch and went to see who was messing with the front door lock. I opened the door, not knowing what to expect. To my surprise, Mish was standing there still holding her keys, looking a little puzzled. She saw me and smiled brightly.

"Are you OK?" I asked curiously.

She just smiled and stepped past me to go inside. That's when she stumbled on the threshold, and I had to catch her. Immediately, I realized that my lovely, steadfast wife was a wee tipsy. I'm not sure if I was more shocked or amused.

I asked her again if she was alright and got a single "Uh-huh" in response. Since she wasn't up for talking and I was tired and had to go to work in a few hours, I decided to call it a night. Mish apparently had a good time and was now home safe, if not a little intoxicated. I hoped that my turn at Ramblers the next evening would go as well.

The next morning, Aaron and I headed to school as usual. I left Mish asleep in bed as I quietly closed the door. On the short drive, Aaron asked me what we were doing for Thanksgiving. Thanksgiving! I had completely forgotten about the most quintessential American holiday. Back home we would have been berated for weeks with reminders everywhere. Since only America celebrates Thanksgiving, and Canada but on a different day, there were no advertisements on the telly or sales at the grocery store on turkey and trimmings. Leave it to a perpetually hungry growing young boy who thinks with his stomach to remind me of Thanksgiving.

I asked around school where the best place to get a turkey was. Surprisingly, most people I talked to had never even eaten turkey before. These poor British souls deprived of the taste of succulent roasted turkey meat with stuffing and cranberry sauce. They had no idea what they were missing.

That night, I reminded Mish that we had some shopping to do. While she pondered how to procure traditional Thanksgiving dinner items, I got ready for Ramblers. I decided that maybe I should represent America a little better and wore decent slacks, a button shirt, and a sweater for good measure. I planned to drink less than my wife did the night before and be home earlier; after all, I still had to teach the next day.

Mish gave me a goodbye kiss and wished me luck as I headed out across the village. I love the crisp, cold air of an autumn night. It is invigorating. The stars were bright in a cloudless sky. I could smell the chimney smoke from home fires in the village. It definitely felt like Thanksgiving despite being in England. This time of year always perks me up for some reason. Maybe it is the pending holiday season with fond memories or just the sense of change, either way, I love walking under a fall sky in the evening.

I found the house down a short lane at the edge of the village. By the bright lights and raucous laughter, I surmised the social had already started. I walked up to the front door and rang the bell. Almost immediately, an older portly gentleman loudly but warmly greeted me and ushered me inside. He put a large hand on my shoulder.

"The American is here!" he bellowed to the crowd.

Straightaway, someone thrust a pint in my hand, and the drinking began.

I was waiting for the day that I had a proper name and would no longer be called "The American." No matter, the beer was smooth and plentiful, so conversation flowed easily. It was a blur of names and faces. I was asked where in The States I was from and what brought me to England. No one had ever been to Seattle, so they had some questions about exactly where it was. Most had been, or wanted to go, to New York. Why do we West Coasters play second fiddle to the Northeast?

One gentleman obviously tried to rile me by continually referring to America as "The Colonies" and me as a "Yank." Another one referred to Thanksgiving as "that American holiday where they eat and eat to get fatter." I bit my lip. This type of dry and caustic humor is annoying and, unfortunately, too common among a certain older generation of English. They mean it in jest, sort of. They are the ones who still faithfully cling on to the glory days of the British Empire and the superiority of everything British. It is vexing, but I learned by now to not get annoyed and let it go. I was not here to enlighten them or defend my country's honor.

Despite one overly nationalistic muppet, as the British would say, I was having a splendid time. I'll admit I am a lightweight. I do not drink that much and only have a glass or two of Guinness or red wine at home. Plus, the alcohol content in Europe is higher than in America, and the pints are larger, too. In a short time, I was feeling the effects of my third pint of English ale.

By the time I finished my pint, I was yawning and ready to head home. Unbelievably, everyone else was still going strong with no signs of leaving any time. No sooner than I downed my last swig from my glass, someone came along, slapped me on the back,

"Let me refill that for you, mate," he generously offered.

I tried to turn him down, but he grabbed my glass and disappeared into the crowd as he went off to find a keg.

I gingerly asked the bloke I was talking to how many pints he had drank.

"I don't know, mate. I guess I'm on my sixth or seventh. Who keeps track," he replied.

What! These people drink like fish. Their poor livers must be in overdrive. The National Healthcare Service must be swamped with organ requests. By the time my anonymous beer keep came back with a fresh pint for me, I was making my excuses to leave. I got several, "It's still early, mate," and "Come on, one last pint for the road!" I raised the white surrender flag and bid a hasty retreat for the door. Britain 2, America 0.

The cold air helped me sober up on the walk home. It was almost midnight, and I needed to be up in a few short hours to teach. I now could understand the initiation that Mish went through at Sweets. I was greeted at the front door by her empathetic smile and wink. I climbed into bed, not knowing if I could handle that much English socializing once a week.

The following morning was a little rough, Albeit. Luckily, it was Friday and I just had to make it through the last day of the week. My colleagues just chuckled when I told them where I had been last night.

"How else did you think we make it through the awful English weather here?" a friend asked me. Good point, I concurred.

Saturday, we decided to go shopping for Thanksgiving dinner. We were determined to put together a traditional meal. After numerous markets, grocery stores, and butcher shops, we still came up empty-handed. The boys were looking more and more famished with each strike-out. They were practically starved-looking when we walked out of the last store in defeat.

We might not have a turkey, but we were still determined to celebrate Thanksgiving. We decided to create a new family tradition on the spot. I asked everyone what their favorite food was. After throwing out cheeseburgers and pizza, we all agreed on seafood. Coming from the Pacific Northwest, we eat a lot of salmon.

We walked over to the local fishmonger and picked out a buffet of fresh seafood. We got clams, oysters, shrimp, crab legs, and, of course, salmon. The boys started to drool. We were going to have a wonderful Thanksgiving after all.

That Thursday, we all pitched in to prepare a grand neo-traditional Thanksgiving feast. Since Thanksgiving is always on a Thursday, I had a convenient excuse for missing Ramblers. Mish still went to Sweets, though she fared better this time.

Thanksgiving was very memorable that year. We had an amazing time and gave thanks for all the blessings bestowed on us: a wonderful home, new friends, and a healthy, happy family. We could ask for nothing more. Being thankful for the little things in life because they actually make a big difference is the key to happiness. Life is good.

Chapter 18 – A Charles Dickens Christmas

"For it is good to be children sometimes, and never better than at Christmas, when its mighty Founder was a child Himself." — Charles Dickens, A Christmas Carol

The holiday season was building to the big finale. Halloween was a smash. Thanksgiving was a gourmet success. Christmas was now drawing near. At least this holiday was celebrated in England. Europeans do go all out for it, too.

We love Christmas. I think most American do, too. I'll be honest, though. Christmas in America has become very commercialized. I know that the corporate takeover of Christmas has been going on for a long time. Stores start putting out Christmas decorations before Halloween now. Soon, we will be able to buy Fourth of July sparklers and Christmas ornaments on the same day.

We are urged to spend, spend, and spend. Even the beloved classic Rudolph the Red-nosed Reindeer was created by the Montgomery Ward Department Store ad department in 1939 to sell more toys. Even St. Nicholas got a huge makeover by the Coca-Cola Company in 1931 to mirror their soda cans. They are responsible for the image of Santa as a big, jolly old man in a bright red and white suit. I almost wish I never knew the truth.

Christmas in Europe is a very welcome and different experience. The closest I can probably describe it is like being in a live Charles Dickens' Christmas Carol. In England, Santa does not shamelessly wear a corporate logo for a suit to promote a product and his sled is not led by a caribou with a genetic anomaly for a nose and huge self-esteem issues. There are no 4th of July Christmas sales either. You are not expected to go into a credit card frenzy debt and mortgage your house or sell a kidney to buy gifts. Amazingly, Christmas here is to be enjoyed with family and friends and reflect on the meaning of the holiday.

We did not even see any tell-tale signs of Christmas until December. Then, almost overnight, villages and towns were transformed into something magical. If you can imagine our quaint stone village with its two small churches, pubs, horse stable, and park decorated in white lights, green garland, red bows, and shiny brass bells everywhere. There were no cheap plastic lawn ornaments or gaudy one-upmanship light displays. It was simple and elegant. I don't think I had ever seen a more beautiful display of the holiday.

The second week of December brought a special and rare treat to the Midlands, snow. We thought Middleton looked fabulous before in its Christmas regalia, but now it was a winter wonderland all draped in glistening white. We marveled at the transformation. As the snow came slowly down, I had a brief image of being in a giant snow globe.

At Aaron and Elijah's school, they were preparing for the annual Christmas pageant and concert. Mish and I remarked how the school called it a Christmas concert and not a Holiday or Winter concert. In the United States, such use of a religious term at a public school would have brought protests, lawsuits, and media coverage. Admittedly, we are not overly religious, but found the lack of political correctness refreshing. Call it what it is, Christmas.

More astonishingly, our village staged a living nativity Christmas Eve. Villagers volunteered to play characters from the Biblical account of the birth of Jesus. They started on the outskirts of the village, where Joseph walked alongside Mary on a real donkey, followed by a processional of Wise Men on horses, carolers with candles, and the local pastor on foot carrying a large cross. Slowly through the dark streets, they walked as the carolers sang traditional hymns. On both sides, people stood in the cold and joyfully watched the small parade. After it passed, we all fell in behind and walked with them to the stable.

At the stable, a rustic wooden cradle was ringed by some farm animals. We gathered around and peered in as the actors recreated the birth of our Savior. Someone passed out small candles that we lit while we sang O Holy Night. Whether you were Christian or not was irrelevant. The whole experience was deeply moving.

The fact that an obvious religious event could take place on public streets without anyone complaining was astonishing to us in a good way. Even more astonishing is that only 20% of UK Christians attend church, compared to 48% in the US. Every village has at least two churches, one Catholic and one Protestant. Yet, they are largely empty come Sunday. Many clergymen rotate among three to five different village churches because they do not have enough of a single congregation at each to service all of them. I pondered this religious tolerance. Do we Americans just like to complain, or do we go overboard to ensure that no one is ever offended?

The service ended and we all thanked the participants as we headed back to our homes to warm up and enjoy the final hours of Christmas Eve. We lit a small fire and enjoyed some hot chocolate next to our Christmas tree.

I thought that we didn't bring over any Christmas decorations, but Mish triumphantly pulled out a small box of precious ornaments and our stockings. Once again, she saved the day. Leave it to a mother to think of such small details. We didn't have enough for the whole tree, so we had to improvise. After we had gotten the tree, we sat at the dining room table and made ornaments from scratch. None of us are particularly artistic or craft-talented, but we enjoyed making them anyway. The boys made old-fashioned cut-out snowflakes, Mish made paper chains, and I drew and cut-out cardboard angels. When we were all done, we looked at our tree with pride, it was perfect.

Now, on Christmas Eve, we sipped from our mugs and admired our handiwork. We truly felt blessed. Without all the expensive décor or mountainous piles of presents, it was still Christmas.

We had an extended holiday break, too, which meant we had time to do some more exploring. To date, we had only traveled in England. We all agreed it was time to cross the channel to the mainland. France, here we come!

The day after Christmas, we packed the family wagon for its longest journey so far. We drove to the port city of Dover on the English Channel, where we could catch the train that would take us under it. The famous Channel Tunnel is often abridged to the "Chunnel" by Europeans. You can drive your car onto a Eurotunnel Shuttle rail car, which will then dive deep under the sea floor for thirty-four miles at speeds of 99 mph. This makes it the longest undersea tunnel in the world. Once aboard the shuttle, you can get out of your car and stretch your legs. There are even loos if you need one. The whole journey from Folkestone, England, to Calais, France, takes just thirty-five minutes.

We stayed the night in Dover at a very unusual B&B. It was the only one available, so Mish booked it for us. The nice older lady showed us to our room when we arrived. She opened the door to reveal a large single room cluttered with an eclectic mix of old and new brightly colored furniture. Everywhere were books, knickknacks, lamps, and other odd paraphernalia. There was a dining area, living room area, kitchen area, study area, and bedroom area, but all in one open space. Luckily, the bathroom was down the hallway and not in the open, too.

Aaron and Elijah, being very inquisitive right away, loved it. They spent the night exploring the oddities and looking through the books. I was too tired to care and was glad that the boys were quietly occupied. Mish and I fell asleep and let them go at it.

The next morning, we headed over to Folkestone to catch a train. The system is pretty straightforward. Huge signs directed us to the France-bound train side, and we drove into line. As we were sitting waiting for our turn to go through the toll booth, two uniformed police officers came walking down the line towards our car. Mildly curious, I watched as they approached.

To our surprise, they stopped at our car and looked at the license plate. One officer came up to my side, knocked on the window, and asked to speak with me. Alarmed, I quickly obliged and rolled down my window.

"What is the matter, officer?" I cautiously inquired.

"Sir, do you realize that you have an unpaid parking ticket from the UK?" he replied politely.

I was taken aback, not knowing if it was a question or accusation.

"No," I lied.

"Well, you do, sir. It's from the city of Nottingham," he stated matter-of-factly.

Busted!

"How do you know that?" I inquired incredulously.

"Our cameras automatically pick up your plate, and the computer runs a routine check on all vehicles leaving the UK," he explained.

Wow, talk about efficiency! They really want to make sure that you don't stiff them before you leave the country.

"What should I do?" I helplessly asked.

"Since you are a UK resident just going on holiday, please pay the fine upon your return," he told me.

I breathed a huge sigh of relief.

"Of course I will, officer. Thank you," I promised.

Big Brother is definitely watching in the UK. It's a good thing that the speeding ticket didn't come up, too.

They have traffic cameras everywhere. Sometimes, you know that you have been caught when you see the bright white flash of the camera as you go zipping by one. Other times, you only know when you get an unexpected letter in the mail accompanied by a picture of you committing an infraction. I love the question they ask in the letter, "Is this you?" I wanted to be snarky and send back, "No, it was not, it was my evil twin," just to see what would happen. Mish talked me out of it for my own good. Bailing me out of an English jail probably would not be an experience she wants.

Thankfully, they let us continue on our way and board the train. We had no further incident and arrived in France ready to explore. The French sensibly have huge signs as you drive off the train, reminding you that you are now driving on the right side of the road. I wondered how big a problem Brits were coming over and having a head-on collision. I was glad to be back driving on the right side until I realized that our car's steering wheel was on the wrong side now. I felt like a mailman back in the United States.

I managed to adapt, but it still felt weird driving from the outside of the lane. Left-hand turns were a little nerve-wracking. With Mish navigating, I somehow managed to get us to our hotel in Caen.

For this first adventure into France, we decided to stay along the northern French coast in the province of Normandy. Normandy holds a particular interest to me as a former Navy man. This is the site of the legendary D-Day landings, where on June 6, 1944, 4,414 Allied soldiers gave their lives to establish a foothold in Nazi-occupied France. Their sacrifice enabled Allied forces to begin the long and fierce push to Berlin and the end of World War II in Europe.

I have read many accounts of that fateful day. I know much of the details surrounding Operation Overlord and the invasion of the infamous five beaches: Utah, Juno, Sword, Gold, and Omaha. All my life I have wanted to see the landing sites and walk those beaches. As we drove, I told the boys about the invasion and the heroism of the men who fought here.

We arrived in Caen and checked into our hotel. The rooms were very small, so we got one for Mish and I and one for the boys. Having a little privacy is sometimes nice. The day was still early and we were all anxious to see the area. I wanted to go to the D-Day Museum first so that we all had an appreciation for what we would see along the coast.

There are several museums dedicated to D-Day and World War II. I recommended the one at Utah Beach, partly because it was the biggest and partly because Utah and Omaha beaches were where my compatriots landed. I wanted to see it for myself.

The museum was unbelievably moving. It really prepared us for going to the beaches. As we walked around, I explained to the boys how the events of June 6th unfolded. They were very captivated by the stories of the soldiers who stormed the beaches, climbed the cliffs, and parachuted against overwhelming odds into enemy fire. According to the museum, the odds of surviving D-Day were 1 in 4. Not numbers I would want to stake my life on.

The next morning, we drove out to the beaches. The largest and most heavily defended beach was code-named Omaha. The daunting task of securing this beach fell to the United States. The main landing force was made primarily of American soldiers from the 1st and 29 Army Infantry Divisions. They landed at precisely 6:30 am on Omaha beach, preceded by heavy naval bombardment. They suffered 2,400 casualties. Consequently, the beach has been forever nicknamed "Bloody Omaha."

Walking along Omaha Beach was a powerful and eerie experience. As we walked along the sand we got a full appreciation for the enormity of the task of those soldiers. First, the beach is extremely wide and they unluckily landed at low tide. Second, there is absolutely no cover at all. We imagined the brave soldiers jumping from the somewhat protection of their amphibious landing craft and making a mad run across the open terrain to the bottom of the bluffs, where machinegun-wielding German soldiers waited. To me, it looked like pure insanity, but it needed to be done. Their heroism that morning cannot be overestimated.

After the beach we headed for the Allied cemetery nearby in Colleville-sur-Mer. The site of all those white marble crosses in unending rows on a field of green grass took us over the top. The full measure of the loss of life was bluntly displayed. Numbers on paper can be meaningless, but seeing the graves laid out before you makes those same numbers very real. As we walked among the headstones, we read the names inscribed on them. Occasionally, we came across one without a name, but instead simply read "Unbeknownst Except to God." We could not help but wonder who was buried there, his name a mystery. Did he have family who wondered what had happened to him? Was he forgotten by all? We truly wept as we walked.

Happy and sad, this is why we came here, to experience things that most people only read about in books. Mish and I know that these experiences will help shape our boys and enrich their development. Hopefully, one day, they will look back and appreciate them.

We cherished our time honoring the soldiers from D-Day, but now it was time to seek out a cheerier experience for all of us. Next on our bucket list was Mont Saint Michel. The island monastery is another UNESCO World Heritage Site and as recognizably French as the Eifel Tower or Notre Dame. It is just a short drive west near Avranches so we decided to head out to it.

The island can only be reached by a half-mile causeway at low tide. During high tide, it is completely inaccessible except by boat. Fortunately, we arrived at the beginning of a low tide. This would give us a few hours to tour the island before we were trapped. I was more worried about our car floating away because the parking lot would be underwater. The difference between low and high tides can be up to forty-six feet. Hopefully, someone would sound a signal to let everyone know the tide was changing.

The citadel is impressive. It has been standing since the 12th century and endured sieges, fires, modifications, storms. Today, it is an actual working commune of monks who support the abbey through tourism. There are 50 shops and restaurants, along with a few hotels on the island. Aaron and Elijah loved the maze of streets that wind their way up to the abbey. Along the way, they stopped in every sword shop they could find, which were many.

By the time we climbed to the top of the monastery we were getting very cold. December on an island in the English Channel is a tad nippy. The only one who seemed not to mind was Albie. After visiting the abbey, we walked back down to find some warm food and drink and get out of the cold air. We found a quaint-looking crêpe cafe, of course, in France, with seductive aromas wafting out of it.

We were afraid that poor Albie would have to wait outside. Mish and I were about to flip a coin to see who got to dog-sit outside in the cold when the waiter came out. "Entrez s'il vous plait," he said. We pointed to Albie. "Le chien n'est pas un problem," he assured us. We gratefully all went inside to enjoy a wonderful, warm snack. Albie loved sitting under our table with his family, too.

We beat the tide and made it back to our hotel. We almost forgot that tonight was New Year's Eve. How cool? Christmas in England and

New Year's in France. The boys went to their room, and we went to ours. The bathroom, like many hotels in Europe, is communally located at the end of the hall. Mish and I took turns and finally settled in bed to await the new year.

I was dozing off when I heard a soft knock at the door. I opened it to find Aaron and Elijah in their pajamas, looking sadly up at me. "What's the matter," I asked. "We went to the bathroom and locked ourselves out of our room," they moaned.

I went down to the front desk to get an extra key, but no one was there. The hotel staff had taken off to celebrate. Since there was nothing I could do, we all piled into our small room and counted down to midnight together. Maybe that was their plan all along.

Our first excursion into France had proven amazing. We learned a lot of history, ate some great French cuisine, and got some more family bonding time. All in all, it was a very memorable Christmas.

Life is not about material stuff. It is about experiences. The greatest gifts we have given our children are ones you cannot buy in a store but ones you can share together doing things. Long after they are grown up, they will remember where we have been and what we have done far more readily than what they have owned.

Chapter 19 - An Unusual English Winter

"There is a tide in the affairs of men, which taken at the flood, leads on to fortune. Omitted, all the voyage of their life is bound in shallows and in miseries. On such a full sea are we now afloat. And we must take the current when it serves, or lose our ventures." – William Shakespeare

Our trip back to Middleton was uneventful. The Christmas break was coming to a close, and school was just a few days away. We felt relaxed and renewed, ready to take on the new year. I found it hard to believe that we were settled in England and life had assumed a new normal.

I was getting so familiar with the roads, the main motorways anyway, that I seldom needed the help of my trusty navigator to get around, although that didn't stop her from sometimes giving input anyway. Teaching here was getting to be like teaching anywhere, mostly. I was figuring out the British system and preparing my students as best I could for their pending exams. The boys were progressing in school and Scouts. They had made friends and were into a routine. Mish was still keeping a horrid schedule because of the time difference between Washington State and England, but she was juggling it fairly well. All in all, life was going well.

We felt at home and even called our little village home. This is the big difference between visiting other countries and living in them. We were now completely immersed in the English culture. Our friends and neighbors were even no longer referring to us as "The Americans." We had real names again.

The days were getting shorter and shorter, and the temperature was dropping lower and lower. Soon it passed cold and went to outright frigid. England was having the worst winter in a half-century, not that we knew the difference. One morning, we woke up to find a foot of snow blanketing the village, which is a lot for this part of the country. We were used to it, so it didn't bother us, or at least the boys and me. My southern bell wife went into indoor hibernation until spring.

My eBay purchase was about to show its true value. Our family wagon had four-wheel drive with all-terrain tires and, therefore, handled well on the icy roads. What it lacked in aesthetics, it now made up for in ruggedness. Unfortunately, the rest of the country was not as well equipped or experienced on winter roads. Driving became an obstacle course where I had to dodge stuck cars, idiots driving too fast, snow drifts, and people sledding on the road.

Apparently, most English rarely, if ever, go sledding, or sledging as they call it here. I had grown up sledding, skiing, playing ice hockey, making snowballs and snow forts, and all other winter childhood activities. Mish, on the other hand, being from a warmer climate, did not have the experience of playing in the snow, along with having cold & wet socks, frost-bitten fingers, and a red, runny nose for half the year. She also never felt the joy of shoveling a driveway before school or carrying in firewood after school. I felt sorry for her.

This was our very first winter in England and I was very excited to re-experience a huge part of my childhood again. I couldn't wait to instruct the boys in all things wintery. We took them to the village park, where there was a steep hill covered in slick white snow just waiting for sledgers. I made two makeshift sledges out of some plastic bin tops, a perfect size for Aaron and Elijah.

We were not the only ones with this idea, however. People from all over the village and beyond had discovered our not-so-secret hill. There were people of all ages out enjoying this rare opportunity. Everyone was having a splendid time sledging, throwing snowballs, building snowmen, and even making snow angels. A little bit of snow turns everyone into a kid again.

Seeing as I was an old pro at all this, I instructed the boys on the proper way to fly down a hill on a sledge. Elijah looked a little intimidated and didn't mind letting his big brother go first this time. Aaron was keen to give it a go. I placed him on his home-made sledge, told him to hold on, and gave a big push. That's when I suddenly realized I might have over-done it.

Aaron shot down the hill like an Olympic bobsledder. All I saw was the back of his head above a rooster tail of white snow speeding down range. I yelled after him to break, but he just kept going. I frantically tore down the hill after him.

I watched in fear as he reached the bottom of the hill, sped across the valley, plowed over some poor, unsuspecting guy, and came to an abrupt stop in a bush. As I ran up to him, he was picking himself up and dusting a bunch of snow off his clothes. He was a little shaken but had a huge grin on his round, freckled face. I breathed a deep sigh of relief. I could feel Mish's disapproving eyes burning into me from the top of the hill. Elijah, now completely terrified, would not get on his sledge. Bright lad.

With that near accident behind us, we decided to go home and try other, safer winter activities. The boys went in the backyard and built a snow-knight. They took a shield, sword, and helmet they got at Warwick Castle and adorned their knight in his armor. They were very proud of him. Albie got into the action, too, and ran around the yard chasing snowballs I tossed at him. How he thought he was going to find a specific piece of snow from all the other snow, I had no idea, but he desperately tried. He would come up for air from digging completely covered in a white snow bear stuck to his fur.

Unfortunately, the snow didn't last long. Within a couple of weeks, it disappeared almost as quickly as it came. The boys' snow knight got down-graded to a squire and then to just a slushy pile with his armor and sword remaining. I will admit I like the snow, but I like it even better if it doesn't last long. We wanted to get back out and explore more of England and Mish would only emerge from her cave if the streets were snow-free.

We checked our must-see list and selected a spot. We decided that we could not come all the way to England without paying homage to one of its greatest sons. The home and theater of the legendary king of the bards, Shakespeare, was not too far away. Who hasn't read, willing or otherwise, such staples of high school English class as Romeo and Juliet, Hamlet, or Macbeth? I am definitely not into tragedies and admittedly bought the cliff notes to pass English Literature, but I do recognize his greatness and substantial contributions to the literary world. It would be another amazing history lesson. Besides, the boys could brag to their friends back in Washington that they were in the guy's house.

Off we went on another Saturday morning on a family adventure. Stratford Upon Avon is an old medieval market town in the West Midlands about ninety miles northwest of London. William Shakespeare was born there in April of 1564, the exact day is unknown. It is also home to the Royal Shakespeare Theatre. This is not the famous Globe Theater, which many of us learned about in school while studying Shakespeare. A recreation of that theater is on the south bank of the Thames River in London. The original Globe burned down just fourteen years after it was built in 1599. The current one wasn't built until 1997, four centuries and seven hundred and fifty feet off the exact mark. The Brits don't advertise that to the unknowing tourists.

We strolled the town looking for Shakespeare's birthplace, which was very easy to find, with signs everywhere directing us to it. The small Tudor farmhouse on Henley Street is original and believed by historians to be the actual place where the bard was born and raised. We took a guided tour of the home to learn something more about the man who is widely considered the greatest writer in the English language.

On the tour, I could not help but ask some serious questions. Honestly, I was not purposefully trying to be difficult. I was genuinely curious. I had learned somewhere that William Shakespeare might have been the pen name of another writer, maybe even a woman.

So, I asked a question about Shakespeare's real identity to the tour guide. The stately gentleman turned to me as if I had insulted all of England. He looked at me sternly over his glasses with English pride in his eyes and staunchly assured me that any such rumors were rubbish and mere fabrications by dolts. OK, I was schooled. Now I know.

I kept quiet the rest of the tour. We left the home and went in search of more Shakespearean artifacts. The small hamlet is very pretty. I noticed more of the long canal boats on the River Avon as we walked along the water. Some were turned into floating mercantile and art studios. We took the opportunity to finally climb aboard one. Inside, they are amazingly roomy, much like an RV but on water. I could totally see us taking one on an extended excursion through the country and stopping at villages and towns along the way.

We went walking through a beautiful little park and found a small art studio in the middle of it. Inside, a local artist was teaching people how to do rubbings. He told us that rubbings were a very old art form common to Shakespeare's time. We looked around at the walls covered with brass plates with raised etchings. Some were simple designs; others were pretty country scenes, famous people, various animals, castles with knights, and even a dragon. The artist instructed everyone to pick a plate. We each eagerly chose one and waited for instructions. He showed us how to scour the plate with a copper stylus and then place a piece of black paper over it. We then firmly rubbed the paper with our hands. When we lifted the paper, the image was left on it. Magic! It was great fun and we all walked away with our own piece of personal artwork as a souvenir.

Since creating art is hungry work, we found the usual village pub and enjoyed a good meal. While we ate, Mish and I chatted about our time here, and the boys quietly devoured their meals. We remarked how amazed we were that as we traveled, much of the history that we learned about in school, which didn't really make much sense to us then, was coming alive here. I actually feel that I could talk somewhat intelligently about European history, art, and literature now. Mish and I knew that boys were getting an incredible education.

Tired out, we headed back to our small home in the village. The snow had all melted, which meant we could resume our daily walks. We love to take evening walks as a family. It gives us time to share our day, discuss whatever is on our minds, and get a little exercise and fresh air. Middleton is an ideal place to do just that.

We really have come to love our little village. We have walked through all its streets and surrounding area. One of our favorite walks is through the adjacent county park. To access it we turn into a break in a tall stone wall, go down a narrow ivy-covered lane, and through an old wooden fence. It is almost like having a secret entrance to a magical world.

The boys usually run up ahead because on the other side of the gate are horses, which is why we always bring carrots or apples on our daily walks. Mish and the boys delight in feeding them every time. Further down the path in a large pasture are cows. For some inexplicable reason, they are infatuated with little Albie.

As soon as they see him, they come running from the four corners of their enclosure and gather around him, mooing. Of course, Albie thinks this is great fun. He has a herd of large bovines coming to his beck and call to pay homage to their lord and master.

The only thing we can think of is that they are trained to obey the shepherd dogs. Looking at our plump fur ball, I failed to see any resemblance to a working canine.

Down the path, a way is a coral of Shetland ponies. We know that these miniature horses have a nasty reputation for being ornery, but as soon as they see Mish and the boys coming around the corner with treats, they become perfect little four-hoofed angels. Albeit, they do start to aggressively push and shove each other to get their fair share of carrots. A plump pony rounder than the rest always tries asserting his large girth and gets more than his share. Mish has to tease the bully with a carrot while Elijah goes down the line, feeding the other ones. He ensures that all the ponies get equal portions.

Today, we decided to walk a little further than usual since we have been house bound by snow. We took a long-cut through a fence and along the edge of another pasture. We learned from our neighbor that a still-standing old English law permits travelers to cross private property as long as they stay along the perimeter of the fields. We took advantage of this and set off across the countryside.

We were passing through a neatly trimmed pasture when we became surrounded by sheep. They were searching for a handout, too. They must have heard from the horses across the way that we had carrots.

Unfortunately for them, we were all out. They were gentle but insistent that we must have something. They nudged and sniffed us all over in hope of finding a treat. Two little lambs tried their best to get in on the action. Elijah knelt to pet them and was knocked over onto his back.

Before he could get up, one of the little guys jumped onto his chest and laid down. Elijah wasn't hurt, just surprised that he had become a mattress. Both were content to stay there for a while, but we wanted Elijah off the cold ground. The lamb was not happy that he lost his warm soft bed and let out a loud "baa" in protest.

We escaped the sheep obstacle and continued our walk. The next challenge was the cow gauntlet. We attempted to cross into a neighboring field but were blocked by curious cows that wanted to know what we were up to and if Albie was here to herd them. We valiantly tried to break through their defense but fell back to regroup.

We formulated a new strategy that involved a lot of shooing and arm waving. The cows were not deterred and just blankly stared at us with their big brown, not-understanding eyes. Defeated, we took another route.

After wading through a sea of yellow mustard weed and traversing a muddy bog, we made it back home. We were famished. Mish made us another one of our favorite meals, steak and ale pie. Practically any dish with Guinness in it is good in my book.

After warm showers to get the mud and farm animal smell off us, we sat down to a hot meal in our little stone house as the light outside faded to darkness. We were as cozy as five little lambs in a manger.

Shakespeare was right. When opportunity calls, you need to take it or forever resign yourself to a stagnant, dull life. Not for the first time, Mish and I agreed that we are eternally grateful for seizing this opportunity to come to England. We dared to take the risk and were now rewarded for the choice.

These past six months in England have been a family adventure that will last in our memories and shape our lives for all time. We cannot imagine now not doing this.

Chapter 20 – The Best Place to Get Italian Food

"The Creator made Italy by designs from Michelangelo." – Mark Twain

Spring break was upon us which meant time for another family adventure. We all agreed this time we would go to Italy. With warm weather, great food, and numerous historic places to see, it was the ideal holiday destination.

Mish had a particular interest in going to Italy because she had been there as a young girl. She was very interested to see how well she remembered it. The boys and I were interested in Italian cuisine more than anything else. I think it is universally agreed that Italians are the best cooks in the world. So, we logically concluded that there would be many incredible restaurants on our trip. Our strategy was to eat our way across the country.

We planned this to be our biggest excursion on mainland Europe thus far. We would fly into Trieste in northern Italy on the Adriatic Sea, take the Eurail to Venice, then to Florence, and finally end up in Rome, where we would fly back to England in ten days. Poor Albie would have to stay behind this time with the dog sitter. He would never know the table scraps he missed.

This would also be our first time flying on the infamous Ryan Air. This ultra-low-budget Dublin-based airline flies all over Europe. The company operates their fleet of Boeing 737s like flying buses. They make regular daily runs from smaller airports in Europe and even allow you to purchase tickets at the gate right before boarding. Do not expect any comforts or amenities, though. The seats are plastic with not cushions, seriously, and no fold-down tray tables or front pockets. Their planes are equipped with the bare minimum allowed by regulations and not one free thin blanket or dollhouse-sized pillow about them.

Ryan Air also charges extra for everything, and we mean everything. All baggage is an extra charge. Picking your own seat is an extra charge. A glass of water will cost you two Euros in flight. They even tried to charge passengers for using the toilet in flight until the European Aviation Board put a stop to the practice.

On one half-full flight, the stewardess made all of us move to the middle of the plane and pack in with no empty seats in between us to better balance the plane for optimizing fuel economy.

Despite all the potential fees, if you are traveling on a budget, then it is the cheapest way to go. We bought tickets to fly from London Gatwick to Trieste for less than €45 a person. Many times, if a plane is not full, Ryan Air will let last-minute passengers fly for free just to fill the plane. You just need to pay the obligatory tax on the complimentary ticket. Be advised, however, they are notorious for late arrivals. Passengers actually clap upon landing on time on their flights.

We didn't mind the sparseness too much. It is a trade-off for flying with a family on a budget. The boys did miss the all-you-can-drink ginger ale and unlimited movies, however. I was glad that they fly newer 737s, made in our home state, so I knew at least they were safe, if not comfortable.

Flying into Trieste was smooth and easy. Ryan Air came through and got us there with no issues. Trieste is not on the tourist map for most vacationers, but it should be. It is a beautiful, picturesque small city on the rugged Adriatic coast. It is authentically Italian. Since the city is not a tourist destination they do not cater to visitors. We found this out when we went to get something to eat.

Traditionally, Italians do not eat supper until after 7:00 PM or much later. Lunch is strictly from 1:00 to 3:00 PM. Most restaurants and cafes are closed between the two meals and, except in large cities like Rome, fast-food and quickie-marts are non-existent. We landed at 4:00 PM. Therefore, we were out of luck and hungry.

We were all starving. The boys, who are always looking to their next meal, were not happy little campers. We tried to make the best of it and walk around to see the sights and forget about our hunger. It really didn't work, but we had no choice. The hours to dinner wore on and on and on. Finally, the clock tower in the city square chimed seven. We dove into the first restaurant that opened.

Not surprisingly, we were the first customers. The very nice host sat us at a table and immediately brought out bread and wine. We don't speak Italian, and he didn't speak English, but that did not seem to hamper him. This was a traditional small mom-and-pop establishment, which meant there wasn't a menu; you were eating whatever they were cooking.

A traditional Italian supper, or cena, consists of ten courses. We started with the aperitivo, which is like an appetizer except you must have wine and you only eat small snacks, like bread with a plate of olive oil or melted cheese to dip it in.

Mish and I sampled the house wine, and we all hungrily gobbled down the bread. I think that the host was not expecting such famished patrons, but he did bring out more bread, thankfully.

The next course is the antipasto. There is no equivalent to this dish in America. It is like a second appetizer or warm-up to the main course. Our plate consisted of cold meats, like salami and prosciutto, sliced cheeses, and more bread. We devoured all of it, too.

After a short break to digest the antipasto, the host brought the primo, or first course. He set down huge plates of pasta smothered in a rich tomato sauce. We all started to salivate a little. The boys love all noodles and dove in. I was afraid to get my fingers too close to them. We didn't talk much except for occasional grunts and moans of approval.

We cleaned our plates and sat back, feeling much better. We sat drinking more wine and listening to the other customers that were now trickling in. Not that we understood what they were saying, but the Italian language is really beautiful sounding. Shortly after, the host brought the second course or secondi. These plates were loaded with baked fish and grilled marinated steak. The boys' eyes grew wide and clearly showed, "There's more!"

Along with the secondi came the contorno. This was a separate side dish of buttered mixed vegetables. We sat back up and started eating once more. The entrees were delicious. Everything was local and homemade. Between the wine and the food, we were feeling pretty good and loving Italy so far.

Just when we thought we were nearing the end of our culinary journey, the host brought out the insalata. We always thought that the salad came before the meal. These were small Caesar-type salads. The boys were not keen on them and had already eaten their vegetables, so they got a pass.

By this time, our stomachs had expanded quite a bit, and we were feeling full. To our astonishment, the host arrived at our table with another course, the formaggi e frutta. He sat down a large plate laden with fresh fruit and a variety of cheeses. I looked at it and put a hand on my engorged stomach. It all looked so good that I couldn't pass it up. I bravely sampled the offering.

Finally, the dolce arrived, my favorite part of any meal. For the dessert course came a rich tiramisu cake soaked in a dark liqueur. No matter how I would feel in the morning, I was going to eat it. Even though it was floating in alcohol, we allowed the boys to have some, too. Hopefully, it would make them sleep soundly.

With the dolce came the caffe. Italian coffee is strong and dark. This was an espresso served in small cups, definitely not the mugs we are used to in America. The bitter taste actually balanced the sweetness of the cake nicely. We did not let the boys have that much caffeine. They would definitely not sleep soundly. They would be bouncing off the hotel walls all night.

We finished all the courses and laid our cups down to rest, feeling very full and relaxed. We were contemplating how to get up and head to the hotel when our host put a tall, clear, ice-covered bottle on the table and produced two shot glasses. This was the final course, the digestivo. I politely told him no thank you in English, hoping he would understand that we were fine.

"From me to you," he told us in English with a heavy Italian accent!

Not wanting to insult him, I pointed to the bottle.

"What is it?" I politely asked.

"Grappa!" he exuberantly replied.

Mish and I had never heard of grappa before. We learned it is a fermented wine-ish drink made from distilling the skin, stems, seeds, and pulp from the grapes after they have been pressed to make wine. I should mention that it is up to 120 proofs. We did not know that. No one told us that. All we knew was that our generous host had bought us an after-dinner drink so we could make an obligatory toast.

He poured the clear ice-cold liquid into three glasses, one for him and one for Mish and I. He held up his glass and yelled, "Salute!" and then downed his shot. We cautiously looked at ours and took a sniff. Instantly, we realized that this was going to go down like liquid fire. Mish and I looked at each other, raised our glasses in turn, yelled, "Salute!" and threw the liquid down our throats. As expected, it burned. I'm not sure who turned redder, but we both were hit hard by the grappa. A hoarse "Grazie" was all I could manage to say.

The whole meal took well over two hours. Most American restaurant owners want to turn over tables as fast as they can to maximize revenue. In Italy, the restaurant hosts strive for an experience. Here a meal is a very social event that your day revolves around. It is to be savored and enjoyed, not gulped down in a rushed feeding frenzy. We finally thanked our host and walked out into the cool night air to our hotel. I was glad that it was a few blocks away. We all needed to walk a little before going to bed.

If we had known that Trieste was such a neat city, we would have planned on staying longer. Unfortunately, it was just an entry point into the country for us. Our train to Venice left early the following morning.

We took a taxi to the train depot and bought tickets to Venice. This was our first trip on the Eurail train system. In the United States, I often here people lament that we do not have such an efficient and wide-spread high-speed rail system as in Europe. We were going to find out if it lives up to the hype. Elijah likes that the trains are red, so it must be good.

The train was indeed smooth and fast. The Italian countryside flew by almost completely quietly. Before we knew it, we were pulling into a station near Venice. At the station we had to switch trains to a smaller one that runs exclusively to and from the island city. It dead ends at the city entrance and heads straight back to the mainland to drop-off and pickup another load of passengers. We reached its terminus and excitedly got off. We were actually in Venice!

Venice is another iconic site. It practically screams Italy. Like many things in Europe, Americans grow up seeing pictures of places like this, but we were really here. Venice can be sweltering and claustrophobically crowded in the summers. This time of year, however, was perfect. The weather was warm but not hot, and we practically had the city to ourselves. Even the train coming in was not fully loaded.

We went straight to our small hotel to drop off our luggage and then out to explore the city. From the first moment we stepped into Piazza San Marco, I was in love. The large public square is framed by St. Mark's Basilica and the Campanile on one side and the Procuratie Vecchie and Procuratie Nuove along the other side. Together, they form a magnificent, enclosed court two football fields long. Napoleon was so impressed he allegedly once referred to it as the "Drawing Room of Europe."

From the plaza we walked between the Columns of San Marco and San Teodoro out to the lagoon which defines the city. We watched in amazement as gondoliers skillfully paddled their long black boats on the water. They make it look elegant and effortless, but I am sure it is hard work. Riding in one was another item on our bucket list. We hailed one nearby and were soon being chauffeured through Venice's famed canals, taking in the whole romantic scene.

Within moments, we were lost in the intricate maze of the city's watery streets. No other city in the world is like Venice. Our gondolier told us about its history as he continued our tour without once missing a stroke. In the open, it may have been still sunny, but in the shadows of the buildings, it was growing dark, and we were growing hungry. Watching the poor guy paddle us all over was indeed hard work and made me hungrier. He put us ashore, and we found a small, quiet café to sit down in for another incredible Italian meal. This one, thankfully, was simply pizza. We were all still digesting last night's dinner. We savored every bight, however. Even the pizza in Italy is better!

Walking back to the hotel, we got turned around in the maze of canals and buildings. The walkways are not very well-lit, so the narrow alleys become quite dark. We found ourselves lost and alone in some places. Elijah began to get a little afraid.

Admittedly, I was getting a little nervous too. By sheer luck, we rounded a corner and saw a familiar landmark. Shortly, we stumbled our way into our hotel lobby and shut out the night. Elijah was greatly relieved.

Three nights in Venice was just about right. There was enough to see to keep us busy but not overwhelmed. We walked over the famous Bridge of Sighs, Rialto Bridge, Ponte della Paglia, and a bunch of other bridges whose names I never learned. Mish kept trying to educate us by looking them up in her guidebook, but after a while, they all blurred together.

We boarded the Eurail train again and headed south for Florence. Mish found lodging at a personal home of a local resident in the middle of the city. We were going for a full, authentic Italian experience.

We pulled into the city, and we were instantly blown away by its beauty. Italy was upping its game. I'm not sure which cities, Venice or Florence, are more spectacular. Both are amazing. Venice is on the warm, azure Adriatic Sea; Florence is at the base of the snow-covered Apennine Mountains. I could not pick one over the other.

Florence has one appellation that gives it bragging rights over any other Italian city. It is often referred to as the "Cradle of the Renaissance" by historians. This is with good reason. The architecture is magnificent. Dominating the city skyline is the Cathedral of Santa Maria Fiore, or Il Duoma for short. The Dome's enormous red roof can be seen from almost anywhere in the city. At the time of its building and for centuries afterward, it was the largest dome in the world. It is still the largest brick dome ever built.

We decided to brave the lofty height and take the dome tour. Visitors to the cathedral can climb a long, steep, narrow staircase to the base of the dome, sitting high up on the outer walls. From there, an even narrower wooden ramp walkway sandwiched between the outer red brick dome roof and the inner painted plaster dome ceiling takes you to the very top of the enormous dome. A small access door allows intrepid visitors onto the copula. Outside, on a small balcony almost four hundred feet above the ground, you are rewarded with an incredible bird's eye view of the beautiful city below.

We all started the long trek up the dome. We were all fine until the rickety wooden planks inside the dome. At that point, Elijah started to have second thoughts. He looked at the single-file line of people hunched over climbing the steep walkway and decided that he was good not seeing the view from the top of the dome. No amount of coaxing could budge him. We certainly weren't going to push the issue, so either Mish or I had to head back down with him. I felt like I had seen enough, too, and agreed to take him. I held his hand as we squeezed and slid by the long file of climbers coming up. We were going against the traffic flow, but there wasn't much I could do except keep saying, "Spiacente."

Once on the ground, Elijah was back to his old jovial self. We looked up in vain, trying to glimpse Mom and Aaron on the top of the dome. When they finally came back down, we decided that we had earned a treat for our effort. Mish knew just the thing, gelato.

The boys and I have never had gelato before. Mish fondly remembered it from her childhood. She found us a gelato shop conveniently right next to the cathedral. Once again, Italians impressed us with their culinary prowess. In America, ice-cream shops crudely put their cardboard tubs of ice-cream in a frosty glass display case up front. The partially scooped containers just duly sit there. In Italy, on the other hand, showmanship is everything. Their gelato is proudly displayed in open ornate trays, sculpted into wavy towers, and decorated with flowers, fruits, shaved chocolate, candy, and other goodies. It looks like art. I could hardly bear the server destroying one of the creations by getting me a scoop, almost. We each chose a different flavor because sharing is caring.

We walked around enjoying our delicious gelato and taking in the ambience of Florence. Mish had heard about the famous leather market and wanted to check it out. After all, she couldn't leave without some fine Italian leather purse.

At the market, we found Porecellino. He is a bronze boar fountain that dates back to 1634. Local legend says that putting a coin in his mouth gets you good luck. In addition, if you rub his snout, you will ensure a return to Florence someday. Superstitious, maybe, but we all rubbed his snout just to be on the safe side.

Elijah was enamored with the boar. He saw a booth selling stuffed Porecellinos and really wanted one. We allow ourselves one souvenir per city. Mish got a wallet, and Elijah got a pig. Aaron and I were fine with gelato.

We had another train to catch early the next morning. Since it was Sunday and most things would be closed, we were going to have to miss the Museo Galileo. This history of science museum is reported to be quite good and has a large display of antique science equipment. More interestingly, it has Galileo's middle finger. I'm not kidding. The legendary astronomer, who was sentenced to house arrest for life by the Catholic Church for his scientific views, left the ultimate parting gift. It is encased in a glass egg on display for all to see. We had to leave Florence but had assured our return by rubbing the pig. Therefore, we would still get a chance to see Galileo's severed appendage in the future.

Our final train stop was Rome. The well-known travel author and fellow Washingtonian Rick Steves has proclaimed that if you only have a chance to visit one city in all of Europe, let it be Rome. We may just agree with him. This famed city is a history lesson, cultural experience, culinary delight, romantic rendezvous, and architectural study all rolled into one non-stop amazing exploit. We wanted to take it all in at once but were not even sure where to begin.

We took a taxi from the train station to our lodgings. Along the way we were gawking and pointing at all the fabulous structures. Mish had been oddly tight-lipped about where we were staying. She had given the taxi driver the address. I asked here again what type of hotel she booked, and all I got for an answer was, "You'll see." I was really hoping she had scored a five-star hotel with all of the luxuries. The last place was nice but a little sparse.

Our taxi pulled up in front of a non-descript building near the heart of the city. Good location, but where was the valet to take our bags and usher us to our suite? At last, Mish let us in on her little secret.

"You need to be open-minded," she carefully said.

Uh-oh, I reflexively thought.

"We're staying in a convent," she exuberantly announced.

"A what?" I said.

"You heard me, a convent," she repeated.

"You mean with nuns and stuff?" I inquired.

"Be open-minded," she sternly reminded me, "it will be an experience. Plus, it was cheap."

Traveling on a budget means you don't always stay in upscale hotels. I was hoping just once we would.

We followed her to a plain wood door with a small brass sign next to it that read, "Casa Santa Sofia." The door was locked, but there was a bell. Mish rang the bell, and in short order, an elderly nun in her full habit attire appeared. Mish showed her our reservation, and the sister welcomed us inside.

The nuns help support themselves by renting rooms to tourists. They only charge a modest fee and provide a nice simple breakfast, too. In return, they ask that you respect their prayer time and curfew hours. The rules did not seem like an imposition, and the rooms were comfortable, if not sparsely furnished. I gave Mish a side-ways look while the sister explained their policies. She looked back with a sly smile. As the old saying goes, when in Rome do as the Romans.

We dropped off our luggage and hit the Roman streets to explore the city. We walked down a narrow alley, turned a corner, and there it was the Colosseum! It took our breaths away. Here was another picture from the history books come to life. Even the boys right away recognized the imposing structure. We quickly purchased tickets and went into the arena.

We stood in the same exact spot where thousands of Romans once stood to watch gladiators fight each other, sacrificial salves, and wild animals to the death. The wooden floor is long destroyed, but you can see the lower subterranean levels where the gruesome spectacles were staged. I explained to the boys how the unwilling participants were kept in jail cells beneath the arena until their time came to meet their fate above in battle. The boys shuddered as they listened to me. This place makes our modern football look tame.

We went to the Forum next. These ruins are all that is left of the heart of the once mighty Roman Empire. For over twelve centuries, the Forum was the center axis that the entire empire revolved around. It was a combination of political venue, public speaking platform, celebratory auditorium, and execution site. Caesar himself would stand here and address the Roman Senate and seek the thunderous applause of approval from his loyal subjects. Some of civilization's most important history happened here.

Just off to the side of the Forum is a lesser visited but still monumentally important site, the Mamertine Prison. According to theologians, both Saints Peter and Paul were imprisoned here. To envision two apostles who were disciples of Jesus Christ chained to the ancient stone wall inside the cell was deeply and profoundly moving. We were seeing Biblical accounts become real life.

Rome is full of places like that, where ancient history is turned into contemporary experience. I wish I could go back in time and tell my high school history teachers, "I get it!" I hoped that at least some of this was sinking into Aaron and Elijah's young brains. When they get to high school, they will be able to tell the class, "Been there, done that."

We spent three days touring Rome. We saw the Pantheon, the Circus Maximus, the Spanish Steps, The Trevi Fountain, and many, many more places. We walked our poor feet to the bone. As we were nursing our sore tootsies over some more gelato, which was becoming a dangerous daily treat, I remarked to our waiter how magnificent his city was.

He shrugged and said, "It is OK."

"Just OK? It's amazing," I replied in shock.

"For you, yes. For me, I have spent all my life here. I see the Colosseum almost every day," he explained.

I guess I could see his point. We lived in the Pacific Northwest. As beautiful as it is, we opted to leave and come to Europe. I suppose any place becomes dull with familiarity. For us right now, however, Rome was still new and exciting. We could not fathom how it could ever become old and boring.

We continued savoring our cold treat while walking around under the hot sun. I noticed a correlation between Elijah eating gelato and his behavior. The more he consumed, the giddier he became. Kids love ice cream, but he was really tickled with it. I asked him how his gelato was. He responded by giving me a sloppy gelato hug and kiss. To my astonishment, I smelled alcohol. Alarmed, I asked him what flavor he got.

"My favorite," he replied with a big grin.

We discovered that he had been getting real wine-infused gelato. Our little boy was a wee tipsy! Oh well, once again, I thought, when in Rome...

We had one last place to visit before heading home, the Vatican. It is on the other side of Rome, so we had to cut across the city to get to it.

Since it was too far to walk, I hailed a taxi and put our lives in the hands of another Italian driver who thought he was Mario Andretti. We held on tightly as he careened through the crowded, narrow streets, barely avoiding parked cars, people, dogs, and anything else unlucky enough to be in his path. Apparently, stop signs, streetlights, and other laws that keep sane drivers and pedestrians safe are optional in Italy. Amazingly, we made it to Vatican City without an accident.

Technically, Vatican City is a separate country from Italy. It is the smallest sovereign nation in terms of size and population in the world. It governs its own affairs, but you do not need a passport to enter.

Stepping into St. Peter's Square, you have no doubt that you are now entering the seat of power of one of the largest religions on the planet. This is clearly the center of the Catholic world. St. Peter's Basilica dominates the small city-state like a commanding lordly figure. In fact, it is the tallest dome in the world.

Walking into the basilica is truly an awe-inspiring experience. Whether you are Catholic or not is irrelevant. You cannot help but be humbled by the sheer grandeur of the church. The dome measures a staggering four hundred and forty-eight feet from the floor to the top and one hundred and thirty-six feet in diameter. It is a monumentally cavernous structure. Aaron and I were fairly sure that you could fly a small airplane around inside it.

Off to the right, when we entered was a small closed-off alcove. Walking over and peering inside, I beheld one of my favorite sculptures ever, the Pieta by Michelangelo. The all-white marble depiction of the

155

Virgin Mother Mary cradling her crucified only son, Jesus, is extraordinarily touching. I really wanted to get closer, but it is shielded by bulletproof glass. In 1972, a mentally disturbed man attacked the sculpture with a hammer and broke off Mary's nose and arm at the elbow. It has been painstakingly restored and now protected. I cannot fathom how anyone could willfully destroy a piece of art or history solely to make a personal political statement. He should cut his own arm off next time.

Numerous other pieces of priceless art adorn the basilica. We tried to see them all. The crown jewel of the Vatican, however, is not in this church. Behind St. Peter's is the famous Sistine Chapel. We had to go outside and all the way around to its entrance. The line to get in was already long and growing. We got in queue and waited not so patiently.

The Vatican Museum planners make you navigate a long and winding maze through the Apostolic Chapel to see other artwork leading up to the grand finale. To be honest, it is very impressive, but we were all now pretty tired and hungry again. Besides, after two or three dozen oil paintings, they all start to look the same.

We toughed it out and were rewarded at the end with Michelangelo's masterpiece. We actually felt very uncouth and self-conscious when we first walked into the chapel. We went from one room through a single plane door into a larger rectangular room where a crowd of people were straining their necks to look upwards. Mish and I followed everyone's lead and looked up, too. The vaulted ceiling was covered in a myriad of random Biblical scenes. The vivid and brightly colored fresco paintings were impressive. There are so many that I lost track of where I was looking.

I leaned over and quietly asked Mish if this was the Sistine Chapel. She wasn't sure either and shrugged her shoulders. Fortunately, other chapel visitors were more artistically savvy, and we discovered from them by quietly eavesdropping that this was indeed the one and only Sistine Chapel. Live and learn. For some reason, I expected a big, elaborate nave with ornate stained glass and large marble columns like we have seen in other chapels throughout Europe. Architecturally, this chapel was small and rather plain. What makes it impressive are the paintings covering almost every square inch of the walls and ceiling.

Michealangelo had quite the imagination and time on his hands. He was the primary painter of the ceiling, but several other artists contributed to the overall work. Combined, they created an enduring triumph of Renaissance art. We marveled at the detail and emotional impact of the frames. As we were admiring the ceiling, I finally found a piece that I knew. The fresco of God reaching out to his new creation, Adam, with their fingers almost touching, jumped out at me. Suddenly, I felt a little less unsophisticated.

We emerged from the chapel back into the bright sunlight. The Vatican is well worth a visit, no matter what religion you may or may not be. Not going because you are not Catholic would be akin to not going to Paris because you are not French. Be warned, however. It is a powerful recruitment tool for the Catholic Church. I almost wished I had been raised Catholic so I could have gotten the full impact of visiting.

Mish's mom is Catholic, but her dad is not, so she is sort of half-Catholic. She does not practice the faith but still felt compelled to pay respects to Pope Paul VI, who was entombed in the catacombs beneath the basilica before we left. He was the Pope when she was growing up, and she felt a special connection to him. I felt obligated to go with her. After all, the Pope is the leader of the largest religion in the world and, therefore, a revered spiritual and political figure worthy of respect from anyone.

There were many followers in the tombs morning various deceased Popes. Some were crossing themselves, laying a flower on a coffin, and weeping sadly. I looked over and saw a tear trickle down Mish's cheek as we went by her Pope's place of rest. No matter how much our logical side rationalizes things, the emotional side always plays a major part in our lives.

We crossed back into Italy and took a taxi back to the convent to spend our last night in Rome. Early the next morning, we caught another taxi to the airport and once again risked our lives on the crazy streets of Rome. Italian taxicab drivers have earned their reputation.

He drove like a rally race car driver who had way too much espresso this morning. He tore off the line and recklessly weaved in and out of traffic and past stop signs. I assured him that we had plenty of time to catch our flight. Undeterred, he continued his maniacal pace through the crowded city streets, all the while muttering expletives in Italian at other motorists who dared get in his way. We held on for dear life. At one point, he went up on a curb to get around a slower-moving truck. I had to pry my fingers off the seat armrest when we arrived at the airport. Mish, Aaron, and Elijah quickly scrambled out of the death taxi, thankful to be alive. Mish paid him, and he shot off again, quickly disappearing into the traffic in search of more victims.

Just when we thought the thrill rides were over, the plane ride back to London was even worse. Ryan Air once again did not disappoint. I'm not sure if the airline's pilots are adrenaline junkies or simply don't care about passenger comfort or sanity. Our plane hurtled through the sky like an out-of-control roller coaster. I swear he purposefully tried to hit every pocket of air turbulence he could find.

Mish and Aaron were having a great time. Every time we dropped, they raised their hands over their heads as if they were on an amusement park roller-coaster ride. I am never quite sure if Mish has nerves of steel or just a care-free attitude towards sudden death.

Meanwhile, I was getting really airsick. Somewhere during the frightful flight, I started to feel extremely panicky. Mish's poor hand was crushed by mine as I held on for the second time today for dear life. My logical side was cowering behind my emotional "O my God, we're going to die!" side. Emotions 1, logic 0.

On a particularly rapid and sudden freefall, Elijah finally lost it. He had been a trooper, but that nauseatingly quick descent broke his last nerve, and he started to cry. Poor Mish had to deal with me on one hand and Elijah on the other.

I swear, when the plane finally bounced onto the runway at Gatwick, I almost cried in relief. Little Elijah looked pretty rough. I felt really bad for him. I hoped that we would be able to get him back on another plane after he regained his nerves. I swore, however, I would not get on another one of those crazy flying contraptions. I didn't mind taking a nice relaxing cruise back to the United States.

Thankfully, we arrived back home in our little village without any further death-defying acts. We all agreed that Italy is an amazing country. Mish's memory served her well; it was as good as she remembered it. The only downside was that none of us wanted to get on a scale. We were sure that we all gained a few pounds. We confirmed that the Italians can cook.

Rick Steves is right; if you only can visit one European country, go to Italy. We think that the Italians have found a better work-life balance. They get the job done but in style and a relaxed manner. We Americans can learn something from them.

Chapter 21 – The Emerald Isle at Last

"There are only two tragedies in life: one is not getting what one wants, and the other is getting it." — Oscar Wilde

Oscar Wilde was one of Ireland's most gifted poets and playwrights. He is known for living an extravagant life. His flamboyant style, coupled with his brilliant wit, won him both many admirers and critics. He was famously imprisoned for being a homosexual. He achieved fame as a brilliant writer and rose to the highest levels of social circles in Victorian London, yet died in exile and poverty.

Fame and fortune brought with them public scrutiny and the need to keep up appearances. Wilde managed it for a time, but the precarious lifestyle and prison existence drained him. He finally succumbed to poor health and died at the early age of forty-six.

Wilde, for me has always been a case study in being thankful for not having certain things, like fame and fortune. He left a quiet life in pastoral Ireland for an exciting life in the big city of London. Yes, he achieved literary immortality, but at a high cost. I love another quote of his, "Be yourself; everyone else is already taken."

After almost a full academic year in England, I was feeling more like me. With the pressures of running a college gone and the need to climb the corporate ladder summarily dismissed, I was feeling more like my old self. I had time to be with my family. I enjoyed teaching again. Life was going well.

More than anywhere else in Europe, I wanted to see Ireland. Not only were some of my favorite writers born there, but also my ancestors. To me, Ireland represents a connection to the past. In some strange, inexplicable way, it hauntingly calls me home. I felt to completely mentally heal, I needed to walk among its green hills and clear rivers to renew my soul.

Mish's parents, Philip and Nancy, were flying out to see us and England at the same time. We decided that when they arrived would be the best time to go to Ireland. We could all experience the Emerald Isle as a larger family. Once again, Mish made all of the travel arrangements. We were wondering where we would be staying this time, perhaps a castle, I hoped.

It is good to see Mish's parents. Every year, we try to get together, either they come to us, or we go to them. Unfortunately, we don't always connect. We lived on the West Coast and they live on the Gulf Coast, which is about as far away from each other as you can get in the continental United States. Mish is close to them, and with my parents gone, they are the only grandparents Aaron and Elijah know. We had not actually seen them in a few years, so this was a special reunion.

There wasn't enough room in the car to fit everyone, so Aaron and I went to get grandma and grandpa. I was proud of myself that I could now navigate all the way to Heathrow Airport and back without help from a satnav or Mish. The family wagon was running well, too. The duct tape still held the body pieces in place, and seat covers hid most of the stains.

We picked them up and turned around for home. Along the way, I got to show off my right-sided driving skills and knowledge of England. They, of course, wanted to see as much as possible in the three weeks that they were going to be here.

We were greeted jubilantly with warm hugs and kisses all around when we got back to Middleton. Mish had prepared one of our favorite English recipes, fish pie. We all sat down at the table and caught up on each other's lives. Having a close family is a blessing. Luckily, we all get along well too.

The very next morning, we took a shuttle to Gatwick Airport. The lure of Ireland and the promise of more castles convinced Elijah and I to get back on a plane.

Once again, we were taking Ryan Air. We are gluttons for punishment, I guess. We warned Mish's parents about the no-frills airline. They soon realized that we were not exaggerating about their bare-bones approach to flying.

Thankfully, the short flight across the Irish Sea to Dublin was smooth. We opted to forgo Dublin this time and head straight for the west side. Mish's father, Philip, had reserved a large van for the trip so we all could comfortably fit with our luggage. I knew who was going to drive, so I put on my good son-in-law chauffer hat and hopped in.

Four uneventful hours later, we arrived in the small seaport village of Kinsale. The moment we pulled into town, my heart swelled with joy. I could not have imagined a more beautiful place if I tried. Brightly colored buildings lined the cobblestone streets, and lush flower baskets hung from the antique gas lamps. The village meandered along the small inlet until it disappeared around the green hills. It looked too perfect to be real, like something out of a painting.

We walked around the village, admiring how clean and neat it was. The Irish take great pride in their towns. The government even hosts a "Tidy Town" contest where villages compete for the title of "Tidiest Town." Kinsale had won the coveted award several times.

In order to learn more about the area, we signed up for a guided walking tour. Normally, I am not in favor of these, but Mish's parents wanted to, so I went along. It turned out to be very informative and fun.

The older gentleman who gave the tour put Elijah in charge of the map. Elijah took his responsibility very seriously and directed us which way to go. He was adorable as he walked up front with the guide, consulting his precious map. We obediently followed, not knowing where we were going and hoping that the guide was checking Elijah's directions.

As the sun set behind the hills of Kinsale, the town took on an even more surreal look. The gas lamps were lit, and wax candles shown in many windows.

We walked past the open doors of pubs with loud laughter and delightful smells rolling out of them. I watched as the moon glistened off the dark water in the harbor and illuminated the small fishing boats bobbing at their piers. Why would anyone want to live anywhere else, I thought?

I could have stayed the rest of my life right there, I think, but we wanted to see more of Ireland and headed further west to the Dingle Peninsula and the famous Ring of Kerry. The Ring of Kerry is a scenic drive that circumnavigates the Iveragh Peninsula in a one-hundred-eleven-mile spectacular loop. It is one of the most beautiful drives not just in Ireland but the world.

Due to time constraints, we were forced to do the loop in one day. I definitely wanted longer, but we were only here for a short time. We were told to go counterclockwise around the peninsula to avoid getting behind the numerous large tour buses which go clockwise. You don't get slowed behind them, but you do get to meet them head-on along the narrow, winding road. If the buses don't scare you, the sheep will.

The Ring lives up to its hype. We passed by rugged coasts, rolling green hills, ancient castle ruins, quaint seaside villages, and old farms. I had trouble keeping my eyes on the road because I kept looking all around, which was a challenge on that road. We stopped many times to get out and admire the scenery and smell the fresh air. Everywhere we looked was just breathtakingly beautiful.

From the Ring, we headed inland to one of Ireland's most famous castles, the Rock of Cashel in County Tipperary. According to legend, the Rock is where Aenghus, King of Munster, was converted to Christianity by St. Patrick himself. The castle sits on an enormous rocky mound in the middle of a large plain. Irish folklore describes how the giant rock originated from a mountain range twenty miles to the north. The Devil was so mad for being kicked out of the area by St. Patrick, he bit the mountain and spat out a huge chunk into the plane below. Hence, the mountain range is called The Devil's Bit.

The castle is an outstanding example of Celtic art. The medieval architecture is very impressive, too. Regrettably, during the Irish Confederate War, English troops sacked and looted the church. Much of it now lies in ruin.

On one side of the remaining outer wall, there is still a tall round tower that looks like something from a fairy tale. From the top, you have a commanding view of the land for many miles around.

I told Mish someday we were going to return to Ireland and take our time to savor every mile of its verdant landscape. She enthusiastically agreed. Having to rush through it this trip was almost cruel. I was exceedingly grateful I had this precious opportunity, however. Sharing the moment with my family was exceptionally special. We would return.

The four days passed far too quickly. Before I could order another Guinness, we were back on Ryan Air and in England. I left Ireland, but Ireland didn't leave me. I got the thing I wanted most from the trip, inner peace. A tiny flame was lit that I knew would never be extinguished.

A psychologist friend told me once that we are all three people in one body. One person is the one we want other people to see. Another person is the one we think we are. The last one is the person we truly are. Most people will never allow themselves the opportunity to get to know the third person. We are so concerned with image and appearance that we hide our true selves from the world and even ourselves.

Be the person you were meant to be, not the person you think everyone wants you to be. I knew now that I had no desire to ever return to my old self.

Chapter 22 – The Big Smoke

"When a man is tired of London, he is tired of life." – Samuel Johnson

London is an amazing city. Since moving to England, we have visited it several times. Each time, we see something new. I'm not a city person, but if I were, I would put London at the top of the list of places to live.

Of course, Mish's parents wanted to visit London while they were here. Now that we were locals, we felt fairly confident that we could show them around the city. There is so much to see and do that one day is far too short. We had to pick and choose the highlights.

We liked starting a tour with Westminster Abbey. Formally titled the Collegiate Church of Saint Peter at Westminster, the large Gothic church is the official coronation site of all English monarchs. It is also the burial place of many prominent British figures. Isaac Newton, Stephen Hawking, Charles Darwin, Mary Queen of Scotts, Geoffrey Chaucer, Charles Dickens, Rudyard Kipling, Ernest Rutherford, King Edwards I, III, V, and VI, King Henrys III, V, and VII, King Richard II, and many other noteworthy persons are laid to rest in the abbey.

Westminster Abbey is also easy walking distance to the Palace of Westminster, which is where the Parliament of the United Kingdom meets.

The first time we were in London, we were walking around the palace and looked up to see Big Ben. Aaron was quick to identify it. It was one of our first moments of sudden realization that we now live in England. Seeing the famous landmark made it sink in. Technically, the structure is properly referred to as the Clock Tower. Big Ben is a nickname for the clock in the tower.

From the Palace of Westminster, we crossed the Westminster Bridge. We wondered why everything was labeled Westminster something or other, so we did a little research. We learned that Westminster used to be the capital of the Kingdom of England and resided within the city boundaries of London. Today, it is just a small government district within the West End region. Now we know.

Across the bridge is a modern iconic piece of the London skyline, the Big Eye. Everyone wanted to ride it except me. I gladly stayed with Albie on the ground. Mish, Aaron, and Elijah have already road the giant Ferris wheel but wanted to ride it again with grandma and grandpa. Once more, Albie and I took a nap on the grass below. Apparently, the view from the top of the wheel is amazing. I saw the pictures so I'm good.

We walked back across Westminster Bridge to watch the changing of the guard at Buckingham Palace. This time-honored ceremony takes place daily at 11:00 AM in front of the palace. The recognizable bright red soldiers with their tall bear-skin hats are not just ceremonial. They provide real protection for the monarch and his or her family. The rifles they carry are quite functional, and they will not hesitate to use them if needed. This has not prevented a few foolish tourists from interfering with their duties by mocking their stiff marching style and trying to get them to alter course or blink. What drives some people to such gross stupidity and disrespect boggles me.

We didn't mess with the guard. We courteously watched as they did their traditional daily routine. Having been in the military, where I marched and stood guard myself, I did not envy them. I empathized with how tedious and tiresome it really is, especially in their uniforms. I knew that they must be dripping with sweat under them. Despite the stifling heat, they were precise and on point with each movement. The whole ceremony took exactly forty-five minutes on the dot. They made it look easy.

We were all getting hungry and looking towards lunch. The last time we were in London, we found an interesting Mexican restaurant just off Trafalgar Square. We were walking by and saw a large brass plaque on a building that read "Embassy of The Republic of Texas." Intrigued, we went in.

We learned that from 1836 to 1845, Texas was an independent nation. Its sovereignty was being challenged from the north by the United States and from the south by Mexico.

Knowing that it would need allies, the Texan president, Sam Houston, sent a delegation to England seeking support. England was more than happy to recognize the independence of Texas from its former rebellious colonies.

In 1845, Texas, fearing for its existence from mounting hostilities by Mexico, finally succumbed and joined the Union. Texas became a state, and the embassy was closed. The short-lived Republic of Texas was consigned to history.

Humorously, the Texas delegation stiffed the building owners with an unpaid rent of £160 when they left. In 1986, members of the Anglo-Texan society returned to their long-lost embassy dressed in full buckskins to settle the outstanding rent debt still owed by the current Republic of Texas. All was forgiven over a few pints.

Today, only the plaque remains. It is now a Mexican-themed restaurant. We loved and missed Mexican food and decided to try it. The food was decent, but the waiters trying to fake a Mexican accent with their English one was hilarious. "Por favor, mate, have a seat." I tried not to crack up.

This time, we opted for a more authentic English lunch and searched for a nice pub. Aaron and Elijah had heard about the Sherlock Holmes Pub and wanted to go there. We found it, but the line was so long we had to disappoint them and went to a less touristy one. Maybe next time.

After lunch, we walked around some more. London is overwhelming. All the museums are free, and there are a lot of them. The best one is simply called the British Museum. It houses many famous artifacts from antiquity, including the Rosetta Stone. It, like many objects at the museum, is highly controversial because they were removed from their original places during the days of the British Empire in the 18th and 19th centuries. Several countries have asked for their items back. So far, the museum has declined these requests. As you can imagine, it is a politically sticky wicket.

We also visited Down House on the south side of London. Mish really wanted to see the home of Charles Darwin. Back in the 19th century, Down House was in the countryside. Today, it is swallowed up in the London sprawl. However, it does still retain much of the country charm that Darwin loved about it. You can walk the same sandy path that Darwin did every morning for hours as he contemplated his scientific theories. Mish made a lap on the path to fulfill a dream of walking in the footsteps of a great idol of hers. The estate offers a unique glimpse into the life of one of the most controversial figures in modern history.

To get around London, we used the Underground. The Tube, as it is called by Londoners, runs under the city of London with two hundred fifty miles of track. It was the first subway system in the world when it opened in 1863.

Every Londoner knows the instruction cautioning you to, "Mind the gap." The boys would mimic saying it along with the polite female computer voice every time we got on a train. The other saying that caused us a chuckle was, "This train will terminate at the next stop." It seemed a little harsh to us. Why not just say, "Stop?"

Mish got a souvenir t-shirt of the Underground rail lines. It showed all the colored rail lines and stops. It actually came in useful one day when we were trying to figure out how to get someplace.

There is much I could write about London. We visited it frequently to sightsee, shop, and go to doctor's appointments. An unexpected find moving to England was Professor Carol Black at the Royal Free Clinic in London. She is the leading researcher on scleroderma.

Scleroderma is a group of rare diseases that involve the hardening and tightening of the skin and connective tissues. The exact cause is unknown. Sometimes it runs in families, other times is does not.

In some cases, just the skin is affected, localized scleroderma. In many cases, however, the disease attacks internal organs, systemic scleroderma. The latter one is particularly troublesome and life-threatening. There is no cure for either. Unfortunately, Mish has the latter one.

A year after we were married, Mish began to develop the beginning signs of the disease. Her fingers would turn blue and cold for no apparent reason, even during a hot summer day. She developed a red rash on her face and started having difficulty breathing. After a few years of misdiagnosis and worsening symptoms, we finally got the answers we needed to fight the disease.

A wonderful doctor in Seattle was able to help put Mish back on the road to a healthy life, albeit we had to make changes to our lifestyle. Mish was put on a strict regime of some heavy-duty medications, like an immunosuppressant and broad-spectrum antibiotics, which caused their own complications. She also had to make diet and exercise adjustments.

Keeping warm, especially her hands, became a paramount issue for her as well. She also had to get used to regular pulmonary and heart tests and blood work. All of this was overwhelming and taxing on her. I worried about her getting depressed and quitting.

She is very strong and a hard fighter. She refused to let the disease slow her down. She was a little nervous about moving away from her doctor, though.

When she mentioned the move to her doctor, the doctor was actually excited. She knew of the clinic in London. She made the necessary calls to set up introductions with Professor Black. We could not believe our luck!

We went to London for Mish's medical appointments and then would tour the city. We are amazed at how things seem to work out. We believe most things, the big things in life, happen for a reason. I'm not going to profess to understand divine intervention versus sheer luck. We like to think that we have a guardian angel who looks after us.

You never know what life will throw at you. You don't even know how long you will have on this Earth. My best friend used to tell me, "If you want to make God laugh, tell him your plans for the future." I used to not believe him.

This is the same friend who would badger me by asking when I was going to marry that cute redhead I was dating. "We're just friends," I would tell him, dismissing his probing.

A year later, I asked him to be my best man at our wedding.

After the wedding, he asked me how many children we were planning on having. "We think that we don't want to have kids," I would say, always getting a little annoyed.

Three years later, we asked him to be the godfather of our son, Aaron. Four years after that, he became Elijah's godfather, too.

Chuck is still my best friend and teasingly reminds me of those times we planned a course for our life only to have our ship go in another direction. Looking back, I would not steer any differently. I love our life, even though it is nothing like I originally planned. Life is funny that way.

I no longer try to plan every detail, only to become frustrated and bitter when things don't go my way. I try to live purposefully.

Ralph Waldo Emerson said, "The purpose of life is not to be happy. It is to be useful, to be honorable, to be compassionate, to have it make some difference that you have lived and lived well."

You do not need to be rich or have all the answers. No time will be the perfect time to start living the life of your dreams either. What is required is the courage to take steps day by day to change and faith that your path will reveal itself in time. That is the key to living well, I think.

Chapter 23 – Where to Next?

"Learn to enjoy every minute of your life. Be happy now. Don't wait for something outside of yourself to make you happy in the future. Think how really precious is the time you have to spend, whether it's at work or with your family. Every minute should be enjoyed and savored." – Earl Nightingale

The school year was coming to a close. Most of my students had passed their exams and were looking to their future with hope and anticipation.

Mish also was winding down her classrooms and trying to get the last stragglers over the finish line to pass. This is the time of year when teachers can breathe a sigh of relief that the end is in sight.

I made another trip to London. A recruiting company for international teachers was having a job fair. I decided to attend and see what the possibilities were.

We could stay in England, but you never know what else is out there unless you look. I have learned to not be complacent and just settle for whatever happens to come or not come my way.

The job fair was overwhelming. I was like a kid in a candy shop. The company set up booths in the large ballroom of a hotel where schools from around the world could advertise open positions. My jaw dropped as I scanned the room. The possibilities were endless!

I walked around in my best suit with copies of my up-to-date resume and searched for schools that needed a science teacher. There were many.

Now that I had international teaching experience, I was much more marketable. I was confident that I could find somewhere desirable.

I talked with administrators from every inhabited continent. A school in Addis Ababa was interested in me. The thought of safaris and climbing Mount Kilimanjaro was strongly seductive. Another school in Columbia looked enticing. We could snorkel in the warm, clear Caribbean Sea and hike the tropical rainforest. Maybe next time, I thought. An Australian school had openings. No, too many poisonous animals.

We had pretty much exhausted England but had not seen nearly enough of the rest of Europe. I narrowed my search for schools on the European continent. Which country, though? As I was thinking and walking, I went by a school from Frankfurt, Germany.

"Germany?" I thought. We have not been there. I hadn't considered it.

I walked up to the gentleman behind the booth, who greeted me warmly and shook my hand. He said, "Are you looking to come to Germany?" in a thick Scottish accent. His accent took me off guard.

"You're not in Germany," I remarked.

"Nay, I'm from Edinburgh. I'm the school director for the school," he explained.

This is one of the many things I love about international schools. People come together from around the world and work at the same school as one unified faculty. Education is universal. It does not matter where you are from.

The director and I chatted, and before I knew it, I handed him my resume and was asked for an interview later that day. Excitedly, I called Mish and asked her how she thought about moving across the channel to Germany. She was as enthusiastic as me.

I walked around some more and finally found a quiet place to sit down, exhausted, and prepare for my impending interview. I really knew very little about Germany. I certainly did not speak German.

What I did know about it was from studying World War II, which isn't the best example of Germany at its finest. I researched the school online and learned enough to probably put my foot in my mouth.

The time came for the interview and I met with the director again and his head teacher. It went well because, at the conclusion they offered me the position. I was not prepared to make a decision on the spot.

Normally, hiring managers tell you they will be in touch and go back to deliberate. I asked if I could talk to my wife before I committed. They completely understood, and we agreed to meet up later.

I called Mish again. I didn't even say hello first. I just triumphantly blurted out, "They offered me the job!" There was a slight pause.

"I guess we're going to Germany," she said.

"Do you want to go?" I cautiously inquired.

"Duh, of course!" she responded right away this time.

That was that. We were going off on another family adventure into the unknown.

Obviously, we had some serious preparations to make. Luckily, we are already residents of the European Union, so we did not have as many hoops to jump through. Thankfully too, the school in Germany was taking care of securing visas and a place for us to live.

Once again, we had to talk to the boys about moving. We were not worried so much about Aaron as Elijah. Aaron usually is up for an adventure. Elijah, on the other hand, likes stability. He has come to love Middleton and his school. He loves all his animal friends and going to the pub for dinner. We were not sure how he would respond to Germany.

I got back from London, and Mish and I sat down with the boys to talk. It was like a flashback from exactly one year ago. Not surprisingly, the conversation went as expected. Aaron was all in, and Elijah was skeptical. I really did feel bad for the little guy. I knew he was very happy where he was. I worried that I was being selfish, dragging him away from his new home.

After debating the subject for a little while, Elijah agreed that he would go to Germany as long as he could take his stuffed animals with him again. I promised him he most definitely could and that we would find more furry friends for him in Germany.

All that was left to do now was the logistic task of moving our personal items. Everything we bought on eBay went back on eBay. Mish did her super-woman thing and got busy packing and arranging our stuff. Bit by bit, the house became sparser as items were sold or packed away.

We ran into a huge problem right away. There was going to be a time gap between my current school ending and my new school beginning for the traditional summer break. Do we stay in England or do we go straight to Germany?

In the end, we decided to go back to our home in Port Ludlow. We needed to check on the house anyway. We also thought that seeing their old home would help the boys by showing them they still had a permanent home. We were just extending our vacation.

Going to the United States caused another huge issue. Where were we going to store our stuff and car while we were gone? We thought about several possible scenarios and finally decided on the most economical one. We would leave everything in the family wagon parked in long-term parking at Heathrow Airport for the summer. When we flew back to Europe, we would fly into London again, pick up the car, and drive to Germany.

Mish and I looked at all the stuff we wanted to take to Germany. We had no idea how to fit it in our car. We pared the pile down to as much as we could, but we had accumulated a bunch of stuff since we were here and did not want to part with much of it. This is where invention becomes the mother of necessity.

I bought a huge duffel bag meant for carrying golf bags and strapped it to the roof with tie-down straps. We crammed stuff in every nook and cranny of that poor car.

By the time we were done every square inch was taken up. We left just enough room for the boys to squeeze in between bags and boxes. We needed to give it a test first, so we all climbed in. That's when Mish noticed Albie staring at us from the house. He had a look that said, "What about me?" *Oops.*

Poor Albie would have to go on Mish's lap for the ride to the airport. I wasn't quite sure if driving with your car filled to the top like this was legal or even safe. I couldn't even see out of my rearview mirror, and Elijah disappeared when we closed the doors.

Before we took off, I looked at our packing job and was reminded of the Beverly Hillbillies.

We took one last walk around the village and said goodbye to all our new friends. Elijah fed his beloved animals again and said goodbye. They would miss the little boys with carrots and apples. We all wanted one last meal in the Red Lion, so we ate dinner there before taking off in the morning. Bright and early, we got on the A1 for Heathrow.

We dropped the car off in long-term parking. The attendant just stared at our car with disbelief.

"It will be fine," I assured Mish, or so I hoped.

With a last glance at it we boarded the shuttle for the terminal.

After a full year, we were on our way back to Washington State. We knew, however, that this was just a visit. In eight weeks, we would be flying back to Europe and a new family adventure in Germany.

Part II

Chapter 1 – Heading Back Across the Pond

"Life can only be understood backwards; but it must be lived forwards." — Søren Kierkegaard

We were on another airplane heading back over the Atlantic Ocean on our way home to England after a nice summer break in beautiful Washington State. Thinking of England as home struck me as kind of odd. After all, we have been living there for only a year. It did feel like home, though. We were all anxious to get back to Europe and resume our new life as so-called "expats."

For some inexplicable reason, I didn't like the label expat. I was very patriotic. I even had honorably served in the United States Navy. I loved my native country and was a proud American. The term expat seemed to imply that I no longer held allegiance to the United States. We were going to go back to the U.S. someday, we just didn't know when. Maybe "temp-pats?"

I leaned forward in my seat and stared out the small plane window. We were flying the usual overnight route chasing the sun as we headed east, so outside was completely dark. I strained to see if there were any faint lights below that would indicate civilization and, more importantly, land. There was only blackness. We must be over the ocean, I thought. Knowing that made me slightly uneasy. I hated to fly.

Next to me, my wife, Mishele, was asleep. Our two boys, Aaron and Elijah, were still wide awake, binge-watching movies and enjoying complimentary all-you-can-drink soda. The cabin lights were dimmed, and except for the soft glow of computer screens, it was dark inside the plane, too. All I could hear was the constant loud whine of the plane's engines as we hurtled through the night sky.

I leaned back in my seat and tried not to think of the flight. Luckily, it was smooth, so I could somewhat relax. My mind drifted to England. We would be landing at Heathrow Airport outside London, picking up our stalwart family wagon, which was hopefully still there, and heading to our new home. I reflected on how we came to be living abroad. Sometimes, it still seemed surreal. We had become a world-traveling family.

I remembered that almost a year ago to the day I quit my comfortable job as a college administrator and convinced my family to move five thousand miles away to a small village in rural England.

At the time it was the most daring decision we had ever made. Looking back on the whole idea, I could see how it probably sounded crazy, even to me.

Now, however, it seemed like no big deal. Doesn't every family move halfway around the world to a never been before place with less than six months' notice?

We had actually done just that, though. I, my intrepid wife, our two adventurous little boys, and a neurotic dog with eight pieces of luggage and four carry-on bags left Seattle and started a new life in a country none of us had ever been to. I started a new job teaching science in a school in Corby, and our boys started in schools as the only Americans around. Mishele continued to teach online for a school back in Washington and somehow managed to adjust to the eight-hour time difference. Despite many obstacles and stumbling blocks, we managed to make it work.

In retrospect, I was a little arrogantly proud that we did it. It took some imagination, a bit of research, and a bunch of hard work and perseverance. My family had agreed to the plan and worked together to make it happen. Our family adventure began and was still going.

The last year had been incredible. As I sat on the plane, I closed my eyes and remembered all the amazing experiences we had. We had learned a whole bunch about many different things.

Now, we can tell the difference between Renaissance and Medieval art, understand what Guy Fawkes Day is, and know not to try to keep up drinking with the British. My only regret was that we had not done it sooner.

I am amazed and remorseful that I had to get so miserable where I was that I started to search for a radical way out. I wonder how many people are pretending to be happy in a job like I was, yet dutifully keep slogging through it day after day, secretly hoping something better will fall out of the sky into their laps. We didn't wait for divine intervention out of the blue to come rescue us. We simply just made it happen.

I wondered, If I really loved my job, would I have started looking for an international position? Probably not. We would have stayed comfortable and ignorant in Port Ludlow but would never have known what we missed. This is a fascinating paradox, stay happy where you are and not know how much more enriching your life could be, or become horribly unhappy and then find a more fulfilling life elsewhere. So, do we first need to be motivated by misery to cause change, and then we can find happiness second? There has got to be a better way because life is too short with no second chances.

I believe that there are three very important key habits that help us live a purposeful life. Firstly, do what you love to do. Why be unhappy? Don't be miserable and just limp along to retirement if and when that comes. Find your passion and follow it. I love to teach. I am deeply committed to education for many reasons.

At the end of the day, however, I simply enjoy being with my students and colleagues at school. I'm sure some insightful psychologist could dissect my mind and figure out what in my past led me to be a teacher. It doesn't matter. It is my passion. I don't care why it is or about anyone else's opinions.

Secondly, have an enthralling, captivating, and gripping future planned. We have a plan, mostly. We are winging our way to England to pick up our trustworthy family wagon at Heathrow Airport and drive to our soon-to-be new home in Germany. Our main goal is to raise our two boys and help them get off to a good start in life by providing them with incredible experiences. Maybe this isn't such an ambitious future, but as parents, it is our top priority.

I identify with a t-shirt I saw which eloquently summed up my life's dilemma, "I never received my acceptance letter to Hogwarts, so I'm leaving the Shire to become a Jedi." How true. Alas, my dream of graduating from Star Fleet Academy has passed. Instead, I now want to live one endless adventure and make a difference in the world around me while taking my family along for the ride. Check, I'm doing that.

Thirdly, make a difference in the lives of others. I never wanted to be a millionaire. Money is not a motivator for me; fortunately, my wife overlooks that one small character flaw. For good or bad, I inherited this nasty altruistic gene which prevents me from looking out only for myself.

Unfortunately, there is no known cure. I am terminally afflicted with being a do-gooder, which might partly explain why I'm a teacher. I'm not perfect by any means, but I do sleep well at night, knowing I have helped many people. More importantly, I am proud of the example I set for my sons.

I seem to be living a purposeful life for the most part, I concluded. I am happy with where I am and excited about where we are going. In a few more hours, we would be back in England and starting a new adventure. Life is good.

With that settled, I fell asleep for the rest of the flight.

Chapter 2 – Déjà vu in London

"Anyone can plot a course with a map or compass; but without a sense of who you are, you will never know if you're already home." – Shannon L. Alder

Once again, our jetliner touched down at Heathrow Airport. The moment the wheels hit the runway I looked over at my wife and smiled; I also released the firm grip on her hand now that we were back on the ground. We looked over at Aaron and Elijah, who were clearly happy to be back in London. I think we all felt a mixed sensation of excitement and déjà vu.

The first order of business was to pick up our trustworthy family wagon. When we left England for the summer, we packed everything that we wanted to keep for Europe in the vehicle and parked it in long-term parking at the airport. It basically became a mobile storage unit for a couple of months. We hoped that it was not broken into or towed away because we were planning on having the stuff in it to start our new home in Germany.

As we rode the airport parking shuttle bus to the lot where we last left our vehicle, we all anxiously looked out the bus windows, trying to be the first to spy it. Elijah's keen eyes picked it out right away, and he let out a triumphant, "There it is!" Indeed, there it was, our 1989 Nissan Terrano turbo diesel in all its glory. Even the duct tape was still in place. The glue that I used on the driver-side mirror held, too. Even more amazing, all our belongings appeared intact. Not that anyone would have looked at our garage sale on four wheels and thought, "Wow, that looks worth breaking into! Those plastic trash bags must be filled with valuable items! Clever how the owners disguised their high-end things in that jalopy." Actually, I was really surprised that the lot attendants didn't have it towed away as a derelict eye sore.

We somehow crammed our luggage into the wagon and made room for ourselves, too. Luckily, our poor dog, Albie, was not with us this time. He would be flying directly to Germany and await us there, hopefully. He probably had no idea where he was being dragged off to now anyway.

I put the key in the ignition and turned it. To my utter surprise, the engine roared to life immediately. I never doubted it for a moment. Our little wagon may not be pretty, but it is reliable so far. I put it in gear, and we were off.

After two months of being back in the United States, I had to switch driving modes and re-adjust to driving on the left side of the road. My brain quickly remembered, and before we knew it, we were heading out of the airport, making for Dover, where we could catch the ferry for France.

Last time we went to France, we went under the English Channel on the train. This time, we wanted a view, so we decided to take the ferry instead.

Both the train and the ferry take approximately the same route. The ferry, however, takes quite a bit longer, 90 minutes compared to 35 minutes. Since we were not in a hurry and wanted to see the beautiful white cliffs of Dover, we opted for the ferry this time.

It was just like old times, me driving, Mish upfront navigating, and the boys in the back trying to behave. England was familiar to us. We had lived here and traveled all over the island. We had become accustomed to living as Brits.

Many native British practices were now routine. Some were very obvious, like learning to drive on the opposite side of the road and knowing how to properly navigate a roundabout. Others were more subtle, like knowing how to select a good pub and staying out of the middle lane on the motorway.

This last nuance of British life is very important to know if you are going to drive on the motorways here. Middle-laners are some of the most despised people in the UK. You would think, by the disparaging looks and vulgar gestures of other motorists, that driving in the middle lane was high treason.

Using the middle lane for passing is perfectly acceptable, but staying in the middle lane for more than a quarter of a mile is akin to insulting the queen herself.

I remembered to stay to the far outside lane with the other slow pokes and keep clear of the race car drivers on the inside. Although we have large turbo-charged V8 muscle cars and enormous 10-lane interstates in the US, we really do drive quite slow compared to Europeans. I'm not sure why that is. I prefer to relax and enjoy the scenery without risking my life on a trip to the store. Besides, the family wagon would only go 65 mph tops, maybe 70 downhill.

We made Dover in due time without mishap. We were all hungry for our first authentic pub meal in over two months. The other nuance of selecting a good pub came in handy. We located a suitable one in short order. Soon we were enjoying our favorite dishes and reminiscing about old times in jolly old England.

During our travels abroad, we have come to learn some truths. The most important one is that home truly is where the heart is. Home is not a physical place. It is a state of mind, and emotional attachment to a place and its people. We had each other and loved meeting new people and seeing different places. Our home was wherever we were at the moment.

Chapter 3 – Arrival in Germany

"Learn from yesterday, live for today, hope for tomorrow. The important thing is not to stop questioning." – Albert Einstein

From the observation deck of the ferry, we could see the French shoreline slowly approaching. We were very excited to be going back to continental Europe. Our other visits there had been amazing, so we had very high hopes. Soon, we would be living almost in the center of the continent in Frankfurt, Germany.

We have never been to Frankfurt, or Germany for that matter. This was a completely new destination for us. England had been strange to us at first too, but at least we spoke the same language, sort of.

None of us spoke a single word of German, however. We did learn that all Germans take English in school starting in 5th grade, which was comforting. They also drive on the right side of the road as in the United States, a plus.

We docked in Calais, France, and straight away got on the road for Frankfurt. Unfortunately, our vintage family wagon was not equipped with a satellite navigation system. I was not familiar enough with the motorways in this part of Europe either, so I relied on Mish and her trusty map to navigate.

Worse, the steering wheel was now on the wrong side of the automobile. We were definitely rocking old-school on the autobahn, but we made it in only six hours flat.

I was given the address of a house that the school had secured for us. It was located just west of Frankfurt in the small village of Eddersheim.

As we neared our new home, we all couldn't help but anxiously stare out the windows surveying the area. This was going to be home for the near future.

Frankfurt sits at the base of The Taunus, a small mountain range. The tallest peak is a mere 2,880 feet. Small compared to the majestic Mount Olympus back home in Washington State, but a welcome sight nonetheless. We loved England, but it was lacking in elevation gains. The mountains ahead looked promising for some decent hiking.

The city also straddles the Main River, pronounced '*mine*,' which flows into the mighty Rhine River and onto the North Sea. The Main is large enough to be navigable by small sea-going vessels, so we saw many strange looking boats traveling up and down the waterway.

European riverboats were new to us. These long and narrow, low boats looked ideally suited for traveling along the maze of rivers that crisscross the continent. I hoped we would get a chance to ride one.

The center hub of Frankfurt is very modern looking, with tall glass skyscrapers reaching up to the sky. It is not at all what we had become used to in England. This city definitely looked new and well-planned. We learned why.

During World War II, it had been a target of Allied air campaigns because of its strategic location on the river. Tons of iron and coal were shipped through the city to make weapons for the Nazi war machine. After the war, Germany rebuilt the city and transformed it into a modern major economic center of the country and region.

This was the white elephant in the room. I'll admit most of my knowledge of Germany stems from my interest in World War II. I'm pretty sure everyone on the planet knows about the whole nasty Nazi thing that happened, except maybe some extremely remote Eskimos who were happily oblivious to that time period. I really wanted to know the true Germany and not the probably biased one I had in my head from history classes and Discovery Channel documentaries. How much could I get away with by asking questions and making observations? We would see.

I did quickly learn, however, that the Germans take their driving seriously. The infamous autobahn was living up to its reputation. I tried to stay in the far-right lane, which was now the slow lane, and grip the steering wheel for dear life. Our poor family wagon was doing its best to chug along at a respectable 75 mph, only to be passed by like we were standing still by fast-moving blurs.

With such legendary car manufacturers like Porsche, Audi, Mercedes, and BMW, it's no wonder why Germans drive like racecar maniacs. Our poor old Nissan was out of its league.

Luckily, before our car died from exhaustion, we arrived at Eddersheim and got off the raceway. We took the next ausfahrt, which is extremely difficult to pronounce without a giggle, and headed into town. We quickly located the house on a short and narrow cobblestone lane in the center of town. It looked too amazing to be true. It was a three-story townhouse with a private courtyard near the park and river.

The business manager from the school shortly arrived and let us in. To our astonishment, it got even better. The school had ensured that the house was fully furnished and equipped right down to details like kitchenware, bed linens, bath towels, and laundry detergent. They even got the boys a foosball table and assorted games and books for their bedroom. Most heartwarming of all was a huge gift basket of German treats and delicacies sitting on the dining room table. We were overwhelmed.

To top off the warm welcome, the school business manager gave me a €500.00 cash advance on my salary to get settled in. Never in the United States would I ever have gotten this type of royal treatment from a school. Unbelievable, they truly value and appreciate teachers here.

We thanked the gracious school representative as she left and marveled at our luck. Just when we thought that the afternoon couldn't get any better, we were greeted by our new neighbors who informed us that the town was having its annual celebration that evening in the park. We surveyed our new home, put our luggage in the bedrooms, and went out to join in the festivities.

The festival in the park was a small-town end-of-summer affair with food, music, games, and, of course, beer. Mish and I savored our first genuine German beer and gave a toast to our new home. The boys ran around looking for food, which they quickly found. So far, our first hour in Germany was going extraordinarily well.

Tired from the long flight and drive, we called it an early night and walked the short distance back to our home, yawning and thinking of bed. Mish neatly unpacked her and my suitcases while the boys emptied theirs on their beds.

Elijah, however, carefully arranged his stuffed animal friends on the shelf by his bed. Satisfied that they were accounted for and in correct formation he proceeded to ignore the rest of his belongings and indulge in the provided games and books.

Meanwhile, Aaron meticulously placed his possessions on shelves and the desk, he claimed. Once finished to his satisfaction, he proclaimed himself room captain and ordered Elijah to finish his unpacking, to which Elijah promptly ignored. Thus, an unstoppable force met an immovable object. I closed the door and pretended not to hear the ensuing squabble. Ah, brotherly love.

Leaving the boys to sort it out, I inspected the house in greater detail. The first floor had a toilet with a sink, a modern, fully equipped kitchen, and a dining-living room combination area.

The second floor was the boys' bedroom, full bathroom, and laundry machines. The third floor held a small loft and the master bedroom. It was more vertical than horizontal living but fit our needs. All in all, it was a comfortable and cozy house.

I was perplexed by the toilets, however. In America, toilets are pretty standard in design and function. They're just ordinary bathroom fixtures that most of us don't give too much heed to. In fact, I don't ever

197

remember examining one in detail until now. What caused me to stop and take a closer look at our German toilets was the shelf.

An American toilet is essentially a bowl of water that you deposit your waste material in. When you flush it, the water is emptied down the drain along with your waste.

Magically, it disappears for good, hopefully. A German toilet has this dry protrusion that sticks out below your bum to catch your waste before it gets flushed. I really wanted to know why.

Since it was late, I did not have a German to ask, so I had to suspend my curiosity until later. Things like this have a habit of keeping me awake at night.

By the time I finished my rounds, Mish was unpacked. We were both exhausted. The boys wanted to stay up and play, which was fine with us as long as they didn't wake me. Luckily, I quickly fell asleep thinking about how blessed we truly are and not about toilets.

German was going to be a new experience for sure. We would need to learn a whole new set of customs, skills, rules, and language. Letting go of our American ways was hard, but we adapted to England. We were now challenged to let go of English ways and adopt German ones.

We accept that life is about change. The ancient Greek philosopher Heraclitus once said, "The only constant in life is change." How true! We mark time by the changes.

Graduating school, getting married, having children, moving, and even death are all momentous occasions in our lives that alter our current reality and force us to adopt a new one. They are also the points in time that we look back on to mark how far we have come. Without changes, life has a tendency to just slip by unnoticed.

Embrace change. Use it to reflect on and learn from, but also use it to inspire your future. Complacency is a horrible disease. Keep looking for opportunities to go further, do more, create new things, and improve yourself. There is a whole world out there to explore.

Chapter 4 – The German Way

"It is nonsense to say that Germans are unable to change." – Angela Merkel

The next morning, we went out to explore the area. We really wanted to get up into the Taunus Mountains and see the legendary natural beauty of Germany. We heard that there was a quaint small town not too far away in the mountains, so we decided to make for it.

Driving on the right side of the car was irritating and a little dangerous. Mish and I decided that although we had become fond of our semi-reliable family wagon, we needed a new car. The fact that we were noticeably the grungiest looking vehicle on the autobahn was a tad embarrassing, too. Germanys take great pride in their automobiles, and we didn't want to look like "that" family.

Since I had bought our vehicle through eBay for a mere $400.00, we had gotten our money's worth anyway. Therefore, I made finding a suitable replacement a high priority.

For now, we still had our little SUV. It faithfully chugged its way up the mountain without mishap. We found the little village of Idstein and started exploring. Straightaway, we all agreed that Germany, at least this small part, was breathtaking.

The Taunus are not the Alps, but they are still proper mountains. They provide a beautiful backdrop for the picturesque village with its timber-framed medieval townhouses and stone walls. Take away the cars and paved roads, and you could believe that you were back in the

15th century. We felt very relaxed and content as we strolled around the village, taking in the ambience of the whole scene.

After peering through the windows of a few delicious looking bakeries and drooling over the decadent pastries, we grew very hungry. Mish suggested a pick-nick lunch in the park, which sounded splendid. We found a small market in town where we selected some lunch items. When we went to check out, our debit and credit cards were surprisingly declined.

Repeatedly, we tried in vain to access our bank account. Mish, who does the finances for the family, could not figure out what was the problem. Not being able to speak German only exasperated the issue. The nice lady at the register did not speak English, so she could only smile a shrug.

Confused and disappointed, we went to leave empty handed. As we turned away, the cashier called back to us. She pointed to our grocery items and gestured to take them. Even more confused, I shook my head.

Apparently, the lady behind us in line paid for them. We were extremely thankful and embarrassed at the same time. We repeatedly thanked her. It was a wonderful gesture from a stranger to foreigners in her country.

We gratefully took our items and resumed our pick-nick in the park. I'm sure that to Germans, this was just an ordinary day in an ordinary town. To us, however, it was amazing. That is one of the marvels of traveling. You appreciate new places because you have never seen them before. You are looking at them through fresh eyes. I thought back at how we probably took for granted how beautiful the Pacific Northwest is, too.

We headed back down the Taunus to pick up some needed supplies for home. We found a grocery-retail store combination, Real, in the next town over from where we live. Real is the German equivalent of Wal-Mart. It has a little of everything at decent prices and ok quality. It's what we needed to start stocking our cupboards and refrigerator at our new home.

As we perused the grocery aisles, we recognized many common staples, like breads, dairy products, and produce, and some stuff that we had no idea what they were. We would need to learn enough German language and culture to shop here, I guess.

I asked passer-byes what some odd-looking items were, and to my astonishment, most understood me and politely answered in decent English. They were more than willing to explain what schnitzel, heringssalat, and rinderroulade were and where to get the best bread and meat.

Already Germans were turning out differently from what we previously thought coming here. They were not living up to their stereotype of being dispassionate and stern automatons. So far, they were truly warm and welcoming.

In our short time here, every German we ran into was polite, helpful, and kind. Had they changed after two world wars, or were they always like this? I was genuinely interested to get to know them better.

On the way to the checkout line, we passed something that caused me to gasp with excitement. There to behold was a spectacle not to be seen in all the United States, a whole long aisle dedicated to fine European chocolates. Chocolate actually has its own aisle all to itself! What a country! I turned down the aisle and fell into an instant rapture.

Shelves upon shelves of delectable chocolates of every conceivable variety lined both sides. I didn't know where to begin. It was Nirvana wrapped in gold and silver foil squares.

Mish hurried me through the chocolaty gauntlet, probably for my own good. I would have spent the rest of the afternoon standing in the middle of the aisle, hypnotized in a diabetic coma. The aisle over, however, was worse. It was beer alley up next.

We had heard that Germans love their beer, but now we understand the full magnitude of their insatiable thirst. There must have been fifty different types of beers on display, most, if not all, of them I had never heard of before. Weihenstephan Hefe Weissbier, Erdinger Kristall, Spaten Oktoberfest, Aecht Schlenkeria Rauchbier, Paulaner Salvator Doppel Bock, Schneider Weisse Aventinus Eisbock, Augustiner Hell, Gaffel Kölsch and a host of other brands that we could not pronounce lined the shelves. There was not a Budweiser or Coors can in sight.

Since we could not read the labels, we selected a beer the only other way, the one with the coolest picture on the bottles. I asked Elijah which label he liked. He pointed to one with a monk on it, Franziskaner. I had mixed feelings over letting my eight-year-old pick my beer, but we were in Germany now, so why not.

Once we were through beer alley, we finally made it to the checkout lane. Mish somehow did her accounting magic and figured out how to get our banking cards to work. This time, we passed the cashier with no issues.

All that grocery shopping made us real hungry again. We walked outside to load our car when we smelled something very enticing. In front of the store was a doner kebab stand. Kebabs originated in Turkey in the 17th century and migrated to Germany in the 1970s.

Today, they are one of Germans' favorite fast foods. Although it wasn't an authentic German delicacy, we were game to try one. We ordered four and watched the server slice off sheets of thin meat from the vertical rotisserie. He folded them into a pita bread sandwich and added lettuce, tomatoes, onions, and olives and smothered it with a white sauce. We drooled watching him make them.

The kebabs tasted even better than they looked. Ok, not a traditional German lunch, but still pretty tasty. Since the Germans embraced them, it looks like we might as well, too. I am amazed at how certain ethnic foods find their way far from home.

Back in America, we are used to borrowing cultural dishes from everywhere, but I didn't think about other countries doing the same. Apparently, even Germans adopt new things.

With our hunger satisfied, we headed home. Luckily, Germans favor full-size refrigerators like in The United States, unlike the British with their tiny boxes. We didn't miss our small one back in Middleton at all. We could actually get a full grocery shopping load for two perpetually hungry growing boys into this one. There was even room for the beer.

Since it was still early, we decided to walk around our little town to get to know it better. We walked down the narrow cobble-stone alley between the houses, went through a gate, and emerged in the park along the river. We were in a great location. The boys, including Albie, could run and run until exhaustion.

Straightaway, Elijah homed in on the ducks. Like a fox he crouched down and bolted off full speed on an intercept course for the nearest flock. These ducks obviously have had little boys chasing them before. They just nonchalantly waddled away and into the river right before Elijah could get to them. They quacked in mockery as they paddled with their webbed feet out into the current.

Undeterred, Elijah went running after another group.

While his little brother tried in vain to catch a duck, Aaron found a tree that needed climbing. He got up just high enough to make mom and I a little nervous. He is our daredevil, for sure. Our two energetic boys can really keep us on our toes. At least Albie seemed content to just sniff around and pee on some new trees. I guess he wanted the German dogs to know that an American canine was now in town.

Our first few days in our new home were going splendidly. We felt oddly at ease so quickly. Maybe this international vagabonding was starting to sink in. We were not intimidated by the language barrier or the new laws and customs. We knew we would eventually figure most things out, one way or the other. At least I hadn't needed an emergency room yet.Unfortunately, Aaron did. I was at school when one of the administrators came and pulled me out of class. He informed me that my wife and two sons were on their way to the emergency room at the local hospital because something had happened to Aaron. He did not know anything else.

Of all the times for our car to be in the shop, I cursed. I had biked to work and had no quick way home or to the hospital. Fortunately, one of the school counselors offered to drive me. I gratefully accepted. We rushed out of the school and into her car. I had no way to contact Mish because we had not set up a cellular phone account yet. So she would not know I was on my way. I hoped she was handling things well and, more importantly, that Aaron was ok.

We arrived at the hospital, and I thanked my ride profusely. I turned and looked at the entrance of the building. All the signs were in German, of course. I looked for some type of clue that would indicate the emergency room. I stopped a woman in surgical scrubs for help. Luckily, she spoke decent English and helped me.

I raced to the ER and found the check-in desk. I tried to explain who I was and that I was looking for my son. The receptionist did not speak English but correctly surmised that I was the father of the only American boy admitted today. She ushered me into the pediatric ward, where I found Mish and Elijah sitting next to Aaron, who was lying on a gurney with an IV in his arm. He looked pale and scared. Instantly, my heart sank.

Mish looked up, both surprised and happy to see me.

"What happened?" I asked breathlessly.

"The doctor thinks he has an appendicitis infection. He collapsed at home in pain and holding his stomach," she replied tearfully.

"What are they going to do, operate?" I asked.

"I guess we are waiting for the doctor to get test results before she makes a decision," Mish said.

I tried to get more information, but no one spoke English. I, unfortunately have had to take Aaron to the ER before. This time was different. I could not communicate with the doctors. I grew frustrated and a little scared. I wanted to know what was going on. This is when living in another country, especially when you don't speak the language, becomes very difficult.

Having your child in the hospital for any reason is nerve-racking, but having him in a hospital where you cannot communicate with the staff is outright terrifying.

As I was running around trying to get answers, the doctor came back. She, thankfully, spoke some English. She was very professional and accommodating and informed us that Aaron would be fine but needed some antibiotics for the infection. We simultaneously breathed a huge sigh of relief. He would not need surgery.

The doctor, however, did want Aaron to spend the night for observation. Mish agreed to stay with him while I took Elijah home. Before we left, I gave Aaron a big hug and told him he was a real trooper. I reframed from letting him know he just caused my hairline to recede another inch. Parenting definitely ages you. I still wouldn't trade it for the world.

The German healthcare system was proving to be very good. The German people, too were proving to be some of the warmest and friendliest people we have met so far on our journey. Germany was turning out different than we expected, but in a good way.

As the old saying goes, "Never judge a book by its cover." I admit I had a vague, unjust stereotype of Germans before coming to Germany. Most of what I thought I knew about Germans came from high school history class, which only mentioned them as the aggressors in the two World Wars, and from movies, which usually depicted them as the bad guy Nazis. I had a lot to learn while we were here. Keeping an open mind, listening first, and asking questions were going to be my new mantras.

Chapter 5 – Our First German Tourist Destination

"People are basically the same the world over. Everybody wants the same things - to be happy, to be healthy, to be at least reasonably prosperous, and to be secure. They want friends, peace of mind, good family relationships, and hope that tomorrow is going to be even better than today." – Zig Ziglar

Teaching was starting off well at my new school. The school is owned and operated by a large international education company for children whose parents work in Frankfurt. The European Central Bank, along with several automobile companies, like Volkswagen, Daimler, Hyundai, Kia Motors, Seat, Skoda, Jaguar, Ferrari, Fiat, Chevrolet, Land Rover, and Maserati, to name a few, have headquarters in the area. Frankfurt also is home to the largest United States consulate in the world.

Consequently, it is the financial and transportation hub of continental Europe. Therefore, the school was built to serve a very diverse and affluent clientele. I was delighted to find that it is a very nice facility with all the amenities you would expect.

The school provided a comprehensive curriculum and standardized testing system, too, which made for a relatively easy teaching gig. I didn't have to plan for classes or create assignments, so I had more time than normally as a teacher. This extra time gave me a chance to get to know my colleagues and try to learn German.

I asked for suggestions about what to do and where to go in the area. I was overwhelmed with the responses. We definitely landed in the middle of the action.

We were very excited to get out and explore our new home, but first, we needed a new set of wheels. Actually, we needed a whole new car. Its time had come. I had been inquiring about used cars and found the perfect one, a Mercedes A-Class. Mercedes does not export them to the United States, so I was unfamiliar with it, other than it was another baby diesel engine with another manual transmission. Europeans love that combination.

Luckily, the dealer took our jalopy, not too enthusiastically, and cash, very enthusiastically, in exchange. We signed the papers, swapped keys, and got ready to go. I gave one last look at the old car. It was our first European car and we had many great memories in it. It's strange how we get sentimental over inanimate objects, but we do. The new car was in every way nicer, but the old Nissan would always be our first international ride.

Our first real family adventure in Germany, we planned for next weekend. According to my sources, there was an ancient Roman fort a short drive north from us. We had seen other Roman structures while living in England and visiting Italy, but we still wanted to see these and learn some more history. I don't think we will ever get tired of seeing ancient things.

I never really got an appreciation from school history books of how huge the Roman Empire truly was. Seeing a colored-coded map in a book doesn't do it justice. How could the Romans control such a vast amount of land without modern communication or means of travel? We have traveled from its northernmost extent in England to its heart in Rome to now an outpost on the continent. All roads really do lead to Rome, I guess.

The Saalburg is a fully restored fort located on top of a ridge in the Taunus. It is the most complete Roman ruin in all of Germany and a UNESCO World Heritage site.

Back in the days of the Empire it was part of a long defensive line, or limes, which guarded the frontier. Today, it provides a rare glimpse into Roman life.

We walked through the main gate and felt instantly transported to the second century. The only thing that was a little anachronistic was the ubiquitous gift shop. It was strategically placed so that we had to pass through it to enter the main compound. We hoped to get through it as quickly and cheaply as possible. Elijah, however, had other plans. His keen eyes right away spied a shelf with stuffed animals on it.

We know how much Elijah loves stuffed animals. He collects them, names them, cares for them, and wants more of them whenever he can. Before moving to England, Elijah raised money to adopt animals through a World Wildlife Fund program.

Usually, he tried to sell stuff he found. I got very suspicious when he would raid the garage or hall closet and ask if we needed some item he triumphantly pulled out. If that didn't yield enough cash, he would peddle painted rocks to our neighbors. Fortunately, they couldn't resist his chubby cheeks and brown eyes looking up at them hopefully.

When he raised enough money, he would excitedly pick an animal from their website, mail in his application with the money, and anxiously await his "adoption kit," which would include an "official" adoption certificate, a picture of his animal, and a small stuffed animal in place of the real thing. We were not quite sure if Elijah did it to help save endangered species or for the stuffed toy. Either way, he was doing a good deed. Coincidently, he got lots of mail from the WWF. He had to be their best customer.

His love of all things furry, feathery, and scaly had not abated with time. He zeroed in on a small stuffed bear in Roman soldier attire standing proudly on a shelf. He made a beeline right for it. His brown eyes gleamed with joy.

I know that I am a sucker for his charm, and he knows it too. Luckily mom is more disciplined and can say no. We do, however, have a family rule that everyone is allowed one small souvenir whenever we go on a major outing. Elijah was quick to invoke this rule.

"Please!" he begged.

I looked at mom, mom looked at me, and I caved first. I gently picked up the bear and handed it into Elijah's eagerly waiting arms.

Straightaway, Elijah created a name for his new friend on the spot.

"I'm going to name you Sir Bearington," he proclaimed.

Sir Bearington it was. Now we could finally enter the fort, and with a Roman soldier to escort us too.

Saalburg is completely restored to the smallest detail, unlike most Roman ruins that are left how archeologists found them. Therefore, much of the fort is of modern construction from the extensive repair work. We actually liked the experience of seeing how it looked over two millennia ago. We saw the garrison barracks for the soldiers, a jail for military deserters and disloyal subjects to the emperor, the armory, and a shrine to the Roman gods. There are even period dressed docents walking around as if this place is all quite normal.

Outside the fort is a short trail that leads to a restored section of the limes. The earthen trenches and stone walls mark the boundary between civilized Rome and the barbaric unexplored lands. We set up a pick-nick near the fortifications and enjoyed pretending we were back in ancient Roman times.

Mish and I relaxed in the sun as Elijah played with Sir Bearington. Meanwhile, Aaron wandered around, looking through the stones and grass, hoping to discover an old Roman relic. I hated to spoil his fun, so I didn't tell him that this place probably has been picked over so many times that anything on the surface was long ago snatched up.

Plus, most treasures you have to dig for anyway. He reminds me of myself when I was much younger. Boys' imaginations are filled with buried treasure and secret places waiting to be unearthed. I left him to his search and childhood.

After eating and resting, we decided to head back down the mountains to Frankfurt. Along the way we discovered an unexpected small treasure after all. At the base of the Taunus is the Opel Zoo. We never pass up the opportunity to see real animals, so we pulled in. Elijah was very excited to see German animals because African lions in America are different from African lions in Germany. Maybe it's their accent?

Mish worried about leaving Albie in a hot car while we went into the zoo. Her fear turned out to be unfounded. To our amazement, they let Albie, a dog, in! I never heard of bringing your own animal with you to the zoo. Albie was extremely excited at the opportunity to see and smell all sorts of things he had never encountered before. He enthusiastically followed after Aaron and Elijah as they scampered from enclosure to enclosure on the hunt for wild animals.

One of the many things that surprise us living abroad is how seemingly universal rules are not really universal. For example, visitor safety is not given the same priority across different countries. Europeans, in general, seem to have a more "visitor beware" philosophy, compared to Americans' extreme paranoia that something bad will happen if we don't blatantly post a dozen warning signs all over the place.

I have my interpretation of this difference. I think that in the United States, we expect or accept that people will do dumb things. Therefore, we need to idiot-proof every public place to protect us from ourselves and from overzealous lawyers. In Europe, on the other hand, they believe if you're that stupid to not heed common sense, then you deserve whatever happens.

Case in point, we straightaway observed that the wild animals at the zoo were not as heavily barricaded behind multiple fortifications as in the US. We remembered that English zoos were the same way. You can get much more up close and personal with the critters here. We found out how much more up close and personal, too.

We decided to take a break from chasing the boys around the zoo. Mish produced some snack bars from her bag and used them, like all good mothers, as bribery to get Aaron and Elijah to stop for a moment. Aaron was sitting on a wood railing enjoying his snack when a small black hand reached from behind him and grabbed his treat.

Poor Aaron was so surprised he almost fell over the railing backwards. We all simultaneously looked up to see that the bandit was a rather large and plump raccoon. He was obviously very accustomed to stealing human food from unsuspecting visitors. He just sat there happily chewing on his ill-gotten gain, staring at us through his black furry mask, which was very fitting for a thief.

Two of his accomplices quickly scampered over to get in on the action. Elijah, of course, promptly offered his snack to the newcomers. I suppose better, more sensible parents would not have allowed their child to feed his snack to a wild creature with sharp teeth and possible diseases. Not us, we fell into the sucker-for-brown-eyes category of parents and allowed him to feed the raccoon. My excuse is that I could not read the German signs that say don't allow your child to feed the dangerous wild animals, please.

We enjoyed our time feeding the German raccoons more than we did the rest of the zoo, even though we have American raccoons in plenty back in Washington State. I wonder if German raccoons and American raccoons would understand each other. After all, humans have different languages around the world, maybe other animals do, too. American cows moo. What is moo in German?

After contributing to the raccoons' human food addiction and musing over animal linguistics, it was time to head the rest of the way home.

Driving through the village to our house, we saw one last stop we had to make. In the center of town was a gelato shop, the perfect end to a perfect day. I parked the car at our house and we walked back to the shop.

We savored the cold, delicious treats and talked about our adventure today. As we relaxed, I watched other families coming into the shop. Whether you call it gelato or ice cream, it is enjoyed by children and adults, the world over all the same. Zoos and ice cream make for a great summer family outing, no matter what country you are from. I am always amazed that people have more in common than they do not.

People are people, no matter where you go. Everywhere we travel we see the same thing, people just trying to live their lives. We all want to have a safe and secure place to raise a family, enjoy ourselves along the way, make enough money to pay the bills and a little more, and hopefully grow old together. I wonder why we can't all just get along.

Chapter 6 – Two Wars

"The greatest gift in life is to be remembered." - Ken Venturi

One of the running jokes in Germany is that if you are waiting for the train and it arrives late, your watch is off. Living here, I can vouch for German punctuality. The whole country seems to function like a well-made watch.

Whatever the reason, Germans are rigid. Rules are rules; they are to be followed without question. I do not think that there is a word for "exception" in the German language. Tell an American the rules and the first thing we will do is try to find a way around them.

This strict adherence to law and order is a double-edged sword for Germans. On one side, it has enabled them to accomplish amazing feats with astonishing efficiency and effectiveness. After a devastating defeat in World War I, for example, they rebuilt their battle ravaged country in less than twenty years to once again become the formidable military force in Europe and wage another war the likes the world had never seen. Not bad.

On the other side, it locks them into blindly following rules without pausing to think about their effect or consequence on people. They are very obedient people. We found this out to be true the hard way.

The original plan to educate Aaron and Elijah while in Germany was to have our boys homeschooled by their mother. After all, Mish is a certified and experienced teacher who is quite capable of teaching them. Plus, the German school system does not embrace multiculturalism at all. Lessons are taught in German and only in German. Since neither boy knows German, we obviously deemed putting them in the local public school would be useless, especially since we are pretty sure that we are not permanently settling here and becoming German. We did not, however, anticipate uncompromising German regulations regarding school.

We assumed that our plan would be ok with the Germans. We discovered too late that German law clearly states that all children residing in Germany will attend an approved public or private school. Homeschooling is forbidden. Oops.

We took the typical American approach to this dilemma, ignore the problem and hope it goes away. Little did we know the persistence of Germans. Shortly, we got an official letter from the local council inquiring why are boys were not in school. Rules are rules.

Once again, we did the American thing and tossed the paper away, thinking that the Germans would give up or the issue would get lost in their maze of bureaucracy. Wrong and Wrong. Germans do not easily give up and they are creatures well adapted to their native bureaucratic environment. As we should have anticipated, the second letter came stating very clearly and concisely that our boys would be in school the following week either by parent or police escort. Darn it!

We went to my school to ask my administration for help, guidance, and a miracle. Amazingly, we did get a miracle, or half of one at least. The school could vouch that Aaron would be schooled independently at home under their supervision. Hallelujah! Unfortunately, Elijah was too young to use this rare loophole. He would need to go to German school.

Needless to say, Aaron was ecstatic, and Elijah was less than pleased. He remained stubbornly defiant to the bitter end. I must admit, I was secretly curious who would win this little international war, the obstinate little American boy or the regimented monstrous German education system. Either way, we knew it was going to be one heck of a fight. We wouldn't have to wait long because the first battle was about to begin!

Since things were heating up on the front lines, we decided to take a break and go to neutral France. One of the many great things about living in Europe is the proximity of many different countries. How cool is it to wake up on a Saturday morning in Germany and spontaneously decide to go to France for the day?

We had a very specific destination in mind for this family outing. Mish's grandfather, Herman Boxtall, died in the Normandy invasion after D-Day. He was buried at an American cemetery in Epinal. One of our intentions while living in Europe was to pay our respects to him. No family member ever has had the opportunity to visit his grave over all these years. We felt it was about time to honor a fallen family member.

Finding Epinal was easy; finding Herman's grave we worried would prove difficult and maybe even impossible. So many brave young American soldiers sacrificed their lives for the noble cause of liberating France that the French felt obligated to bury them on their soil. We did not know how well records were kept from that time period. No matter, we decided to go anyway and hope to find his resting place.

We drove into the cemetery and were immediately awestruck. Only Arlington National Cemetery in Washington, D.C., rivaled this place in solemnity and grandeur. Thousands of bright white crosses stood resolutely at attention on a field of bright green grass marking the graves of brave men who perished here. An American flag proudly waved above the grounds, reminding visitors that although this was French soil, these were US soldiers.

The cemetery was absolutely silent as we walked up the long marble steps to the memorial building. Before we got to the top, a man in a neatly pressed suit and sharp haircut came down to greet us. He warmly welcomed us and introduced himself as the director of the cemetery. We explained we were looking for a relative who we believed was buried here but did not know anything other than his name and approximate date of death.

The director promptly guided us into the memorial, where he ushered us to a seat in his office and offered us coffee or tea. He informed us that he could probably locate the grave and started searching on his computer. Within a few moments, he had indeed located the grave. We were astonished and thrilled. We were hoping, but not expecting, to actually find Mish's grandfather's grave. Mish was over the moon excited.

The director took us in his golf-cart straight to the grave. The four of us quietly approached the cross the director specified. When we reached it, we could clearly read engraved in the smooth white marble, "Herman Boxstall." Finally, after over eight decades, members of his family had arrived to pay respects. Mish openly wept. Even Aaron and Elijah, as young as they were, understood the significance of the moment and looked down with sad eyes. We stood there for some time with bowed heads deep in our own thoughts.

The director gently broke the quiet and kindly asked us if we would like him to buy some flowers in town for the grave. We were very appreciative and accepted his gracious offer. He got back in his cart and sped away out of sight. We remained behind talking about what this cemetery and grave signified. For all of us, especially our two young boys, the visit had a significant impact. It is hard to put into words what we felt, but it was deeply spiritual and bonding.

In a short time, the director came back with the promised flowers. Mish placed them respectfully on the grave, and we all said a prayer. We said one last goodbye and allowed the director to take us back to our car. We thanked him over and over for his dedication and compassion for the honored dead and their families. He simply smiled and said he was happy to help and that it was his privilege to keep their memories alive.

I can only hope that when I die my family and friends will keep me alive in their hearts and memories. We cannot take anything with us nor control what happens to our possessions after death. We can determine, however, how we will be remembered when we die by the way we live our lives. Death is inevitable, forgotten does not have to be.

All the trite and cliché sayings about not being able to take your material possession with you after you die and only your legacy matters are true. Period. The memories we imprint on the ones we leave behind are all that is truly left of us after death. Your legacy will be written by them. I tell our boys, and remind myself, to make those memories as good as possible during your life so they endure after death.

As we drove away, I thought how amazing it was that after the deadliest war in human history, we were now living happily in our old enemy's country. A generation has passed since the conflict ended, and now it is relegated to the history books. However, at the cemetery it seemed so real that victory might just have been won. I suppose time does heal all wounds.

Our little war with the German educational system seemed very insignificant now. My frustration was routed in a lack of understanding and tolerance of another culture and its history. The German government was doing what they felt was needed in order to prevent another radical ideology from being born by tightly controlling the shaping of young minds so madmen could not. The visit to the cemetery sparked this epiphany. Although I did not necessarily agree with the methods, I now understood the intent. Maybe Elijah would have to lose his little war after all.

Chapter 7 – Tepees in Germany?

"The necessity for rules and strictness is a way of dealing with an enormously powerful impulse: Germans are among the most emotional people on the planet. Maybe it has to do with the fact that, as a nation, they are always drawn back to nature and the forest." – Simon Rattle

On a gorgeous Sunday, we did our favorite family activity, taking a long walk and getting gelato. The sky was a vibrant blue, there was a crisp breeze in the air, and the leaves were just starting to change to their autumn brilliance. There was no better time to explore a new path.

We headed out along the Mein River. A well-maintained path followed along the water through the forest. This seemed like an ideal route to take. The boys stampeded ahead of us, with poor Albie straining at his leash, desperately wanting to keep up with them. Mish and I walked side-by-side, chatting and enjoying the moment. Simple times like this give us great pleasure.

As we rounded a bend in the path, I noticed a very strange sight, tepees! Standing neatly in a small field were five authentic Native American tepees, complete with horses, a small log cabin, and fire circle. The anachronistic scene caused us to stop and stare in bewilderment. Not only was it out of time but out of place, too.

My curiosity got the best of me, and I had to find the reason behind this surreal Western display. We never would have imagined coming across something very iconic historical American in modern Germany.

Not seeing any "kein Betreten" (No Trespassing) sign, we went through the wooden gate into another world.

I noticed an older man in authentic-looking Native American dress feeding a horse on the far side of the encampment. I left Mish and the boys to explore the tepees while I cautiously approached the stranger. When I reached him, he looked up smiling friendly.

"Hello sir," I started. "I'm an American who just moved to Germany with my family. I couldn't help but notice this place as we walked by. May I ask what it is?"

"This is our camp," he replied simply in English with a slight German accent.

I think he saw the utterly confused look on my face and continued.

"We are descendants of Native Americans who moved here long ago. This is our way of keeping our culture alive and sharing it," he explained.

I was taken back. I never considered Native Americans expatriating to Germany. Who knew? An idea suddenly came to mind.

"Would you consider allowing a local Cub Scout Pack from the international school to come and visit to learn about your culture?" I eagerly asked.

The man smiled broadly and his eyes gleamed with pleasure.

"We would love that," he replied. "We very much want to have people come visit to appreciate this place, especially young ones."

I was over-the-moon thrilled! I could not believe our luck. I was the new Cub Scout Leader for the Pack and was looking for ways to give my Scouts a taste of good old American pioneering spirit. Eureka! My mind raced with ideas of how I could make this a once in a Scouting experience. I was already imagining camping in a real tepee with real Indians doing real native crafts.

The nice gentleman even gave me a pamphlet with contact information so I could get in touch with them. I thanked him profusely and hustled back to Mish and the boys, who by this time had gone into every tepee and were now petting the horses. I triumphantly told her about my find. She was as amazed and ecstatic as I was. Being my Assistant Pack Leader and cohort in crime, she knew that I would be roping her into this next little adventure anyway. It is a very good thing she loves me and tolerates my crazy ideas.

We continued with our walk delighted in how the day, and living in Germany, was going so far. I was enjoying teaching at the international school. It was very different than the English one I just left. Instead of one nationality, I taught to an international body from over twenty countries. At first, I was concerned that teaching to such a diverse multicultural audience would be problematic with the language barriers. My fears were put to rest the first day. All my students spoke excellent English. Some of them even spoke three or more languages. I am embarrassed to say that I struggled to learn French after four years of school. I still cannot *parle Francais* without making a mess of it.

I learned that German students are required to learn English at about age nine, along with their native tongue. Later, in secondary school, they can pick up a third language too if they want, which most do. Many Germans, therefore, are tri-lingual by the time they graduate secondary school. Unbelievable! We were struggling to pick up enough German just to get by.

The downside, for us, of having Germans speak our language was that we were never forced to learn their language. Everywhere we went, everyone accommodated us by speaking perfect English. This proved too convenient. Bit by bit, I let my German lessons slide. I promised myself I would not leave here until I was at least conversational in the language.

Elijah, on the other hand, was going to have to learn German. We acquiesced to the German educational system's demand that he be put in a German elementary school immediately. Needless to say, Elijah was not happy about this. He had lost this battle. Unknowingly to us in his clever little mind, he was plotting a counterattack.

After our walk, and obligatory gelato, we went off our separate ways to get ready for a new week. The three-story town house we lived in was working out splendidly. On the first floor were the kitchen, dining area, and living room. Mish or I could cook meals without disturbing, or being disturbed, by anyone else. Our bedroom was on the third floor. The boys occupied the entire second floor, so we could peak in on them quickly as we went to and from the kitchen and our area. This arrangement was working well, except for one slightly annoying flaw. Our only bedroom window looked straight across the town square to the church steeple. Every time the church bell clock tolled, its ringing had a clear path through our window. Its sound wave reverberated around the room. Sometimes, German reliability was truly annoying. Sleeping in on Sunday mornings was nearly impossible.

Despite bells echoing in my head, I usually got a good night's sleep. It's amazing what you can get use to when the need arises. I once slept under the steel flight deck of an aircraft carrier for two years. When I laid on my back, my nose was actually less than six feet from Navy jets landing above me. The noise was unbearable. I could even see the overhead warp and flex with each touchdown. After a while, I could tell what aircraft landed by the distinct impact it made. After a few weeks of exhaustive shipboard life, I slept like a baby through flight operations. Luckily, that conditioning seemed to apply to bells too.

Other than some misgivings with the clock tower keeper, we were settled in and enjoying our new life. Once again, we were successfully adapting to a new country. I bought a bicycle and started to ride to work. I got there early enough to swim a few laps in the school pool, shower, and get some coffee before my first class. This exercise regimen helped offset the heavy German food and baked goods I was consuming.

I was amazed at how many Germans were following similar daily workout routines. No matter what the weather, we would always see people out and about running, biking, or Nordic walking. Despite drinking a lot of beer and eating a lot of bread and schnitzel, Germans were a fairly fit bunch. Not that I am comparing them to us Americans with our drive-through fast-food couch potato lifestyle.

German health and fitness, we found went to a whole other level. Our neighbors introduced us to the German spa. Spas in America and spas in Germany are two very different things. American spas mostly cater to women. They offer manicures, pedicures, massages, and other self-pampering stuff. German spas are something altogether different.

Spa in German is "heilbad," which translates to "healing bath." German towns with the prefix "Bad" in front of their name indicate that they are spa towns. If you look at a map, you will see many Bad something on it. Germans really like their spas.

Spa culture in Germany is important to understand before you visit one. We, however, went in blind. First and foremost, Germans believe in co-ed changing rooms where both men and women are openly naked. This wouldn't have been a problem for me, I think, except when I took our two boys into one to put on their swim trunks, and there were nude women of all ages standing around. I had a dad moment where I felt the overwhelming urge to cover their young, inquisitive eyes.

"Eyes straight ahead, guys," I warned them.

Once out of the locker room, things got much better. No spa, fitness center, or recreation place looked like this. Under a huge glass dome were multiple swimming pools. The main pool was irregularly shaped and rimmed by a beach complete with real palm trees and a giant waterfall. Beach chairs were scattered all around with people working on their tans under UV lights. While outside was cold and snowy, inside was warm and humid. We stared in disbelief at this miniature tropical paradise. Germans know how to do a spa!

Off the main dome were fitness rooms with weights and cardio equipment, a massage parlor, a sauna, which we avoided because it is fully nude with mixed genders, and a cabana for refreshments. The boys straightaway ran to the faux beach and jumped into the warm water. We were really going to like this German spa culture.

Germany has very strict regulations on water quality. They do not use chlorine to disinfect their pools. Instead, they have ultra-efficient, of course, water purification systems that keep the water better than most natural springs. Consequently, the water is crystal clear and does not burn your eyes or dry your skin. We were in Heaven.

Spas are another manifestation of the German love of all things nature. For Germans, the great outdoors, forests, rivers, mountains, are not just nice things to look at, they are necessities. Throughout their history, forests, and woodlands have been at the heart of stories, legends, and fables, where wolves prowl on unsuspecting young girls in red hoods, lost siblings stumble onto ginger-bread houses occupied by hungry witches, and mystical castles harbor evil queens with talking mirrors. German children grow up knowing the forests as part of their culture. It runs in their blood.

France has Paris, the City of Lights, England has London, The City of Royalty, but Germany has the Black Forest. Although Berlin cannot compete with other European cities in architecture and design, the rest of Europe cannot compete with Germany's magnificent landscape. It is no wonder why Germans are nature lovers, the country is beautiful.

Germans' love of their homeland is evident everywhere. You will be very hard pressed to find a piece of litter, some graffiti, or an ugly billboard detracting from the natural scenery. Everywhere we ventured was unbelievably clean and orderly. To see the land defaced would wound any German, regardless of class, deep in the heart. They could no more willfully destroy their wild lands than they could harm themselves. Their staunch devotion to the environment was an inspiration to us. I think the rest of the world could learn from them.

Maybe the Germans' love of the land is why some Native Americans ex-patriated to Germany. Many Germans certainly are fascinated with them, too. They seem to have an overly romantic vision of Native Americans communing with nature and living as one with it. We found this kindred spirit notion between two extremely disparate cultures amazing.

We found out just how remarkable this relationship was on our Cub Scout camp out at the Native American village we discovered. Mish and I meticulously planned the event. Ok, she did all the work while I rallied the troops. Either way, we had about a dozen eager young scouts with their parents pumped up to go. I was excited.

When the big day arrived, we caravanned to the village hoping for an incredible experience. We were not disappointed. Our hosts went all out.

The tribe greeted us in full regalia. Their costumes were authentic down to the minutest detail. They smiled broadly with her arms stretched out in a gesture of welcome. They obviously were pleased to have guests to entertain and share their culture with. Our young scouts' eyes lit up with excitement as they entered the compound and saw the spectacle before them.

Our hosts built a large roaring campfire in the middle of the teepees. Already, there was one Native American sitting in front of the fire rhythmically beating on a deerskin drum. Another host had set up an archery range for the scouts to practice their woodland skills while still another had saddled the small ponies for the scouts to ride. We were over the moon impressed. This was going to be a fun evening.

First things first. At the beckoning of our hosts, we all gathered around the campfire. The elder chieftain led us in a song of welcome and praise. He then showed us how to do a traditional dance. Not surprisingly, the young scouts, without hesitation, jumped right in and began dancing and singing. We chanted and paraded around the fire as the bright orange flames reached up to a star filled sky. Already, we were immersed in the imaginary world of the American Old West.

It really was a special evening for all of us. Our hosts eagerly shared their passion for their culture and heritage with us. The scouts readily absorbed it all. They practiced archery, rode horses, learned songs and dances, listened to old tales, and made new friends. This is what Scouting is all about, giving young boys real experiences that will last a lifetime. I am always proud and humble to be part of it with them.

After we ate a delicious meal of roasted meat cooked on an open grill, we sat back around the fire and just enjoyed the quiet evening. Eventually, sleep started to creep in on us. We did one last song and dance before bed and thanked our hosts again. As I went to check that the scouts were all tucked snug in their tepees, I glimpsed Elijah, still dancing around the fire by himself in a trance-like state. I am never sure what goes on in his little head, but he seemed to be content to dance away. I went over and broke the spell.

"Time for bed kiddo," I told him.

He yawned and nodded in agreement. I escorted him to his tepee and made sure he was all set for the night. I went back to the fire to find Aaron sitting in front, tending it by himself.

"I'm going to stay up and watch the fire," he informed me.

I let him. He is old enough and very responsible to look after himself when we camp. Also, I know he is a very self-reflective young man who likes to be by himself sometimes to contemplate. I made one last survey of the area and headed off to find Mish and contemplated some sleep myself. The camp fell into a peaceful silence.

The next morning, I woke up and roused the boys. Aaron was still dutifully sitting by the fire, which he had kept going all through the night. Being good scouts, we cleaned the camp and offered to help with any needed chores before we departed. Scouting instills the practice of leaving a place cleaner than you found in the scouts. We always remember this, but in Germany, this seemed redundant.

Germany, Native Americans, Scouts, they all seemed to blend nicely together here. They all have the same core value of being stewards of the land. Instead of dominating and fencing out nature, we should live as one within it.

This concept is in stark contrast to the well-ordered Victorian gardens of England we just came from. The English do not appreciate nature the way Germans do. The English want a tame, subjugated nature with man as master of all he surveys. The Germans, on the other hand, love the raw, wild side of nature where it can be both beautiful and dangerous. Maybe this is one of the reasons they do not relate to each other well. I must admit, I side with the Germans on this.

We need nature. We all need from time to time to break out of our self-imposed exile in modern society and feel the freedom of the open wilderness. On some deep subconscious level, it beckons to us to come back to our roots. In losing our artificial urban existence we find ourselves again. I never thought this would be clearer than living in Germany. Apparently, Germany has several lessons to teach me.

Chapter 8 – A Very Snow Globe Christmas

"Es ist Zeit zum Feiern und zum Versammeln. Ich hoffe das du deine Zeit mit den Personen verbringen kannst die dir am meisten bedeuten. Ein frohes und festliches Weihnachtsfest!" (It is a time for celebration and gatherings. I wish that you may spend your time meaningfully with the people close to your heart. Have a wonderful and merry Christmas!) – Traditional German Christmas toast

It was getting to be Christmas time! Christmas is special all around the world, but it is extra special in Germany. It is so special that the Germans celebrate it on two days, December 25th, Christmas Day, and December 26th, St. Stephen's Day. In fact, they even start celebrating it on Advent Sunday, the four Sundays before Christmas Eve. It is a season of rich, time-honored traditions, warm family gatherings, and lots of delicious food and drink.

We could scarcely believe that school was half over and a new year was just around the corner. The weather in Germany had turned from cool to cold to downright freezing almost overnight. The autumn was glorious with all the brilliant fall colors, but too short. Now, the grey sky ominously looked like snow was on its way.

We had skipped one of the most quintessential German autumn traditions, Oktoberfest. While most towns celebrate this traditional folk festival with zeal and a lot of beer, the original and largest takes place in Munich. Since we had heard that most of the festivities were geared towards adults only, we opted to skip it.

I know it is sacrilegious to say while living in Germany, but we're really not big beer drinkers, and I only drink Guinness anyway. I'm worried they might deport me if they find out. Besides, being around loud drunk people is not something I enjoy. From what I heard from colleagues at school who attended, I don't think we missed anything, except maybe a hangover.

Instead, our sights were set on enjoying all the Advent family traditions leading up to the big finale, Christmas. One of the best-known and anxiously anticipated holiday events is the Christkindlesmarkts or Christmas Markets. These holiday bazaars originated in Germany in the Middle Ages and have been an integral part of the season ever since. We soon found out why.

We went to our first market in Frankfurt on a brisk Saturday afternoon in early December. We had heard of the famed Christmas markets, but nothing compares to actually being at one. They set a very high bar for holiday cheer. Wow! It was like being at Santa's workshop.

The plaza in downtown Frankfurt was filled with small wooden sheds forming a maze of small shops, all decorated with strings of white lights and green and red garlands. As we walked down the narrow avenues, we were treated to a plethora of holiday delights. There were all sorts of novelties for sale. We gazed at the myriads of crafts in admiration while the smell of freshly baked treats tantalized our noses, and the melody of Christmas carols filled our ears. We didn't know where to look first.

The boys and I instinctively followed our noses to the nearest bakery shop. We gaped with tongues out at the giant cookies and pretzels. Mish caught up with us shortly. She knew where we had gone and just shook her head and rolled her eyes in mock disapproval. Her teasing wasn't going to stop us from a little holiday indulgence. The boys and I each picked a treat; Aaron carefully scrutinized all of his options, Elijah went straight to the biggest item, and I opted once again for the chocolatiest. We now had some sustenance to continue our trek. After all, holiday shopping was hard work; we needed to keep our energy up.

Mish, meanwhile had discovered her preferred holiday treat. A shop introduced her to a traditional holiday drink, Gluhwein. The name literally translates to "glow wine." It is usually some type of mulled wine with spices served hot in cute little mugs. After a few sips, Mish realized where it got its name from. The concoction caused her to have a warm feeling inside and a slightly rosy complexion outside on her cheeks. It's the perfect drink for walking around the markets in the cold.

Now that we all had something to soothe our taste buds, we continued our way through the market in search of more holiday goodies. German craftsmanship is legendary for a reason. We marveled at the care and attention to detail the artisans gave to each piece. The wooden toys were especially beautiful. Some lucky young boys and girls were going to find them under their Christmas trees this year.

In the center of the market was the crown jewel of any Christmas festival, the tree. Majestically standing a good fifty feet tall was one of the most spectacular Christmas trees we had ever seen. It had been meticulously decorated with colorful giant lights and ornaments all the way to the top, where it was crowned with a large bright star. It towered over the little market sheds and lit up the whole plaza. The whole scene was something out of a Christmas Carol. Even the Grinch would get into the holiday spirit here.

The Christkindlesmarkts truly are something special. They are in stark contrast to the over-commercialized phony displays at shopping malls in America. They are an authentic tradition. No plastic, neon, made in China, gaudy displays here. This was as genuine as it gets. For some reason, that nostalgia stirs some deep emotions of true joy and satisfaction in us. People need a sense of belonging to the past. It gives us a sense of continuity, which is very comforting.

After getting a little taste of German Christmas, we opted to go for the ultimate in holiday ambience and planned a trip to Rothenburg ob der Tauber in Bavaria. Rothenberg, we have been told, is the most German of German cities. We were anxious to see for ourselves.

Rothenberg is one of only three remaining intact "walled cities" in Germany. It is completely enclosed by a two-mile stone and timber rampart that was used to protect the medieval town from invaders. Inside the fortifications, the town blossomed and prospered to become the second largest city in Germany in the 12th century. Today, it is an anachronistic little village frozen in time, but still retains the cutest German town award.

The drive to Bavaria is fairly bland and uninteresting. Once you get to Bavaria, however, everything changes. Berlin may be the capital of Germany, but Bavaria is its heart. It is a land of awe-inspiring beauty with dense alpine forests, rushing waterfalls, fantastical castles, and adorable wooden chalets dotting the green hillsides. The scenery looks like it just leapt right out of a fairy tale book.

As we neared Rothenburg, it was getting dark. At the northern latitudes the sun sets relatively early this time of year. Having lived in England and Seattle, we were very accustomed to short winter days. Knowing this, however, did not stop any of us from yawning loudly despite the early time. We were anxious to get to our hotel and relax. Even Albie looked ready for bed. Oh wait, that's his normal look.

We found the hotel almost by accident. It was tucked down in a narrow alley with only a small sign above the door to distinguish it from all the other old buildings. Since it was dark, cold, and drizzly, we decided to settle in for the evening to get a good night's sleep. The next morning, we awoke refreshed and headed out to explore the historic city on foot.

It was cold, but the clouds had dried up, and a little bit of blue sky poked out through the grey above. First order of business, find coffee. We stumbled upon a small quaint bakery with delectable-looking pastries in the window. Germans know how to bake. They are master artists who use wheat as their medium. We had trouble deciding on just one breakfast delight from all the mouth-watering choices. As usual, Elijah was first to order. I'll give it to him, he has a decisive mindset.

Now that we had hot drinks and warm treats, we were content to leisurely stroll around the city. Immediately, we were struck by how adorable and fantastical the city looked. We got the odd feeling we had been transported overnight while we slept to another time and place, and when we woke found ourselves in a storybook. The colorful plaster and wood timber buildings neatly lined the cobblestone streets, which meandered tantalizingly out of sight down narrow lanes and alleys. Colorful flower boxes adorned windows, and gilded wooden signs hung above intriguing doorways, inviting passersby to come in. Everywhere, there were holiday decorations cloaking the city in holiday splendor. Some wayward snowflakes drifted down, completing the scene. I really felt like we were in a giant Christmas snow globe.

We walked into shop after shop, never knowing quite what to expect. There were candle shops, boutiques, hat shops, glass sellers, candy stores, a metalsmith, toy stores, and, of course, stores selling Christmas paraphernalia of all sorts. In the city plaza they even had set up their very own Christmas Market. Self-control was the key to navigating through this holiday shopping gauntlet otherwise, you could easily empty your wallet.

Thanks to Mish keeping a firm grip on our finances, we didn't overindulge too much. We promised the boys that they could pick out one Christmas decoration each as a keepsake. Aaron found a hand-carved nutcracker in the form of a Boy Scout, fitting for our young Scout. Elijah picked a beautiful wooden candle carousel that had a snowy woodland scene with animals around Santa Claus, also fitting for our animal lover. We hoped that these would become heirloom items they would treasure forever and pass down to their children. Maybe someday, a young child will reverently place the Boy Scout nutcracker on a table at Christmas, and his parents will remind him that his great-grandfather got that in Germany when he was his age. These were holiday traditions in the making.

Right now, however, we were living in the present and enjoying being together as a family during Christmas in this special place. We listened to carolers in the plaza as we browsed the market, looking at more wondrous creations. All this walking caused us to work up an appetite, so we went in search of something to hold us over until dinner.

We had read about a Rothenburg traditional pastry called a schneeball. Essentially, they are strips of pie crust clumped into a ball, deep fried, and covered with various confections. They sounded amazing. The boys seem to have an uncanny ability to sense sweets a mile away. They quickly located a bakery that sold these sugary concoctions. Showcased in the baker's window must have been at least a dozen variations of them. Unfortunately for Elijah, they were all the same size. He had to default to his second criteria of picking sweets, which was the one with the most frosting. Once again, Aaron carefully considered all his options, and I got one smothered in chocolate. You get sticky fingers eating them because you peel off the dough strips layer by layer. Oh well, it is a price we were willing to pay.

As the sun set, holiday lights started to come on, which transformed the city into a twinkling display of Christmas splendor. The whole city took on another and even more storybook look. Thousands of bright little white lights trimmed all the buildings, gas streetlamps illuminated the walkways, candles flickered in windows, and above it all, a giant Christmas tree lit up the plaza.

Even though we were all getting a little tired from walking all day, we wanted to see the city all over again lit up. First, however, we needed food. We found a quaint restaurant off the main plaza and sat down for dinner. I have to admit, I am not a huge fan of German food. We've had schnitzel in just about every way imaginable and were looking for something less German. Luckily, the restaurant catered to a more international customer and served a variety of suitable dishes. Having non-German food in the most German of German towns was probably not very authentic, but it was more satisfying.

After more walking and window shopping, we finally called it a day and headed back. Rothenberg is very special, especially at Christmas. I really have a hard time explaining why, though. Maybe it's because it reminds me of a favorite childhood Christmas tale. Maybe it's because its nostalgic charm harkens to a simpler bygone era. Maybe because it's easy to pretend you're in some fairy tale story while you're there. I'm not sure. No matter what the reason, we did thoroughly enjoy our time exploring the city. It made our first Christmas in Germany very memorable.

Making holidays special is important. The times you have as a family in the present will form the foundation of traditions and memories in the future. We want our children to look forward to

Christmas even when they are older, not because of presents or time off but because it reminds them of fond times as children. We try to build the memories now so our children can relive their childhood every Christmas time.

Chapter 9 – The White Elephant in Germany

"Those who do not remember the past are condemned to repeat it."
– George Santayana

Christmas Day was fast approaching. The boys were getting anxious for the winter break from school, as were Mish and I. I know Elijah definitely was looking forward to escaping from German school for a while. I dropped him off in the morning yesterday and wished him a good day.

"Off to another day of torture," he snarkily replied and waived as he walked up the steps of the school.

Great, I thought. I'm mentally scarring my kid for life. Someday, he'll need therapy over being forced to attend German school, and it will be my fault. Children definitely know how to lay guilt trips on their parents. Elijah was an expert.

Our little village, Eddersheim, was covered in a thick blanket of pure white snow. We only got one short snowfall that came and went while living in England, but here in Germany, it snows and stays. The boys loved going out and playing in it. Even Albie enjoyed frolicking in the stuff. His dense coat seemed to keep him pretty insulated, along with some fat he had put on for the winter. The snow would stick to his fur and build up in a thick layer. When he came inside after playing with the boys, he looked like an Abominable Snow Puppy. Mish would have to thaw him out so he didn't freeze solid. Boys, two and four-legged, will run around in the cold all day and risk frostbite if you let them.

We were really enjoying another European Christmas. Germany has taken the holiday to a whole other level. We had been to a few Christmas markets but were not tired of them yet. Mish learned that the oldest one was in Nuremberg. I had wanted to see this city and checking out the original German Christkindlesmarkts was a good excuse to go.

Nuremberg has a long and storied history in Germany. The city dates back to at least 1050 AD. It developed around an imperial castle built by German King Henry III, Duke of Bavaria, who became the Holy Roman emperor. Thus, the city was dubbed the unofficial capital of the empire, making it a very important location.

The Nazi party was well aware of the city's historical significance. Their decision to host large Nazi propaganda rallies at Nuremberg was no coincidence. Hitler's blatant attempt to link the old empire with new Germany was not lost on the German people. The now infamous rallies drew thousands of people from around Germany.

I have seen many old black and white photographs in history books of these rallies with Hitler in front of giant swastika flags, stiffly giving the Nazi salute to rank upon rank of well-ordered soldiers marching past. Those haunting images epitomized the power Hitler wielded. And they took place right here in Nuremberg. Despite the Christmas spirit, I had a macabre desire to stand where Hitler did when he preached German superiority to transfixed crowds of misguided followers. I wondered if some left over evil presence still lurked in that place.

Nuremberg is only a few hours' drive from home, so we decided to make it a long day trip. By this time, we were accustomed to the high-speed autobahn and I was thrilled to have a car that could actually keep up, mostly, with the frantic flow of traffic. The new German-made Mercedes family wagon was quite at home on its native roads. I wasn't brave enough to get in the left lane, but at least I no longer hugged the right shoulder.

We made it to Nuremberg in short order and set off to explore a new city. We found the Christmas market straight away. It would have been impossible to miss. It was by far the biggest and most extravagant one we had been to. The typical makeshift village of wooden huts stretched around the city center and out of sight. We were now seasoned marketgoers and knew exactly what to do. Mish got her usual Gluhwein, and the boys and I got our obligatory pastries, and we set off into the fray.

Some of the merchandise is normal at every market, like touristy ornaments and keepsakes, but there are also unique crafts exclusive to every market. You never know what you will find, which makes it like a holiday treasure hunt. Nuremberg certainly had its share of distinctive artisans. We found many things we really wanted to buy but kept it to a few precious items. After all, our hands were already full of tasty treats.

In the center of the market, we found an ice-skating rink. I was thrilled, but Mish was very dubious, which was understandable. I grew up in Connecticut playing pond hockey every winter while she spent her childhood frolicking on warm sunny beaches. To me, the ice was a sacred arena to do battle with sticks and a puck. I think Mish regarded it as a place to break something, like your head.

I was undeterred by my wife's reluctance. The boys had never been on skates and were eager to try, probably because I assured them it was fun. Aaron is more outgoing when it comes to trying new activities and anxiously put on his rented skates. Elijah, on the other hand, is more cautious. He eyed the rink and skaters carefully, scrutinizing whether it was a safe place or Dad was nuts. Eventually, he too put on his skates and headed onto the ice, too.

Luckily, the rink was very tame. All the skaters had to skate, shuffle, slide, or crawl in a counter-clockwise rotation around the ice. Aaron carefully and slowly merged into the flow using the skating techniques I told him. Elijah ignored all of my advice and barreled off after his brother. Unfortunately for him, the laws of physics still applied. His little legs shuffled in a blur of motion, but he went nowhere except finally down. Unfazed, he got right back up and went at it again, only to end in the same position. This time, he grudgingly crawled over to the wall, carefully stood up, and tightly hugged the guard rail for support as he made his way slowly in pursuit of his big brother. We love his sheer tenacity.

Mish and I sat this one out and just followed the boys on the outside as they navigated their way around the rink. We tried not to cringe, or laugh, too much when they fell. After a few laps, they were exhausted and exited the ice. Aaron agreed to try it again sometime; Elijah decided once was good. Fair enough, they tried something new and reminded me of my younger days learning to skate and play hockey. Children are good for that.

The boys' rosy, red cheeks and fading sunlight told us it was time to start heading home. Before we left, however, I wanted to check out the old parade grounds. I didn't want to ruin the Christmas spirit, but since we were here, I thought it would be worth a look.

I was very surprised to learn that the Reichsparteitagsgelände, the former Nazi propaganda complex, still survived. After the war, Germans made a huge, concerted effort to obliterate everything Nazi from the country. In fact, it is illegal to display anything Nazi related or do the Sieg Heil, the Nazi style salute, in public. A Berlin man taught his dog named Adolf to give the banned salute. The obedient German shepherd raised its right paw on command. He got off with a warning, but the owner was sentenced by a local court to five months in jail. Germans take Nazism seriously, which is why I was surprised that they kept one of the most flagrant symbols of Nazism around.

So, in what seemed to be a very anti-Christmas family activity we went off in search of Hitler's old stomping grounds. We didn't have to go far. They are located just outside of the downtown area. The sprawling complex consists of athletic fields, stadiums, a lake, park grounds, and the Kongresshalle.

The Kongresshalle, or Congress Hall, was purposefully built to be the home of the National Socialist German Workers' Party, or Nazi party for short. It was inspired by the Roman Colosseum and designed to awe onlookers with its power and grace. It was to be Hitler's new seat of power. However, like all of the buildings on the grounds, it went unfinished. The outbreak of the war halted all construction, and with the Nazi's defeat, Hitler's dream never fully materialized.

Across the small lake, Grober Dutzendteich is the imposing Zeppelinfeld. That is what I really came here for. It was the center of Nazism. From it, Hitler spread his evil gospel and showcased his power to the world.

We pulled up alongside the massive edifice. I looked at the enormous grey concrete structure with awe and a little reverence. The giant swastika adorning the top had long since been blown apart by the victorious allied forces and the enormous red flags no longer draped the front façade, but it still was a ghostly reminder of the power of the Third Reich.

From the massive grandstand, Hitler commanded respect. His virulent speeches captivated audiences with their seductive messages of hate and conquest. Like some perverse chess grandmaster, he looked down at his pawns to see his cunning strategy play out. In a loud chorus his minions exuberantly responded "Sieg Heil!" at the end of each tirade. I could imagine the ferocious echo of their voices reverberating across the field. The thought sent chills down my spine.

Mish either did not share my fascination with this place or did not want to dampen the Christmas spirit, so she stayed in the car with the boys. Alone in the silent cold, I walked up the concrete steps to the viewing platform. I had the very real and eerie sense of ghosts of the past watching me as I ascended the once hallowed place.

Upon reaching the top I turned and looked out on the expansive parade field below. It was empty now, but once tens of thousands crowded in to see their exalted leader. To address an audience that huge and have them look up and idolize you would have been an ego booster of epic proportions. It is no wonder why Hitler got drunk on power. His mega-rallies helped feed his insatiable ego. I felt very vulnerable and small standing on the same spot, though. I guess my need for adoration was filled in my humble life.

On the drive back home, I talked with Mish about the juxtaposition of Christmas and Nazism. I thought that they were two competing forces that if they tried to exist at the same time and place would explode. Heavy thinking, I know. She is ever my sounding board and patiently listens to my ramblings, especially when she is trapped in the car on a long ride with me. I was perplexed with Germans, again, and needed to reason it out.

I knew from history that Hitler did not seize power in a coupe; he was democratically elected as Chancellor of Germany. The Nazi Party won the majority of votes by a landslide in the election of 1933, placing Hitler decisively in power. His beliefs and agenda were very clear from the start, violent antisemitism, extreme nationalism, and swift revenge on those who wronged Germany. The German people knew this, yet still overwhelmingly endorsed him. Why?

I see Germans at Christmas time enthralled with the holiday season and all it stands for, peace on Earth and goodwill towards man. They are generous and warm people. How could these same people with one hand applaud a monster and with the other hand celebrate the birth of the Savior?

I know The War was a while ago, but not that long. There are still millions of Germans alive today who were affirmed Nazis, many fought against the Allies in bloody battles and fervently supported the war effort and Jewish persecution. People change, but that much? Questions like this keep me preoccupied sometimes, sometimes too much. Mish didn't have the answers, and neither did I. We speculated on possible reasons but couldn't come to a firm conclusion. At least the deep conversation made the miles pass.

Living in Europe has opened our eyes to new paradigms. Nationalism is different here than in the United States. We call it patriotism, but it's the same thing. I grew up being taught that loving your country was a good thing. As children, we obediently said the Pledge of Allegiance facing the flag every morning at school. We proudly stand at ball games for the National Anthem. On the Fourth of July, we get teary-eyed during the fireworks show. So, why here did patriotism, or nationalism, cause so many problems?

I like to think that I have a fairly good knowledge of history. I know the historical facts of how things went down in Germany after World War I. In a nutshell, the victorious Ally's harsh punishment of Germany through the Treaty of Versailles sowed the seeds for a second round. France and Britain did not expect Germany's revenge to come as quickly and violently, and the United States hoped to stay out of another expensive foreign war at all costs. Those and other factors allowed the

Nazi movement to grow unchecked until it was too late. That still, however, does not explain why people would embrace a radical and, to a large degree, illogical ideology.

Nazism is the huge white elephant in the room in Germany. Everyone knows it existed and amazingly still does, but no one talks about it. It is not a subject you just casually bring up at a social gathering. "So tell me, Hans, why were your parents Nazis?" That would not go over well. Yet, I still wanted to ask it.

One day at school, a group of my students were talking about the upcoming World Cup games. I have learned that American football fans' enthusiasm for their team pales in comparison to the fanaticism of German "football" fans. Their passion for their national team knows no bounds. This year was especially intense because Germany looked very promising to take the World Cup Championship. I really don't care about "soccer" but I cheered on the team anyway, partly because I wanted to fit in and partly because I wanted to see how crazy this place becomes if they win.

I casually mentioned to my students how proud they seemed of their national team. I truly only meant it as a passing observation. However, one of them took it a little sensitively and responded that, "Americans are the most obnoxiously proud people in the world." I was taken back. I let the comment be, but it did give me pause to think. I never considered my American patriotism obnoxious or more fervent than any other country's national pride. Maybe I am wrong.

I keep informed on current events back in the United States. Many of the stories on the news seem too familiar, but now I look at them through a different lens. I am an outsider looking in instead of being immersed in the action. Even though it is my homeland, it seems remote and detached from my everyday life. I feel that I am looking at old problems through new eyes. I didn't anticipate this type of epiphany from merely living in another country.

The happenings back home have me greatly concerned. I can see some scary parallels to the rise of Nazism in Germany and the extreme nationalism brewing in America. Some politicians are blaming immigrants for my country's problems the same way Hitler blamed the Jews. They are espousing white Anglo-Saxons as the true inheritors of our Founding Fathers like he did the Aryan race in Germany and Austria. It's as if they read the Nazi propaganda playbook: scapegoat a select fringe group, place your group on a virtuous pedestal, cry your group is under siege, vilify and discredit any and all opposition, and then use your perceived plight as an excuse to seize power. It worked once, so it will probably work again. Nothing changes, I suppose.

I do not want my gloomy thoughts to cast a shadow over Christmas. Even though we may be living in darkening times, right now is bright and hopeful. I take solace that evil was defeated once and can be again. We were going to make this the best holiday season so far. The Christmas spirit lives on eternal.

Irish statesman Edmund Burke wrote in a letter to a friend that, "The only thing necessary for the triumph of evil is for good men to do nothing." How true! History does not have to repeat itself. We have the power to learn from the past and take a different path for the future. We can learn a lot from each other if we allow ourselves to see through each other's eyes.

Chapter 10 – The City of Light

"A walk about Paris will provide lessons in history, beauty, and in the point of Life." – Thomas Jefferson

In my favorite movie of all time, Casablanca, Humphrey Bogart longingly tells Ingrid Bergman, "We'll always have Paris." There are so many famous quotes, movies, books, paintings, and fond memories attributed to Paris that there has to be something special about this city. We were headed there to find out.

The last time we were in France was over the winter holiday break last year. We toured the north coast from Calais to Mont Saint-Michel but never ventured far from the English Channel. This time, we were going to cut through Eastern France and go straight for its heart, Paris. The drive was less than six hours from Frankfurt, so we knew we could take our time and enjoy the French countryside.

To have breakfast in Germany and later that day lunch in Paris is one of the many things that make living in Europe grand. If you wanted, you could even have dinner the same evening in Luxemburg or Switzerland. The variety of cultures in an area slightly smaller than the United States is amazing. Every family outing was a different experience. Someday we hope that the boys will reflect back on this time and appreciate their unique childhood. If nothing else, we have given them the world as their neighborhood.

We set out early because we wanted to maximize our time in Paris, plus Mish wanted to do a pit-stop in the French city of Reims. Reims is

255

famous as the city that the legendary Joan of Arc liberated so that Charles VII could be crowned King of France in its historical cathedral, and it also happens to be in the center of the Champagne region. I am not sure which reason was the more motivating factor for Mish's desire to stop there.

One motivating reason for me to stop in Reims was 20th-century history. A bit of historical trivia I knew was that this city was where, on May 7, 1945, Germany unconditionally surrendered, marking an end to war in Europe. An obscure general, one of the last still alive, General Alfred Jodl, representing the German High Command, signed the papers. For his trouble, he was found guilty by the Nuremberg Trials of war crimes and hanged. Some people just can't get a break.

Road trips have been a great way for our family to connect. We have our rituals when we start off. I must have my mocha, iced or hot, depending on the season. Mish brings books to read and snacks for everyone, the boys gather some games and books to fight over, and Albie comes resigned to another long car trip. I'm not sure if he cares or not because he sleeps twenty hours a day anyway. Once we buckled into our assigned seats, we were ready to set out once more on an adventure.

We make it a point to educate ourselves on our destination. We've learned more about European geography and history while living here than we ever did from schoolbooks. Mish is very good at enlightening us with bits of trivia as we drive, too. She usually starts with, "Did you know…" followed by some obscure piece of knowledge that only a Jeopardy champion could answer. "What was the Celtic tribe that first founded the city of Paris in the 3rd century B.C. for $500, Mish." Of course, the answer is the Parisii. Everyone knows that.

On this particular trip we were schooled in the history of the Grand Est region of France. Did you know true Champagne only comes from this region? By international trademark, it is illegal to call any other sparkling wine Champagne. Not only does it have to come from this region, the vineyards have to use a specific grape and follow very strict rules in order to use the Champagne label on their bottles also. All along, I thought I was toasting New Years with the real stuff. I feel uncouth now. We promised ourselves that we would pick up a real bottle of Champagne while we were passing through the region.

The region is very pretty. We drove up small, wooded mountain ranges where, from the crests, we got breathtaking views below of bright green valleys filled with vineyards and tidy Tudor homes along silver ribbons of small rivers. It is definitely a land stuck in time. I doubt that the scenery has changed at all in a century, which is a good thing. Not all change is good. I wonder if the residents knew, or cared, that we were very appreciative that they forsook the modern world so the rest of us could longingly admire their lifestyle.

Driving in Europe is mostly a pleasure, aside from the motorways of the UK and the Autobahn of Germany. It is an experience to be enjoyed, not just a means to get somewhere as quickly as possible. There are no ten lane mega-interstates cutting straight across the country as in the US. Our highways were largely built after the automobile was invented. Here, roads follow old horse and cart trade routes from city to city as they meander across the countryside. If you want high-speed transit, you take a train. If you want to really immerse yourself in the culture, drive.

We were definitely feeling very immersed in French culture. I was trying, none too successfully, to practice my long disused French. My high school French teacher would not be pleased with my poor pronunciation. I could imagine her just shaking her head and saying, "Monsieur Luc, vous devez pratiquer plus." I never was a very good language student anyway.

Soon enough, we were on the outskirts of Paris! The quaint pastoral landscape quickly became overrun with crowded urban life. For the most part, all cities look the same from their peripheries. There are always the uninspiring generic buildings, warehouses, factories, and lower-end apartments surrounding the actual city. You are obliged to drive through this vast outer defense as you penetrate deeper towards the center. It's a city's core that differentiates it from all others. Paris's core is, without a doubt, a special treasure hidden in the center of a sprawling, bland urban area.

As the roads started to connect, traffic increased accordingly. Parisian drivers are not known for their courtesy. I had to switch to offense driving mode to keep from being run off the road or into something. Mish hung on to the armrests with an iron grip. We knew we were getting very close to downtown.

We rounded a group of high-rise buildings and caught our breath as we got our first glimpse of the Eiffel Tower! There it was in all its steel grandeur, rising high above the city. I know that many Parisians apparently did not like Eiffel's contribution to the 1889 World's Fair, but I'm glad they got over it. The tower truly is magnificent. Due to very strict zoning laws in Paris that keep buildings no more than seven stories, the tower dominates the city skyline at an impressive 81 stories. Even the boys instantly recognized it and were awed.

Mish had scored a small hotel very close to the Eiffel Tower, so the tower acted as a beacon for us to navigate by. We used it and Mish's map reading to find our lodging. Parking was another challenge. All cities are parking nightmares, but Paris takes it to another level. We saw cars parked perpendicular to the curb, cars parked up on sidewalks, cars parked in the street, and cars parked so tightly up to other cars, the driver would never be able to get in. Amazingly, no one seemed to find this a problem. If there are parking police in Paris, they must be the busiest police in the world.

Luckily, the hotel had reserved parking for guests. We found our spot and checked in. The day was still early, so we wasted no time in heading back out to experience all that Paris has to offer.

For some unknown reason, Aaron got it in his head that he needed a French beret in order to properly experience Paris. He really wanted a picture of himself wearing one on a bike under the Eiffel Tower. Odd, but we obliged. Finding a beret in Paris is a fairly easy task. Next to our hotel, we found a souvenir shop with a sky-blue beret. Aaron was thrilled. Now we could get on with exploring the city.

The weather was perfect for a walk in this beautiful city. Mish, ever our travel guide, looked for points of interest. She steered us along a meandering path to the Rodin Museum. I will admit I did not know who Rodin was. Mish was surprised. Apparently, he should be on my list of artists for trivia night.

When we walked into the sculpture garden of the museum I had an instant epiphany.

"He's the guy that did The Thinker," I exclaimed!

I immediately recognized the famous statue of the solitary, heroic-looking man with his chin on the back of his hand, deep in thought. Even the boys recognized the bronze sculpture. I made a mental note to remember the sculptor's name. You never know when it might be a Trivial Pursuit question, or you need to toss it out at a party to sound cultured. Rodin, I got it.

Elijah and I preferred one of Rodin's other works more, The Gates of Hell. The monolithic piece depicts a smaller thinker solemnly sitting above giant iron doors adored with tortured souls. On top of the whole sculpture are The Shades, three figures with bowed heads pointing as one to the inscription, "Lasciate ogne speranza, voi ch'intrate" ("Abandon all hope, ye who enter here"). Sculpture or not, I would not walk through those doors for anything.

That was enough of an art lesson for one day. We casually walked backed to our hotel for dinner and an early turn in. Tomorrow will be a busy day.

The next morning, we headed out early with a busy agenda. Up first was the Louvre. We knew that touring the world's largest art museum would take time. I wasn't sure, however, if I really wanted to see 783,000 square feet of art. Since none of us are huge art aficionados, we agreed to just hit the highlights. I know that skimming through the Louvre is probably like reading the cliff notes of a famous novel, but to be honest, after a while all the paintings start to look alike to my untrained eye. I go into cultural overload and my brain shuts down. After all, I didn't even know who Rodin was until yesterday.

The Louvre did live up to its reputation. The enormity of it is staggering. We were quickly lost in its cavernous halls. This is one of those places where I think hiring an expert art tour guide would be very beneficial. Mish tried her best to educate us and point out significant pieces, but I soon tuned out. I tried to fake interest and nod occasionally so as to look somewhat intelligent. I hoped the boys were getting a good art appreciation lesson, at least.

The one piece of art I was excited to see was Leonardo da Vinci's masterpiece, the Mona Lisa. I knew that one. We knew when we found it by the throngs of visitors surrounding a small roped off area. We were obliged to wait our turn to glimpse the smiling mystery woman. When we finally got to the painting instant disappointment hit.

"It's really small," I said, stating the obvious.

It really is a lot smaller in person than you would think. It is only 30 inches by 21 inches. For some reason, I thought it would be much larger. Hanging on the wall by itself made it appear even more diminutive. I wasn't sure what else to say. My excitement for finally seeing the most famous painting in the world was tempered by my letdown for its size. It was a very anticlimactic experience. I guess I will stick with science and math. I was ready to leave now.

Unfortunately, Mish wanted to get our money's worth out of the tour, so we plodded onward to see more stuff by some famous artists we never heard of. We all gave our very uninformed opinions of various pieces nonetheless.

Elijah recognized a famous sculpture that I was not aware was in the Louvre, Winged Victory. He was greatly impressed with the Hellenistic piece. I must admit, it is very dramatic and conveys a sense of triumph. Luckily, no one knows who carved it so I didn't have to feel embarrassed that I didn't know either.

Once free of the maze of oil-painted canvases and marble sculptures, we emerged back into the sunlight of the real world. We felt more cultured, we agreed. We also agreed the Louvre can be a mind-numbing experience for the more artistically challenged types, like us. We will definitely hire a guide next time.

From the Louvre, we walked to Notre Dame. The medieval Catholic cathedral sits on the Île de la Cité in the middle of the Seine River. It is not the tallest, largest, or oldest cathedral in France, but it is certainly the most famous. With its innovative flying buttresses, tall spires, ornate stained-glass windows, and numerous sculptures, it is the epitome of French Gothic architecture. In addition, some of the most important relics in Christendom, including the Crown of Thorns, a sliver of the true cross and a nail from the true cross, are preserved there. It is definitely worth a look.

Inside the massive nave you feel the history and majesty of the church. I don't care if you are Catholic or even a Christian, architectural wonders such as this leave anyone in awe. The combination of engineering, design, and worship all come together beautifully in one magnificent edifice. Sadly, the original designers never got to see their master plan achieved because the cathedral took one-hundred-eight-two years to complete. Imagine starting a project knowing that not even your children would see it finished. That is dedication. In contrast, the Empire State Building was erected in less than two years. Expectations have definitely changed over time.

Our next must-see structure, the Eiffel Tower of course. Most monuments I have seen tend to appear smaller in real life than the pictures of them. The Eiffel Tower, however, was the opposite. I did not expect it to be this big! It truly dominates the city. As we walked up to it, it got bigger and bigger until we were straining our necks looking at its top. The four massive steel support arches that form the base are simple, yet impressive in size and design. The add strength to support the colossal weight of the structure while giving it a touch of elegance. Eiffel knew what he was doing.

Before getting in line for tickets, Aaron reminded us about his photo-opportunity. He had a beret, and we were under the Eiffel Tower. All we needed was a bike. I looked around, and sure enough, there was a plethora of bikes littering the park. Aaron spied one that fit his vision. I walked over to the owner and explained the situation. Luckily, he agreed to loan us his bike for an impromptu picture. We snapped several photographs to be sure that Aaron got the look he wanted. Success! Now we could get in line.

Since we were off-season, there was hardly a line to go to the top observation platform. At nine-hundred-six feet off the ground, it is the highest observation deck in the EU. Have I mentioned I do not like heights? I really do not like heights. I almost wimped out but couldn't let this possibly once-in-a-lifetime opportunity go by. So, I swallowed my fear and got into the small, creaky elevator with the family and a host of strangers and slowly ascended the tower.

Luckily, for the long ride up, I was in the back of the steel cage and couldn't see the ground drop away below us as we went up. Once we arrived at the top, I was able to unpack myself from the sardine can of an elevator and take a look around. That's when I suddenly realized how high we actually were.

I intrepidly looked out the observation window and was instantly awe-struck by a breathtaking view of Paris, and then I looked down. I heard Mish wince with pain, but I kept staring down, transfixed by the altitude and wondering if the tower would continue to stand, at least until we got back down.

"You're crushing my hand," Mish chided as she tried vainly to break free of my tight grasp.

I just kept looking down.

"Seriously, you're crushing my hand," she repeated with more earnestness. I finally realized what I was doing and released her poor hand. She rubbed it and laughed with the boys at my acrophobia.

"Are you going to be alright?" she asked, still laughing.

"Huh? No worries. I'm fine," I lied.

Secretly, I wanted to get back in the claustrophobic elevator and head back down immediately. Instead, I plucked up my courage and stood my ground while Mish and the boys looked out at the view, albeit away from the windows and as close to the center of the platform as possible.

The sun was setting, and bit by bit, the lights of the city came on in the growing dusk. The brightly lit boulevards that crisscrossed the dark below gave Paris the nickname of the City of Light. Day or night, it truly is a magnificent city.

Mercifully, they got their fill of Parisian cityscape shortly, and we packed ourselves in the elevator. I was very impressed by the tower's design. I admired the steel latticework through the glass windows of the elevator car, which helped take my mind off the height. This was built a hundred and twenty-five years ago. Impressive, I thought. I remarked to Mish about how forward-thinking Eiffel and his team were in their time. She just smiled knowingly back. Lucky for me, she overlooks some of my quirks.

Back safely on the ground, we took in the cool Paris evening. We decided that we would go back to the hotel via a long walk through the city. Everywhere, people were out and about. Delicious aromas wafted from open-air bistros. Loud music leaked out of trendy nightclubs. Parisians casually strolled along the boulevards. We let the aura of Paris envelope us. We could easily see why Paris is addictive.

The next day, we made for the infamous Catacombs. The boys said they really wanted to see them. I was not so sure they knew what they were getting into. This vast underground labyrinth below Paris is the final resting place for over six million Parisians. Technically, it is called an ossuary, which means a place where you put the bones of deceased people. In other words, it is a creepy dark tunnel filled with real skeletons. Despite my fatherly concerns, we went anyway.

The entrance to the Catacombs is a small, nondescript green building on the other side of the city. We would have missed it if it weren't for the long line of people waiting to go down into the dark caverns. Despite the crowd, the boys pleaded to go so we obliged and got in line too.

The line moved slowly, but eventually, it was our turn. Aaron went first, followed by Mish, Elijah, and then me. I looked above the doorway that led into the depths as we passed through. Inscribed on the arch was the warning, "Arrête! C'est ici l'empire de la Mort." Great, even I could translate that, "Stop! This is the empire of Death."

Not heeding the message, down we went. Almost immediately, the air changed. In the tunnels, the air was cold and moist with a musty smell. The floor was uneven and rough, which made walking a little hazardous in the dim light. Undeterred, Aaron forged a path for us through the maze of tunnels.

His confidence, however, wavered when we reached the first gallery. He came face to face with a wall of real human skulls. From floor to ceiling, they were neatly stacked on top of each other, forming a macabre display. Aaron halted in his tracks and stared wide-eyed. Bless his heart, he tried to be brave but succumbed to fear and let his mom go first from then on.

Elijah started out fine. He desperately wanted to prove himself as a courageous explorer who could face anything. However, in the catacombs, you are literally surrounded by actual human remains. They are not props. That reality set in on Elijah, and his courage started to erode, too. He soon was getting panicky. Mish and I couldn't subject them to any more of this ghoulish torture. We ushered them as quickly as we could in the cramped tunnels past other visitors and back into the light. Once more, we had succeeded in traumatizing our boys. Someday, they would probably need therapy for this, I thought.

We decided that we had enough of dark underground places and would stay in the open sunlight from now on. So, we headed to a garden area with living things for a change of scenery. Once back in the land of the living, the boys quickly recovered from their ordeal. Aaron tried to play it off as no big deal. Elijah, on the other hand, flat-out admitted he was terrified and was adamant that he would never go down there again. We'll see who has nightmares first.

We ate a traditional French lunch of bread, salami, cheese, and grapes on the lawn of the Luxembourg Gardens. Even without the usual French wine, the meal was amazing. Sitting on the green grass while sampling our delicacies, we admired the beautifully manicured gardens. Sharing simple times like this as a family are what makes life meaningful and special. I wouldn't trade them for anything.

Our time in Paris was unfortunately coming to too quick an end. On the way out we had one last landmark to see, Versailles. I think everyone has heard of the opulent mansion on the outskirts of Paris. It has been the home to French kings from 1682 to 1789. It is also where the treaty ending World War I was signed on June 28, 1919. The palace itself is known for way over-the-top extravagances. We were anxious to visit it.

To get to the motorway leading to Versailles, we had to go around the Arc de Triomphe. The enormous marble monument is spectacular. The chaotic twelve-lane roundabout surrounding it is terrifying, however.

The French have an interesting approach to roundabouts. Basically, it's every driver for themselves. You approach the roundabout, speed up, and dive in, expecting everyone else to make room for you, which they may or may not. It is a cacophony of blaring horns and revving engines swirling around the steadfast arch. To exit this crazy amusement park ride, you dive to your right for your exit and once again rely on other drivers to allow your passage. Good luck. It is no wonder that most French cars show battle damage.

Somehow, and not due to my driving skills, we successfully navigated the roundabout unscathed and made our way to Versailles. The palace is just a short twenty-minute drive southwest of Paris, but feels like you are going out into the remote French countryside. It is a pleasant contrast to the noisy hustle and bustle of the city. Back when King Louis XIII built a hunting lodge on the grounds in 1623 it was practically desolate.

When I think of Versailles, I think of the famous Treaty of Versailles that officially ended World War I. I remember learning about the treaty in high school, but nothing about the actually place. I knew it was a unique and extravagant palace that had special significance to the French, but nothing else. Here was another chance to visit an historical site that I learned about in school. I was in for a real treat.

Mish, on the other hand, has heard of Versailles' expansive gardens and opulent décor. She was anxious to see the splendor of French Baroque architecture at its finest. As usual, she had already lined up the highlights for us to see with the most expeditious tour route. It works for me.

The boys, Aaron and Elijah, were once again just happy to be going somewhere new, and with the possibility of getting food along the way. As we pulled into the parking lot at the palace, Elijah was already asking when and where were we going to eat lunch.

"We just had breakfast," I reminded him.

"I know, but I'm hungry. So can we get a snack now?" he persisted.

"Probably," I assured him as I rolled my eyes.

"Knowing your dad, definitely," my wife chimed in.

Meanwhile, poor Albie had to sit in the car and wait for our return. He had a look that clearly stated, "I want a snack too." Sorry, no dogs allowed.

The first word that came to mind when seeing Versailles is over-the-top. Ok, that's three words, but it is hard to describe the entirety of the place in a single adjective. Magnificent, awe-inspiring, spectacular, grandiose all fall short. It is so overwhelming that it's impossible to focus on any one aspect of the vast estate. We allowed Mish to guide us. With tour book in hand, she enlightened us on everything we gawked at. Once again, I had no idea what anything was, so I was thankful to get some schooling. At least I could walk away with a fact or two tucked away in my head to later impress someone with.

Shortly, I was with Elijah that it was snack time. Outside the estate, we found a little café and ordered some drinks and sweets to replenish us. This has been an unbelievable experience, I thought as I sipped my coffee. Aaron and Elijah received a whole semester art class of information in four days. They saw the real deal, too, not just boring pictures in a textbook. As a bonus, they learned some French history and geography too. Happy that we could offer this experience to our children, we headed on the road for the drive back home.

Chapter 11 – More Castles

"Everything is theoretically impossible, until it is done." – Robert A. Heinlein

You would think that after seeing dozens of castles, you would get bored of them. Nope. They are still way too cool and impressive to pass up. Maybe because they don't exist in America, or maybe because they represent a romanticized time, or maybe because they resonate power and strength, or maybe all three, but no matter the reason, we find them fascinating. We couldn't pass up the opportunity to visit another one. Rick Steves, the famous world travel writer, proclaimed Burg Eltz his favorite castle in all of Europe. That is a high compliment indeed. We had to check it out for ourselves to see what made it top of his list.

The castle is near the German-Belgium border west of Frankfurt, so for us, it is only about an hour and a half drive. We decided that this would be a great day trip to see the castle and hike some of the nature reserve that surrounds it. In Germany, you are never far from a magnificent hiking opportunity. We can't get enough of them.

You can drive almost right to the front door of the castle or, if you are more intrepid like us, opt to park in the nearby town of Karden and hike in. We thought that coming across it while walking through the forest would be more dramatic, so we donned our walking gear and set out. This time, Albie got to go, too. He loved walking in the forest and eagerly jumped in the car.

The walk through the reserve is beautiful. The path leisurely follows the winding Elzbach River downstream towards the castle. Every turn in the river, we peered through the trees to see if it was there yet. On one bend, Elijah, who is always up in front leading the way, cried out triumphantly, "There it is!"

It certainly was there. Sitting tall and stately on an outcropping of rock surrounded on three sides by the river sat Burg Eltz. It was an imposing site. The stone ramparts rose above the trees and were topped with white turrets trimmed in red that starkly contrasted against the blue sky. Any would be invader would think twice before attempting to attack it.

The castle was built in the 11th century to help defend trade in the Moselle River valley below it. Amazingly, it is still owned by the same family today, which makes me very envious. I have always wanted my own castle. I'm not picky, I'll take a wee one somewhere in Ireland.

Since I don't think that I will be getting my own castle in the foreseeable future, I have to be content touring someone else's. Burg Eltz does not disappoint and allows you to get a glimpse of what living in a fully functional, semi-modernized castle is like. The family actually maintains their private living quarters in part of the castle while opening up the rest of it to visitors. Most of the public areas have been kept to the authentic time periods when they were built, so you can also see what early life in a castle was like. I would definitely take the updated, renovated side. German winters in a drafty castle with only an inefficient fireplace to heat it must have been brutal. My castle would need to have central heating and cooling.

I can see why Rick Steves likes this castle so much. It is big enough to be a legitimate stately castle but small enough to seem personal and cozy in a way. In the living spaces, the walls have been coated with white limestone plaster and stenciled with colorful patterns. The rooms are all fully furnished and neatly decorated, too, so it doesn't feel drab and cold. You could really see someone living here.

We wandered around Burg Eltz and marveled at how it was built. Like all the castles and cathedrals we have visited in Europe, they were all built without the aid of modern technology, so no cranes, bulldozers, jackhammers, power saws, or drills. None. It was all done purely by manual labor and true craftsmanship. I wonder if anyone could duplicate their construction today. Our modern-day skyscrapers are impressive, but to be fair their builders had a lot of help.

I once read an article in an engineering journal that argued we could not build mega structures like Hoover Dam or the Golden Gate Bridge today in the United States. The author claimed that with environmental regulations, labor unions, budget constraints, and government oversight, builders would be too handicapped to even start the project. He concluded that is why America is no longer building colossal structures, like in some Asian countries. Consequently, we are falling behind.

I wasn't aware we were in a race. I would not want to go back to the days when many of America's great construction projects were attempted around the turn of the twentieth century. Workers were treated as expendable, and the environment was not even considered. Ironically, many people were hurt and killed working to build monolithic testimonials of human achievement. Still, it is impressive to see what can be done when getting the job finished at all costs is the goal.

We had a wonderful lunch on the castle lawn and enjoyed the breathtaking scenery. I highly doubt that the original builders had tranquil family picnics in mind when they built this impregnable castle for protection in times of conflict. I suppose it once served its purpose and was now serving a different one. I think they would be happy to know that their hard work and sacrifice have not gone wasted, and after nearly a millennium, their achievement still has a purpose.

We walked back along the same path to our car. The sun was starting to set behind the hills, casting a slight orange glow in the valley as the river bubbled along in its path. The soothing atmosphere caused a few yawns as we neared the end of the trail. Even Albie seemed to be half asleep as he trotted alongside. It had been a wonderful day.

As I drove back home, I couldn't help but think how amazing and surreal our life was. We just hiked through a beautiful forest to see a magnificent castle. How many families get to do that on a random Saturday? Not too long ago, moving here seemed like an impossibility. Yet, here we are living the dream. I feel extremely blessed.

Chapter 12 – Berlin

"The greatest cultural extravaganza that one could imagine." – David Bowie

The school year was going along well. Teaching at the international school in Frankfurt was a very easy assignment. It is what we call in education a "canned course." The school provides teachers with their curriculum and books. Every Friday, the students are tested on the material using a computer exam system, so I don't grade anything. The students know what is expected and do what they are supposed to, mostly. Compared to the United States, I have almost nothing to do before or after school.

That didn't stop some teachers from complaining, however. We teachers are used to being in control of almost every aspect of our curriculum. Taking that burden away doesn't sit well with some of my colleagues. I look at it as easy money. I know I am not here to change their system, so I roll with it. Plus, it gives us more time to see the country.

Teachers are teachers no matter where the school is. Some things are just universal. While some of the faculty sit around during break complaining about their plight, I choose to learn about them and their countries. The staff is an eclectic mix of nationalities, ages, and academic disciplines. I truly love to learn about their experiences and garner any suggestions for where to travel next.

The younger teachers, no matter their nationality, all rave about Berlin. The older ones, mostly with families, are at best ambivalent about it. I really wanted to know why. We have not been to Germany's capital yet and were mulling over a visit soon. Since it was a six-hour drive from us, we wanted to know if it was worth the trip and, if so, where to go in the city with kids.

Since Berlin is a major city with a long, rich history in Germany, we decided that we couldn't pass it up while we were here. I had another break coming up, so Mish set to work planning our excursion. I was really interested in two things in the city, the infamous Berlin Wall and the equally infamous Reichstag.

The drive from Frankfurt to Berlin is pretty boring to be honest. As we headed north, we left the beautiful mountains and forests behind for the vast coastal plain. The landscape started to look more like the American Midwest with rolling hills of grass, lots of cows, and an occasional wide river. The only noticeable difference was the large wind turbines.

Long boring trips like this are where I love the autobahn. With miles of flat smooth roads and plenty of visibility, I set the car cruise control to "get us there fast" and eased back in the seat. With one hand firmly gripping the steering wheel and the other tightly holding onto my coffee, I watched the odometer slowly count to our destination. The regular passing of large trucks that shook our small car and other automobiles with their cruise controls set to "give it all she's got" kept me from dozing off.

After what seemed like much more than six hours, we finally arrived in Berlin. Since we decided on going almost the day before, Mish was forced to find a hotel on a last-minute booking. What she managed to secure was not in the best part of the city. To be honest, it was downright sketchy. I was thankful that she found us a place for the night, but worried that our car might not be there in the morning. With no other option, we checked in.

The room was acceptable. It was nothing to rave about but clean and orderly. As long as our car wasn't stolen, it would be fine. The next morning, we would head into the city center to see for ourselves what all the hype is about Berlin.

The first thing I did when I woke up was check on the car. Luckily, it was still where I parked it on the street. I joined the family at breakfast and was happy to report that we still had transportation. Mish was happy to hear that because she had our day planned. She unfolded a city map to show me where we were headed first. She wanted to enter Berlin the classy way, through the Brandenburg Gate.

We were off season, so the city was not overrun with tourists and sweltering in heat. Finding parking near the gate was easy. The city seemed a little empty without throngs of people clamoring to get the perfect selfie with every statue and monument within ten blocks. Traveling when there are not crowds is one of the many perks of living abroad.

As we walked toward the gate, our anticipation built. We had been to the Arc de Triomphe in Paris and were expecting as grandiose a memorial here in Germany's capital as well. We rounded a corner, and there it was. Immediately, our excitement was dashed. It is small, real small, compared to France's arch, and not as ornate. Let down set in.

"Maybe it seems small because we are still a couple of blocks away," I offered hopefully.

It didn't get any bigger as we approached it. To be fair, the Brandenburg Gate was built first. Frederick William II of Prussia commissioned it in 1788 to help establish Berlin as a cultural center of Europe on par with London and Paris. The Arc de Triomphe was commissioned by Napoleon Bonaparte in 1806 to celebrate all who died in the French Revolution and Napoleonic Wars. Napolean, not to ever be outdone, ordered his arch to be the biggest in the world. Unfortunately, he was overthrown and exiled to the island of Elba and never saw his arch completed. Fredrick, at least, got to see his arch. So, I guess building it to a more reasonable size to be completed in your lifetime might have been a better idea.

We walked through the famous gate and were impressed with the giant bronze statue of the quadriga on top. The history of the gate was not lost on us. Since its construction, it has been the backdrop for many important events. I remember watching old videos of President John Kenedy in 1963 giving his famous "Ich bin ein Berliner" speech in front of it and twenty-four years later seeing President Ronal Reagan challenge Soviet President Mikhail Gorbachev with "Tear down this wall" with the gate in the background. There is no denying that what it may lack in physical size, it more than makes up for in historical magnitude.

While I was trying to give this history lesson to Aaron and Elijah, something caught Elijah's eye and off he scampered. In the Pariser Platz square in front of the gate a young woman street performer had something far more entertaining than me, giant bubbles. Elijah ran over to her captivated by the floating iridescent blobs as she created them one after the other. She smiled as Elijah gawked at them. She knew she had a captive audience. She handed him her hoop so he could make giant bubbles, too. Elijah was so excited that he forgot all else. Soon, he had drawn a small crowd that watched him giddily make bubbles. Great, we come all the way to Berlin and his favorite memory will be the bubble lady, I thought. Oh well, I tossed a couple of dollars in her hat and eventually got him to give her back her hoop.

We continued through the plaza and entered Berlin's city center. We passed many more entertaining street performers. Once more, Elijah was awestruck. This time, he was enamored with a group of performers who walked around with giant fantastical stick puppets. He ran up to them and one of the puppets reached out its long arm and patted him on the head. He would have followed them if I had not had something even more enticing to lure him with.

A vendor was selling giant chocolate donuts. Everything in this city, except gates, must be huge, I thought. They smelled delicious. Aaron wanted in on this action, too. Mish rolled her eyes and got her wallet out. She held up three fingers and paid the man. She knows me. With giant donuts and chocolatey lips, we headed off to the next site.

We roamed the city and found part of the infamous Berlin Wall that was left standing as a reminder of the Cold War. It was coated in many layers of graffiti and looked out of place. If you didn't know its significance, you probably would wonder why this dilapidated relic was not torn down. Mish and I very much remember it and what it symbolized.

Parked along the opposite curb was another blast from the past, a row of Soviet made Lada's. These iconic small automobiles were the people's car of the former U.S.S.R. Sturdy, economic, and no frills, the Lada was the main stay of the Soviet working family. Millions were made over their long production run. I have seen many of them in pictures and movies, but not in real life because they were banned from being imported into the West. They invoke images of Cold War spy movies, like James Bond. I had to get my picture taken with one.

Just passed them, was Check Point Charlie. This was the only gap in the entire wall where someone could cross between east and west Berlin. During the Cold War, it was heavily guarded by both sides. No one passed through without thorough searching and necessary documentation. I got chills walking through the gate. This would not have been possible when I was growing up. Now, it still seemed like I was doing something forbidden.

Next to the checkpoint is a very cool museum that tells the story of the wall and the numerous daring attempts to get through, over, under, and around it. We looked at the photographs of some of the ingenious methods some people tried in desperation to escape east Berlin, some successful and some not. From homemade hot air balloons to hidden compartments in automobiles to narrow tunnels, everything was tried. I explained to the boys why these people risked their lives. This was another incredible learning experience for them. This time, Elijah actually paid attention.

As we left the museum, I took one last look at the wall and was reminded how glad I was that an awful chapter in our history was closed. I sincerely hope we are done with wall building, whether it is to keep people in or out. It is a barbaric practice that should be left in the past.

Next up was the Reichstag. This was another historical opportunity for us. As we walked to it, I reminded the boys about our trip to Normandy and the allied invasion. I explained to them that the building we were about to see burned down in 1933. Hitler claimed that it was an act of arson by communists who were planning a violent overthrow of the government. He used the fire as an excuse to seize absolute power by passing emergency legislation to supposedly protect German citizens. In reality, he abolished the constitution and paved the way for the rise of his Nazi regime.

Even though it was nothing more than an abandoned shell, Allied Forces heavily targeted the ruins as a symbolic demonstration of resolve to defeat Nazism once and for all. The Red Army, who entered Berlin before Patton's 2nd Armored Division, seized the Reichstag on May 2,

1945, and planted the Soviet flag on its charred remains. That act effectively ended World War II. Victory in Europe was declared six days later.

In the 1960s, the Reichstag was rebuilt and given a clear glass dome to replace its destroyed marble one, but largely went unused since the country was divided during the Cold War. After Germany reunified in 1999, the building once more became the seat of the German Bundestag. It was the primary thing I wanted to visit in Berlin.

The building is actively used as the seat of the German government. Consequently, the line was fairly long and the security was very tight to get inside. I got in que while Mish and the boys with Albie sat on the large grassy lawn in front to watch more street performers.

When it was my turn to enter, I called over for the boys. Mish stayed with Albie. We would have to switch off since no dogs are allowed inside. The three of us climbed the ramp that wound its way around the inside of the large clear dome to an observation deck at the top. From that vantage point we could see Mish and Albie sunning themselves below. The whole building is very stately and impressive despite all it has been through.

I tried to imagine what it must have been like in those final days of the war. The city was in ruins and burning. Explosions and gunshots filled the air. Allied and Axis forces fought block by block for control. Looking out over the city today from the top of the dome, you would never realize the carnage and destruction that took place. I sincerely hope, however, that we never forget it.

Chapter 13 – The Alps

"The mountains are calling and I must go." – John Muir

With Berlin checked off our long to see list in Germany, we could start planning our big spring break trip. Since that was a few weeks away, I had to actually work for a change. School was going very well. My problem is I can never leave well enough alone. There is always more that can be done in teaching.

I had convinced the school to order some model rockets for me and formed a club. None of my students had ever built or even seen a model rocket. I had built several as a boy and passed on my passion to my sons. Aaron especially loved rockets. He and I built and launched many of them, the highest going over two thousand feet. I'm pretty sure we broke some FAA rules along the way.

When the rockets finally arrived all the way from the U.S., we set about building them. Every day at lunch, my flight crew came in and diligently worked on their rockets. Aaron, by this time, was a master rocket builder and took on a very challenging rocket with detachable gliders. Even Elijah built one with the help of mom. The excitement grew every day as they neared completion.

When all the rockets were completed, inspected, and deemed flight worthy by mission control, aka me, we scheduled an afternoon for launch. The countdown began. I was amazed that we had caused a little buzz at the school. Word had spread about the rockets and many students and staff were just as eagerly awaiting the launch day as the club.

Finally, the day came. Luckily, the weather was cooperating with clear blue skies and no wind. Stopping the countdown is never a popular decision. I gave the thumbs up for launch. The club members readied their rockets and semi-patiently waited in line for their turn to launch as a small crowd gathered in the school play yard.

I let Aaron have the honor of going first. The seasoned veteran placed his rocket on the pad and expertly hooked it up to the ignition system. He backed a safe distance away and waited for the final countdown. I gave the "all clear" sign.

"10-9-8-7-6-5-4-3-2-1… launch," the other rocketeers yelled in unison!

Aron pushed the button, and the rocket propellant ignited. With a flash of fire, the rocket lifted off the pad, soaring into the sky, trailing a plume of white smoke. Within seconds, it was lost to view. Everyone looked up and strained their eyes to catch a glimpse of it.

Someone shouted and pointed. We all looked and saw the telltale sign of a bright orange streamer. The rocket slowly descended to the ground a few hundred feet away. All the kids temporarily forgot their rockets and excitedly ran to help with recovery efforts. Aaron retrieved it and proudly held it up in triumph. It was our first successful launch.

After that, the excitement magnified tenfold. The growing crowd joined in the countdowns and clapped as the rockets blasted off. One after the other, we launched a dozen rockets, some successful and some not. One landed on the school roof. Another one didn't deploy its parachute and hurtled into the ground in a spectacular crash. Most of them, however, were amazing flights. I was very proud of each of the students.

My school director came over to congratulate me on a successful and memorable extracurricular activity. I explained to him that this was my sneaky way to keep enjoying my childhood hobby. He just laughed and told me to keep up the good work. In actuality, I am very happy to bring something new and different to my students. Their energy is what keeps me teaching year after year.

With the rocket launch done, it was time to go on break. We have been planning this trip for weeks. The one thing I wanted to see more than anything else in Germany was the Alps. They were another spectacular location I have seen many pictures of and always wanted to visit. This trip was my chance.

Mish planned a drive from home to Munich and, from there making a huge loop through Fussen, across the Austrian border to Innsbruck, on to Salzburg, and then back to Munich. Along the way, we were going to visit Neuschwanstein Castle and drive through the picturesque Tyrol region of Austria. All total, we would be gone for a week. This was going to be our grandest adventure so far in Germany. We were all very much looking forward to it.

We set out early in the morning and headed south to Munich. The drive along the autobahn is fairly boring but efficient. We were not interested in anything anyway and wanted to get to our destination quickly, so once again, I set the cruise control and settled in with my coffee for a long drive.

Four hours later, we pulled into Munich. Where Berlin is the capital of Germany, Munich is its heart. It is the third largest city in Germany and the capital of the state of Bavaria. All Germans have a deep-rooted love for Bavaria. With breathtaking mountain vistas, tall dark forests, raging glacier fed rivers, and adorable timber-framed houses, it is as picturesque as you can possibly get. The region is someplace that harkens back to a fairytale like time.

The boys had been somewhat patient during the long drive but now wanted to get out of the car. Every once in a while, I had to peer in my rearview mirror and give them the "don't make me come back there" look. Elijah likes to bait his older brother, which Aaron falls for. The promise of some gooey streusel cake put a stop to it.

We arrived at the hotel and quickly stowed our bags, and headed out to see the city. The first order of business was food. I had to explain to a very persistent Elijah that after dinner is always implied when he gets his reward. We are not fans of German food, too much pig and potatoes for us seafood loving Pacific Northwesterners. However, we were eager to try some of Muich's specialties. One in particular, weisswurst, is a must eat here, we were told.

Basically, weisswurst is a small boiled white sausage that is eaten as a snack, usually in the morning. Being late in the day, we weren't sure if we would find it. We underestimated the German love for all things pork and found a food stand right away selling them. Mish ordered four servings. The man handed them over the counter to each of us on small paper plates. Apparently, they come in pairs. I looked at my two critically. They didn't look appetizing. I bit into one. Their taste matched their appearance, bland and rubbery. I tried some spicy mustard to make it more palatable, but that only made it taste like a mustardy pencil eraser. I ate them out of sheer hunger. Mish gave her two to the boys, who devoured everything.

Feeling guilty that we snubbed our noses at one of Bavarians' favorite foods, we walked around looking for something more suiting our tastes. Each to their own. At least we could say we tried it.

We stumbled across a small restaurant on the Marienplatz Square that served a variety of acceptable dishes and sat down on the outside veranda. We had incredible luck. Across the square was the famous Rathaus-Glockenspiel. Normally, it only rings twice a day, 11:00 AM and 12:00 PM. From March to October, it also rings at 5:00 PM. I looked at my watch. It was 4:45 PM. Amazing timing!

The Rathaus-Glockenspiel is the largest clock of its kind in the world. It was built in 1908 into the tower of the newly constructed Town Hall to celebrate Munich's history. It is two stories tall with 43 bells and 32 life-size animatronic characters that reenact the stories of the marriage of Duke Wilhelm V to Renata of Lorraine in 1568 on the top tier, followed by the story of the Schäfflerstanz, or coopers' dance, on the bottom tier. The whole performance takes fifteen minutes. We ordered our food and waited for the giant clock to strike 5:00.

Exactly on time, the bells started ringing and the show began. A royal entourage paraded around, knights on horses jousted, and dancers twirled. They have been doing this same performance for over a hundred years. It is truly a wonderful example of fine German craftsmanship.

When the show and dinner ended, we walked around some more, enjoying the sites and getting Elijah his streusel. Munich is a very beautiful city. We are only spending the night this time but will be here again in a few days at the end of our loop. Tomorrow, we will head to the most extravagant castle in the world.

The drive from Munich to Neuschwanstein Castle is less than two hours, which meant we could get there before the crowds if we left early. So, right after breakfast we set off on the next leg of our trip. As we drove south, the Alps got bigger and bigger enhancing the anticipation.

King Ludwig II could not have picked a more beautiful location for his castle. The site is near the Austrian border on the northern extremity of the Alps, overlooking a large lake and the hilly countryside below. His father, King Maximilian II of Bavaria, had a small estate known as Hohenschwangau Castle, built on the ruins of another medieval castle on the shore of the lake as a second residence. The young prince spent his summers exploring the area and fell in love with it.

When Ludwig became king, he began a series of very extravagant construction projects, one of which was a personal retreat to get away from the political commitments of Munich. He decided on a specific spot he fondly remembered from his boyhood, where two medieval castle ruins lay. It was above his father's castle on a rocky outcropping that was separated from the main mountain by a steep gorge with a cascading river below. From that high perch, he had a commanding view for many miles.

The first foundation stone was laid in 1869, and construction began. King Ludwig financed the enormously expensive project, $55 million in today's dollars, with his own money and extensive loans rather than public funds. His romantic vision of an expansive complex got out of control. He let cost and time budgets run rampant and quickly ran into trouble with his parliament. The end result was that the government disposed of him in 1886 and forcefully evicted him from his beloved castle. The next day, poor Ludwig was found dead under mysterious circumstances in the shallow water of the lake, having lived in his castle for only 172 days.

The castle was largely incomplete at the time of King Ludwig's death. The Bavarian government opted to hastily and more thriftly complete a simplified version of Ludwig's plan. Once finally finished, it was immediately opened to paying visitors to help pay off Ludwig's hefty debts. Sadly, no one else has ever lived in the castle.

When we arrived, we looked up to see the enormous white castle stately standing out against the dark green trees on its loft perch. It is a very impressive sight. If Ludwig's goal was to impress, he nailed it. No other castle in the world looks as fantastical. It is so fairytale looking that Walt Disney visited it and used it as his inspiration for Cinderella's Castle in his parks.

We decided to stretch our legs by walking up to the castle rather than taking the shuttle bus. It sounded like a good idea, but by the time we reached the top, we were exhausted. The castle was too enticing, so despite our soar legs we climbed up the stairs and toured the castle with its many steps. It does not disappoint. If this is the scaled-down version of Ludwig's dream, I would love to know what he originally intended.

Room after room is adorned with intricately painted walls, real gold accents, and luxurious tapestries. From the large courtyard, we gazed up in awe at the tall ornate spires topped with colorful flags fluttering in the wind. It is no wonder he went over budget. I guess if you are going to build a castle, do it right.

We continued exploring the grounds, becoming more impressed with each new sight. The grand finale was hiking up to Queen Mary's Bridge higher up the gorge. From the middle of the bridge, we looked down to behold the majestic castle in all its glory. I really felt sorry for poor Ludwig that he only spent a very short time in it. I could definitely live here, providing I had a staff of servants to attend to me.

We left the castle eagerly wanting to see more of this amazing area. The drive from Neuschwanstein to Innsbruck promised to be just as incredible. After a brief stop at the castle café for coffee and treats to refuel us, we were off again.

I cannot put into words how beautiful the Tyrol region is. The drive over the alpine passes underneath tall snowcapped mountains with rushing glacier fed rivers alongside is breathtaking. We wound our way through dense forests, past roaring waterfalls, and by grassy alpine meadows. Everywhere we looked was more incredible than the last. I cannot believe that people are lucky enough to live here.

We pulled into Innsbruck after dark, tired but elated with the journey so far. After a good night's rest and hearty breakfast, we walked around the city. Innsbruck is a big city with a small-town feel. It is the capital of the Tyrol region and arguably the center of one of the most magnificent areas in the Alps. Surrounded by tall snow-capped mountains and bisected by the mighty Inn River, it is in the perfect location for all outdoor activities. Large gondolas lift people high up the steep mountainsides all year long to explore the alpine wilderness. It is a nature lover's paradise.

I think I could stay in places like Innsbruck the rest of my life. Just walking around the city invigorates me like nothing else can. As I walked around sipping my coffee, I took it all in. The fresh smell of the clean, crisp alpine air was intoxicating. It is times like this when I feel completely present in the moment. The worries of the future, the regrets of the past, and the troubles of today are swept away by the intensity of the sensations I feel here. I don't want to leave and have those negative thoughts return. Unfortunately, I know we cannot stay here forever, frozen in this moment. At least for a brief time, however, I can get a respite from the real world. I continued to sip my coffee and savor the time I had.

Aaron wanted a traditional Bavarian hat to add to his growing collection. We found a millinery shop, and he selected a green wool Tyrolean hat with a feather in the brim. He felt very snazzy and walked around proudly displaying his find. With his blond hair and blue eyes, he fit in perfectly with the natives. I smile when I see our boys acting naturally, free from peer pressure and societal stereotypes. They are just enjoying the moment too.

We headed out of Innsbruck for Salzburg. Salzburg is famous for the birthplace of composer Wolfgang Amadeus Mozart, and the real Von Trapp family immortalized in the Sound of Music. It is also one of the most well-preserved medieval cities in Europe. It sounded enticing enough to drag us away from Innsbruck.

Like its sister city, Innsbruck, Salzburg sits at the base of the Alps, straddling a large river. It is smaller than Innsbruck but packs a lot into it. We weren't sure where to start first. So, while Mish studied the map, the boys and I opted to find something to eat. Getting great food in any European city is like shooting fish in a barrel, easy. You can't throw a stone in any direction without hitting someplace tasty. Salzburg was no exception. Straight away, we found a street vendor selling enormous warm pretzels. They are one of Mish's favorite go-to snack items, so I ordered four. She was still looking at the map when I brought them back and handed her one. As we munched on our salty treats, we picked a destination.

We decided to walk along the Getreidegasse. It is the main shopping street in Salzburg. It is lined with traditional businesses and quaint cafes with ornate cast iron signs hanging above each of them. As evening fell, soft yellow light from numerous gas lamps illuminated the store fronts giving them an old-world look. This street has probably not changed much in the last few hundred years.

Why, in America, we have to make every city look identical with the same stores marked by gaudy, cheap plastic signs lit with neon is beyond my comprehension. In the name of progress and convenience, we have lost something. Ironically, all the people I have ever talked to that have visited Europe love it for its authenticity and history but go back to the U.S. and resign themselves to living in tacky, over-commercialized cookie-cutter towns. I have a disdain for soulless tract home communities and ubiquitous chain stores that have taken over in America. I think we will regret the corporate takeover of our lives down the road if we already don't. For now, we live in Europe and get to benefit from enjoying places like Salzburg.

Mish once again found us a quaint little hotel in the city center. We wandered there to tuck in for the night. We were all tired from the car ride and walking around and needed a good night's rest. Tomorrow will be another adventurous day with new sites.

In the morning, we walked up the long, steep drive to the Hohensalzburg Fortress. The imposing medieval keep is the largest castle in Central Europe. From its tall parapets, we got a three-hundred-and-sixty-degree view of the surrounding area. Inside showcases an impressive display of medieval art, weaponry, and other artifacts. It is a beautiful castle, but I will still take Neuschwanstein.

We spent two days in Salzburg, seeing the sites. All of us have watched The Sound of Music, so seeing some of the locations from the movie was fun. I honestly had no idea the musical was based on actual events, and the Trapps were a real family. Learning that made seeing them even more interesting.

As with Innsbruck, our time in Salzburg was too short. Before I was ready, we had to get back in the car and head to our next stop. I wanted to see another famous World War II site. This one was particularly infamous and has been on my bucket list for a while.

Perched high on a steep rock outcropping a short drive south of Salzburg is the infamous Kehlsteinhaus, or The Eagle's Nest. Built in 1939 for Hitler's 50th birthday by his Nazi Party, it is the ultimate evil villain lair. At a cost of $247 million in today's dollars and twelve lives lost in construction, it came at a very hefty price tag, too. The Nazis used the spectacular facility to impress important guests and as a symbol of their perceived dominance.

It does impress. To reach the aerie requires walking from the carpark through a four-hundred-foot marble lined tunnel cut through the solid granite mountain to a gilded Venetian mirror clad elevator that whisks you forty stories up the center of the mountain to the top. When the elevator doors open, you are treated to a breathtaking panorama of the Bavarian countryside six-thousand feet below. If you want to make a statement to awe your guests, this does it.

The Nazis also dug, with slave labor, over four miles of tunnels that connect a vast network of chambers and buildings to the nest. They added backup generators, a secure water source, and tons of supplies to complete the impregnable fortress. It is no wonder it survived several

Allied attempts to destroy it and its notorious owner. Even an RAF squadron of 359 Avro Lancaster bombers on a daylight raid were unable to hit the elusive target. Consequently, it is completely intact, so you can visit it today as it was in 1939.

The side excursion to The Eagle's Nest was another mazing opportunity for an invaluable history lesson for Aaron and Elijah. This time, I think they will be much more interested. The place is the stuff of fictional James Bond spy movies, except a real villain did lurk there.

We arrived and took the shuttle bus up the steep winding mountain road to the tunnel entrance. Enormous, thick iron doors opened into the mountain. As we walked along the long echoing tunnel, I could see why the Nazis chose this location. We were inside a solid granite rock formation hundreds of feet deep.

At the end of the tunnel, we reached the elevator. A huge car that could carry more than fifty people quickly lifted us the four-hundred and seven feet to the top in forty seconds. It came to a sudden stop, and the doors opened. We stepped out into The Eagle's Nest.

We looked around in awe. We were actually in the once ultra-super-secret hideout of the world's most notorious villain, Adolph Hitler. However, instead of strategic maps detailing world domination hanging on the walls and soldiers in Nazi SS gear striding around barking orders, there are only bare stone walls and tourists casually eating in the restaurant or taking pictures on the veranda. If you did not know the dark history of the building, you never would guess what went on in this very place seventy years ago.

We joined the other tourists in the dining room. It was surreal to be eating pea soup and drinking beer in the very room where Hitler entertained guests and relaxed with his mistress, Eva Braun. If these walls could talk, I'm sure they could divulge some scary, dark secrets about the evil plans that were developed here. I shuddered a little and tried not to think too much about it and enjoyed my lunch instead.

I noticed a worn antique leather chair next to the huge stone fireplace. I vaguely recognized it from old black-and-white photographs of this place before the war. I got up and walked over to examine it more closely. To my astonishment, the display card said it was one of the original pieces of furniture used by Hitler. One of the waiters saw me looking at the chair and offered me a seat. I was shocked.

"Really?" I said.

"Ya, no one is here. I will take your picture," he replied.

The place was largely empty, so I took him up on his generous offer. I removed the card and eased myself down onto the leather cushion. I was actually sitting in the same seat Hitler occupied. My butt and his butt touched the same spot, I thought in amusement. It was the highlight of the trip for me.

After taking in the amazing views, we headed back down the elevator, through the tunnel, on the bus, and to our car. I absolutely love this region. It has so much to offer that you could not do it all in one lifetime, let only a very short vacation. We had one more stop to make before arriving back in Munich. This one was even more infamous than The Eagle's Nest.

Mish and I had talked about it and decided that we could not pass up the opportunity to visit the site of one of the worst atrocities in human history. Despite we were on a family vacation, we were going to visit a Nazi concentration camp.

Why visit such a horrific place on a family holiday? It is not to walk around taking selfies or buying souvenirs. We feel it is to pay respects to the thousands of people who were senselessly murdered there so that type of barbarism never happens again. That is why the German government left some of them standing. They are a tangible reminder to the world and to the German people themselves what happened.

Dachau is only fifteen miles northwest of Munich, so it would be the last stop on our epic adventure. On the drive we prepped Aaron and Elijah as best we thought for the experience. Mish and I were not sure how unsettling it may be for the boys, especially Elijah. We agreed we would not force them to go if they really didn't want to. Both said they would try it, so off we went.

The parking lot was nearly deserted when we arrived. We were not sure if it was because this was a weekday off tourist season or most people shy away from this place. Either way, we got out of the car and walked into the visitor center. Inside, it was solemnly quiet. Our voices echoed in the large concrete room so much that we instinctively lowered them to a whisper. Mish picked up a free self-guided audio tour speaker and led the way.

The first exhibit chronicled the history of the camp from its opening in 1993 to its liberation by American forces in 1945. So, for twelve years the camp housed over 200,000 prisoners from over thirty countries. The first groups interned were political dissidents arrested for opposing the Nazi regime, then came criminals for forced labor, followed by Jews, and lastly prisoners of war captured on the battlefield. We will probably never know the exact number of prisoners executed here, but best estimates claim at least 35,000 lives. Even more staggering to learn is that this is only one of more than a thousand such camps the Nazis maintained as part of a vast network.

As we continued, we moved into the actual areas where the unfortunate prisoners went through the sterile indoctrination process of the camp by ruthless Nazi guards. The tour took us from where they arrived all the way to where they lived and died. Silhouettes of faceless new arrivals are painted on the walls to help humanize their experience. Their almost ghost-like appearance adds to the morbidness of the scene. This is where we started to feel the intensity of the camp.

I looked down at Aaron and Elijah and saw that they were getting a little scared. Aaron was slightly pale and silent and Elijah, with wide glazed eyes and half open mouth, blankly stared at the pictures. I knew this was a little too emotional for them. I reassured them that this place and these events all happened in the past and there was nothing to be frightened of.

The boys were being troopers until the next exhibit on the tour. We entered a stark, bare room with two thick iron doors on either side, one in and one out. The sign above the entry door read "Brausebad," which means "Shower Bath." The docent closed both doors to give the full effect of the chamber. He pointed to a small metal hatch on the far wall and explained that is where the camp guards dispensed cyanide gas to kill everyone inside. He then pointed to the deep scratches in the concrete around the doors from the fingers of desperate prisoners clawing to get out as the lethal gas burned their lungs. The guards would wait for the screaming to stop and then ventilate the room, gather up the bodies for cremation, and repeat the process with another unsuspecting group. They did this all day long, every day, for years.

The emotion of reliving that horrible experience was too much for poor Elijah. I looked down to see him shaking as tears flowed from his red eyes. I gently picked him up and carried him out of the room. My heart broke to see him like this. All I could do was try to soothe his fear. Very shortly, Mish and Aaron came to join us. The boys had enough.

Worried that we had scarred our boys for life again, we didn't push them any further. Mish and I took turns finishing the tour. I walked around the camp alone first. Being by myself in a mostly empty concentration camp was even more intense.

I found my way to the crematorium where the prisoner's bodies were unceremoniously disposed of. Three large brick ovens stood side by side in a large building off to one side of the camp. They looked like benign giant pizza ovens at first. When I got closer, I read the brass markers that told the number of prisoners cremated in each one, over 3,000 each.

Even with the furnaces burning 24 hours a day, they could not keep up with the demand. The guards had to resort to burying the excess bodies in a large open pit behind the camp. No tombstones, no names recorded, no respect for the dead. It was more than barbaric. Sadness, anger, and remorse churned around inside me. I left wondering how anyone could do that to another human being.

I returned to the family and let Mish take her turn while I stayed with the boys. Thankfully, they seemed in much better spirits. Shortly, Mish returned. She had the same disbelieving look I probably had when I came out. We were very glad that we experienced the camp but were more glad to leave it. It is definitely one of the most memorable experiences that has left an indelible impression on all of us.

I decided we need to end the trip on a happier note. I had been noticing brochures for luge rides in the area and thought they would be a good idea. These crazy contraptions are basically semi-steerable skateboards riders sit on to careen down the sides of mountains on narrow concrete tracks. Apparently, they are very popular with thrill-seeking Bavarians. I'm not sure why I thought putting my family on one was a good idea.

Easily enough, I found us one nearby. Mish and Arron were all in immediately. Elijah looked at the steep slope and speeding cars, unsure. I reassured him it was safe, and because he was too small to ride alone, he would sit in my lap. He was not persuaded. I felt he had enough trauma for one day and agreed to hang back with him. While Mish and

Aaron took the ski lift up to the starting point high on the mountain, Elijah and I went to find something chocolatey. I was cool with that.

Elijah and I found our treat and went back to the viewing area to watch the daredevils get their adrenaline rush. We watched as riders flew down the track at break-neck speeds. Every once in a while, one would take a turn too fast and tumble off the track and into the grass. I winced as they got up, brushed themselves off, and got back on the track. Elijah munched on his treat and laughed each time. He was no dummy.

Many riders later, Mish came flying down the track with her red hair flying behind her and a huge smile on her face. She is an adrenaline junkie, for sure. She whizzed by us like a pro and was soon back out of sight. Following on her heels was Arron. He, too, looked very thrilled as he skillfully drove his car down. Like mother, like son.

Elijah and I walked down to meet them at the finish line. When we got there, they were hooting and high-fiving each other. I was glad they had a good time. By the time we got back in the car, Dachau was a fading, but not forgotten, memory.

We stayed in Munich for the night to revisit the charming city and see more of its attractions. Early the next morning, we began the long trek back home to Eddersheim. So far, this trip has been the highlight of our time in Germany. The Bavarian region is nothing short of spectacular. We can see why all Germans hold it dear in their hearts.

I suppose what remains in my mind, however, is the stark contrast between the incredible natural beauty of the land and the unbelievable ugliness of the human crimes committed there. I do not know when or if Germany will ever live down the infamy of the Nazi atrocities. It is sad that their ghosts still haunt the country no matter where you go. Maybe it is for the best, so we do not forget the lessons learned from that horrible time.

Chapter 14 – Time to Move Again

"Don't cry because it's over. Smile because it happened." – Dr. Seuss

We intended to stay in Germany for longer, perhaps two to three years. Regrettably, things did not work out that way. Elijah was not learning anything in German school, not even German. Aaron was not being academically challenged doing online school either. Their education was a growing concern for Mish and I.

We had few options. I managed to bargain with my school to allow Aaron free tuition. I liked the school and thought it would be a good fit for him. Unfortunately, the German government would tax the "free" tuition as income. At a 40% tax rate, the cost would be unaffordable for us. So much for that fringe benefit. We also could not figure out what to do with Elijah. The German government was adamant on their prohibition on homeschooling, and we could not afford to put him in a private international school either. We truly were at a loss as to what to do.

Looking for options, I hopped on a plane to London to attend an international teacher's job fair. I have been to one before, so I knew what to expect. I brought my best suit, made copies of my resume, and put on my game face. I hoped someplace good needed a pretty decent science teacher.

At the fair, I walked around once again, overwhelmed with options. I handed out several of my resumes and talked to numerous school administrators, the first day. By the second day, I had secured offers in Valencia, Spain, Cartagena, Columbia, and Addis Ababa, Ethiopia. They all sounded amazing.

I ran into a friend of ours who, at the time, was the superintendent of a school district in Ulaanbaatar, Mongolia. Over drinks, he gave his best sales pitch to lure us to his high school. I was very flattered, but I know geography. Mongolia is isolated and cold, very cold. In winter, daytime temperatures rarely exceed -4° F, and nighttime can drop below -40° F. That is frigging cold! I had to politely decline his generous offer.

Back at the convention, I looked for more opportunities. While I was talking to another school in Germany, the director of a small private international school in Costa Rica approached me. She made me an offer that sounded very tempting. I now had five solid offers on the table. I found a quiet nook and called Mish.

She was as overwhelmed as me. All the schools sounded amazing, except maybe Mongolia. We deliberated on the phone for a while, carefully weighing the pros and cons of each location. We have been living in Europe and love it, and there are still many places we want to visit here. Going someplace completely different, like another continent, also sounded intriguing. What to do?

After agonizing over the options, we finally reached a decision. Costa Rica, it would be. It won out because it was on our bucket list to visit someday, and warm tropical weather sounded very enticing after a brutally cold winter in Germany. Plus, it was someplace completely different from what both of us were used to. It would be another exciting adventure for the family.

While I signed my contract, Mish told the boys. Animal-loving Elijah was thrilled at the thought of all the exotic wildlife Costa Rica offered. Aaron seemed ambivalent and would go anywhere. Since the boys were in, we were all in agreement that the next move would be back across the Atlantic to Central America. Now, we had to make preparations.

We were finally leaving Europe. After living in two countries, we had come to think of it as home. We definitely had seen much of it, but there was still so much more. We promised ourselves that we would return someday and explore it more and revisit old haunts. For now, however, we wanted to make one final short trip to say goodbye.

We had made friends in England and wanted to see them before we left. So, we planned a long weekend in London to rendezvous with them. In particular, Aaron wanted to say goodbye to a special friend, who happens to be a girl, one last time. Our young Casanova was smitten with a young English lass named Pippa, whom he still writes to. He didn't want to get an international reputation as a love-them-and-leave-them type.

By now, we knew the six-hour drive to Calais, France, fairly well. In Calais, we would board the ferry and cross the channel to Dover, England, and then drive two hours north on the M-20 to London. Easy trip, or so we thought.

We arrived in Calais and drove our car onto the large ferry as planned. Unfortunately, poor Albie had to stay alone in the car for the voyage while we went topside to enjoy the fresh air and view along with a snack. We figured he would curl up in the backseat and go to sleep. He knew we would come back and lavish him with attention and probably a treat. He leads a pretty secure life.

The crossing went very smoothly, and before long, the familiar white cliffs of Dover came into view over the horizon. We were packing up our stuff when a message came across the ship's public announcement system.

"Would the owner of a blue and grey Mercedes license plate 7JUP6 please report to the Purser's Office? Thank you."

"Great. What has the mutt done this time," I said out loud.

I figured Albie had become lonely and annoyed that we weren't back yet and started loudly barking up a storm. He probably set off all the car alarms on the automobile deck. I imagined car lights flashing and horns honking with Albie in the middle of the commotion, happily wagging his tail in approval of the attention he was getting. I looked at Mish, who just shrugged and headed off in search of the Purser.

At the Purser's Office, none less than the ship captain himself was waiting for us. That dog must have really screwed up this time, I thought. I was deciding on clever ways to punish his furry butt as I walked up to the captain.

"Are you the owner of the car with a dog in it?" the captain politely inquired.

"Yes, what did he do?" I dejectedly responded.

"May I see his papers, please?" he requested.

Mish rummaged through her bag and promptly produced Albie's European pet passport and handed it to the captain. He thanked her and took the small booklet. He carefully examined the document and returned it to her.

"I am afraid your dog is denied entrance to England," he concluded.

"What?" decried Mish. "He is a European citizen and lived in England," she continued.

I'm not sure of the legal status of dogs as "citizens," but I knew when Mish was about to stand her ground. She is very meticulous and does not like being told no on matters she is well-versed in. I learned she was usually right and knew when to back down. The captain, however, appeared to be adamant that Albie's documentation was amiss and invoked his authority on the issue.

"What are we supposed to do?" demanded Mish.

"The four of you may enter the country, but the dog cannot," replied the captain.

Mish looked at me with smoldering brown eyes. She was not happy that she lost this battle. I was not sure what to do. Obviously, we could not leave Albie on the ship alone to take the voyage back to France. He would not understand to wait on the pier for three days while we chilled in London. There was only one solution.

"I will take Albie and the car back to France while you and the boys take the train to London," I offered Mish.

She looked hesitant.

"Are you sure?" she asked.

"Yes. It will be fine. We've already paid for the hotel and can't get our money back. Plus, Aaron is looking forward to seeing Pippa," I assured her.

With the decision made, I told the captain our plan. He informed me that I would need to drive our car off and back on again to re-register it. Thankfully, he arranged for a ride to the nearby train for Mish and the boys. I turned and said goodbye to the boys and told them to be good, and kissed Mish.

"Albie and I will have some bonding time," I jokingly said as I walked down the ladder to the automobile deck.

Ours was the only car left on the ship. It looked very small in the large, cavernous hold. I climbed in and was instantly greeted by Albie who had no clue as to the unintentional trouble he had caused. He looked at me with eyes that seemed to say, "Where is everybody?" I scratched his ear to let him know that everything was ok.

"It's just you and me boy," I told him and put the car in gear and drove down the ramp and off the ship.

Meanwhile, unbeknownst to me, Mish and the boys were being taken to the train in a police car. It was the only option the captain had. Elijah rode on Mish's lap up front while poor Aaron got put in the back behind the wire cage partition. I cannot imagine what onlookers must have thought as the three of them were driving away under police escort. I later learned from Mish that Aaron was a little traumatized by it all. Poor guy, not even of legal age, and already has a rap sheet.

Unaware of what my family was doing, I set sail back to France. On the crossing, I debated on what to do for three days by myself, plus Albie. After some thought, I decided to go home to Eddersheim and wait for Mish and the boys to return when I would drive back to Calais to pick them up. Oh well, c'est la vie.

Once back in France, I began the long, unexpected drive home. Twelve hours of driving in one day was wearing on me. As I approached Belgium, I could feel my eyes grow heavier and heavier. I did not want to get into an accident, so I did the responsible thing and pulled into a rest area outside Brussels. I pulled the car into a nice, quiet, secluded spot away from the lights of the all-night mini-mart and put the seat back for a snooze. Almost instantly, I was out cold.

I woke up in the pre-dawn early morning needing to pee. I had left the window open about halfway and the cool air felt refreshing. I rubbed my eyes and yawned. It was still dark outside, but I could just glimpse the first light from the rising sun. I looked in the back to see Albie still sound asleep. Apparently, his bladder is bigger than mine. I got out of the car and stumbled over to the mini-mart hoping that they had a restroom available.

Luckily, their restroom was open for business. After relieving myself, I splashed some water on my face and then got a coffee to go. I felt refreshed enough to drive the rest of the way home. As I walked back to the car to continue the drive, I saw another car pulled up tightly against my driver's side. A young man was peering into my car trying to coax Albie into his car through the open windows of both vehicles.

I ran across the empty parking lot spilling my hot coffee all over myself. My running and cursing must have alerted the man that the dog's owner was coming to the rescue. Startled, he quickly got into his car and sped away. I reached my car out of breath, but relieved that Albie was still inside. I could not believe that someone tried to dog-nap poor Albie. I was actually very shaken. What kind of low-life would do such a thing, I wondered? Pets are part of someone's family. My relief had turned to anger. I was furious now.

I got back into the car and hugged Albie. He had no idea how close he had come to being taken from us. Still fuming, I got back on the motorway and headed into Brussels for a fresh coffee. We had not visited Brussels yet, so I was not familiar with it. I knew, however, that it would have a city center where I would find a café.

I found the city center easy enough and parked the car. This time, I took Albie with me. He needed to stretch his legs and relieve himself too. Plus, I felt he deserved a treat for the trauma he might have felt if he had been aware of what almost happened to him.

We strolled around Brussels for a while taking in the city. I sipped my new coffee and Albie sniffed everything he could and marked his turf accordingly. It is not as nice or big a city center as other European cities, but it was still a nice stop. As I was getting in the car, I decided to head back to Calais and wait for the family there. It would only be two more nights anyway, and I was exhausted from driving. Albie and I could crash in a hotel somewhere and watch movies and order takeout.

I found a reasonable hotel near the port and did exactly as planned. It was a relaxing two days with nothing to do, except wait. Aside from some short walks, we didn't even leave the hotel. It may not have been the most exotic weekend I've had, but it was refreshing, and I didn't run into any more dog-nappers.

Sunday afternoon came, and it was time to reunite with the family. I hoped that they had a better time than me. I anxiously awaited for the ferry at the terminal. I watched as the ship appeared on the horizon and got bigger and bigger as it slowly approached. The deck hands skillfully moored the ship to the pier and extended the gangway. As soon as the gate lifted, a flood of people poured off the ship.

I squinted to see Mish and the boys. Almost all of the guests were off and the flow of people had slowed to a trickle, but still no sign of them. I started to get a little nervous. At long last, I saw them walk across the bridge. Relieved, I called and waved. They heard me and waved back. I never felt so glad to see them as this time. It was the first time we had ever been separated in different countries.

Albie and I met Mish and the boys at the ferry terminal entrance. We gave huge hugs and kisses all around. I grabbed Mish's bag and lead the way to our car.

"You would not believe the trouble we had. I hope your weekend went better," Mish remarked.

"Oh yeah," I replied. "At least you didn't have to thwart dog-nappers."

Mish looked at me quizzically.

"I'll explain on the drive home," I told her.

It had been a longer weekend than anticipated. All I wanted to do was get back and begin the process of moving. Tomorrow morning, I will need to set things in motion.

I gave my school director my resignation. He was very disappointed but understood. He told me that should I ever want to return, there would be a position for me. His generous offer made me feel both sadder to leave and happy to know I was thought highly of. We shook hands and I went to say goodbye to my colleagues.

Mish readied our household for another international move. This was our second one, so she had experience now. She sorted our belongings into four piles: take, sell, give away, and donate. With all our souvenirs, the take pile was by far the largest. We would not get away with just two bags each this time. We assured Elijah that all his stuffed animals would be going with him, none needed to be put up for adoption. Aaron, however, might need to wear all of his hats at once on the plane.

I found a buyer for our car. One of my American colleagues who was planning on staying for several years in Germany really wanted it. Mish loved the car, but it was not possible to ship it to Costa Rica, not for a small fortune, at least. When we got to Costa Rica, I would need to find us another vehicle. We agreed he could have it the week before we left so I could be there to help transfer the paperwork since I had experience with the convoluted German DMV system. Also, he needed a few lessons on how to drive a stick-shift.

The only slight snag in the moving process was Mish found out at the last minute that she was being summoned to her school's graduation. It was a mandatory all-hands-on-deck event that she could not get out of. Since her school did not know she was living in Germany, she could not use living out of the country as an excuse. So, she would need to fly back a week before me. We flipped a coin to see who got to keep the boys. I won the toss, she got them.

I would be on my own without a car in a mostly empty house for the last few days in Germany. It didn't sound like a fun time. I'm sure I could find something to do to occupy my time and hopefully stay out of trouble.

The German national football team was in the finals for the World Cup and football fever was at a very high temperature. The country last won the coveted FIFA title in 1990. In the previous World Cup championship four years ago, they took third place. So, Germany was hoping that this was going to be their year for a fourth championship title. Everywhere we went there was World Cup fanfare. Since I would be alone, I figured hanging out in a pub watching football on the television and getting into the spirit would fill the time nicely.

When the day arrived, I took Mish and the boys to the airport in Frankfurt. Dropping them off and saying goodbye, only temporarily, was harder than I expected. For some odd reason, watching them leave instead of me leaving was harder. I do not like being by myself and being left behind only amplified the feeling of loneliness. I drove back to what was our home and walked down to the local pub.

The next morning, my friend took our car. Now, I felt even more isolated. I could feel a little depression start to seep in. With nothing left to do except finish the last week of school, I went running after work and then back to the pub. The week seemed to slowly crawl by.

On the second to last morning before leaving, I got up to go to my last day of school. To my utter dismay, when I reached into my jacket pocket, I didn't find my wallet. Immediately, panic set in. Thankfully, I still had my passport safely tucked away in my briefcase. I had identification, but without my wallet, I didn't have money. Aside from not being able to buy a pint at the pub that night, I had no way to buy food or pay for a ride to the airport. Plus, somebody might be running around Germany having a free extravagant holiday pretending to be me.

I hated to do it, but in desperation I swallowed my pride and called Mish to tell her I screwed up. Sometimes, a husband has to do what a husband has to do. She was very understanding and went into problem solving mode. Dealing with fixing my messes is one of her many strong points. She called our bank and put a hold on my cards and alerted them to possible unauthorized use. Next, she looked into wiring me some money so I could at least eat. Afterwards, she chided me for not being more careful.

While I was waiting for Mish to work her magic, someone knocked on the door. A stranger greeted me and asked if this was mine. In his hand he held up my wallet. A wave of relief washed over me. Saved! I grateful took it. To my astonishment, all my cards and identification were inside. I could not thank him enough. I offered him some money for finding it, but he refused. He just said I was welcome and walked away. Miracles do happen. I don't know if that man realized what an angel he was. I called Mish to tell her to re-activate my cards, I was hungry.

With the last, hopefully, excitement over, I was ready to leave Germany. I went to bed for the last time in our house, thinking about all that had transpired in our time here. With streusel and the Alps on my mind, I fell asleep.

My alarm went off and I shot up in bed. I needed to shower, dress, and finish packing in time to meet my ride out front. I waited out in the cool morning air hoping my driver would show up as planned. Right on time, my taxi pulled up. With one last look at the house, I tossed my bags in the trunk and climbed in. The driver asked where I was going.

"The airport please. Departures," I answered.

The drive from what was now our old home to the airport is only twenty minutes. I had just done it a week ago and now it was finally my turn. The driver parked on the curb under the sign for international departures and got out to help me with my luggage.

"Danka," I said as I paid him.

I turned around and went into the terminal through the automatic sliding doors to check in. This was it, I thought as I stood in another long airport line. The next time I am on an airplane, it will be our flight to Costa Rica. I wondered what adventures we would have there.

Part III

Chapter 1 – A Different Continent

"Variety is the very spice of life, that gives it all its flavor." – William Cowper

Back in Washington State we were enjoying the familiarity of home and the magnificent Pacific Northwest summer. Being home was both comforting and a little disconnected at the same time. After living in Europe, we had grown accustomed to the customs, routines, and quirks of the continent.

Living on the other side of the Atlantic Ocean had changed us. Driving around home was different now. I tried to put my finger on exactly what was altering my perception. The mountain scenery was still spectacular. Everything looked the same. Maybe it was the over-commercialization with signs advertising everything everywhere? Maybe it was the abundance of potholes I kept inadvertently running over? Maybe it was the lack of charming little villages? Maybe the excitement of seeing new places was gone? Maybe it was a combination of all of these. No matter what the cause, the travel bug was starting to bite again.

We committed to going to Costa Rica. As the summer waned, the anticipation grew. Central America would be a whole new experience for all of us. As much as we loved Europe, we were eager to try another continent. The thought of a tropical paradise with crystal clear waters, lush green jungles, exotic animals, and erupting volcanoes was sounding better and better every day.

We cherished the summer and spent the precious time reconnecting with home as well as making all of the necessary preparations for another big move. Our house needed some tender love and care, so in between hiking the breathtaking Olympic Peninsula and strolling around Seattle, we whittled down our home repair list. Everything was going well until my clumsiness tripped me up again.

One bright morning, about two weeks out from departing for Costa Rica, I had a small accident. After sweeping out the last load of fresh mulch for our yard from my truck bed, I jumped down to the driveway. The fall was only about three feet, but it was enough time for my right foot to curl inwards on the way down. Instead of the bottom of my foot landing on the hard surface, it was the side of it. My ankle did not transfer the force of impact smoothly and snapped. The pain was immediate and severe.

Instantly, my ankle turned reddish purple and swelled to the size of a small elephant's foot. I almost blacked out from the shock. I knew I had screwed up pretty badly. Off to the local urgent care we went, again.

First mistake, don't go to urgent care facilities unless you have no other choice. No offense to the medical staff at these places, but they simply are not equipped to deal with anything more severe than some stitches or sprains. My poor ankle needed more than they, or me, realized at the time.

The very nice people at the urgent care x-rayed my ankle and determined it was indeed broken. One of the bones had cracked down the middle. They gave me a pressure boot, a pair of crutches, and some prescription strength painkillers and sent me home. I hobbled away, hoping it would heal before we left.

Second mistake, never leave an injury to heal on its own. Get a follow-up from a doctor as soon as possible. No more than three days later, I was limping along in my garage, working on more chores, when I suddenly and unexpectedly got a sharp stabbing pain through the middle of my back. It was so severe that I collapsed onto the concrete floor and was unable to get up. My wife's ESP must have been triggered because she appeared quickly to check on me. She also has taken me to the emergency room one too many times to know not to leave me alone for a long period of time without checking. Apparently, I am accident-prone.

All I really remember is the paramedics coming, giving me an IV, and stuffing me in the back of their ambulance. I woke up a day later in the hospital. Much to my relief, Mish was sitting next to me, holding my hand. I asked the obvious question, "What happened?"

"You had a blood clot," she solemnly informed me. I could tell that she was a little shaken.

Shortly, the doctor came in and told me that the ankle break had ruptured the blood vessels in the right leg, causing blood clots to form. One of the nasty little buggers had made its way to my lung. Evidently, I had dodged a bullet.

Two days later, I was released from the hospital with a box full of needles filled with some anticoagulant medication and a prescription for rat poison. Twice a day for two weeks, I needed to jab myself in the stomach with the shots. Once I ran out of them, I was supposed to start the poison. The poison is called Warfarin and was actually first developed as a poison to kill rats, great.

I am not squeamish about needles. However, I must admit that I did not like the idea of injecting myself, so my wife did. It's a very good thing she loves me. I don't think she was too keen on the idea either, but she hooked me up. It was an odd way to do couple bonding.

Two weeks of the Lovenox shots left my poor stomach looking like it had been used as a punching bag by Mike Tyson. Mish had a hard time finding an area that was not black and blue to inject me towards the last few doses. We were both very glad when she administered the last shot. Unfortunately, that meant I needed to start the Warfarin next.

Somehow, we got the necessary things done before our move date. Mish, Aaron, and Elijah had to pick up my slack while Albie kept me company on bed rest. We talked about canceling the move altogether. I even called the school to see if pushing my start date back was an option. In the end, we decided that continuing with our grand plan was best. The only problem, however, was my immobility.

Mish came to my rescue again. She arranged for my medical insurance to pay for a knee scooter. Crutches were too hard to navigate with my other issues, not that she thought I was too uncoordinated for them, I'm sure. All I had to do was learn how to use it while teaching classes and not run over someone. We were back on course!

Luckily, Costa Rica's laws on pets are much laxer than European ones. I did not have to do any creative documentation on Albie to get him into the country this time. One violation of international law was enough. He would be coming with us once again.

Finally, the morning came when we took a last look at our home and boarded the airplane. This time, we would be heading south, not east. It was a comparatively shorter flight than to Europe, but still nine hours in the air. We were all now very accustomed to international flights, so we settled in for the long haul. Albie, we hoped had also become used to lengthy flights and was comfortably relaxing in his travel kennel somewhere in the bottom of the plane.

Right on schedule, we were wheels down in San Jose, Costa Rica! We eagerly looked out the cabin windows at our new home. Right away, we zeroed in on all of the tropical and lush greenery. This was definitely not Europe. We were in Central America.

My new school director arranged to pick us up at the airport, which was very thoughtful. We had two excited boys, one traumatized dog, a load of luggage, and me on a scooter. Thankfully, she brought the school van to collect us. Once we were all in, she had the driver take us to our new home.

Originally, we were going to be staying in a small apartment near the school, but once again, luck was on our side. A prominent family who had children in the school I would be teaching in owned a large farm with a small guest house. The school director had arranged a deal so we could stay there instead. We had no idea how much of an incredible experience this was going to be. A new adventure was about to begin.

The driver spoke English and chatted as he drove. The first thing he wanted us to know was that Jurassic Park the movie was not filmed in Costa Rica. It was mainly filmed in Hawaii. The fictional Isla Nublar used in the opening shot is not real either, so we couldn't visit it.

Apparently, many Costa Ricans were disappointed and even outraged at the misrepresentation of their country in the film. The capital, San Jose, is not on the ocean and is not the little shanty town it is portrayed. The most egregious thing Steven Spielberg did was make Costa Rica an island. Unforgivable.

I had to inform Aaron and Elijah not to bother looking for dinosaurs. That didn't deter them from searching anyway. You never know.

As we drove the half-hour from the airport to the farm, we gazed out the van windows at a strange new world. What we saw both elated and depressed us. The beautiful thick green vegetation covering steep mountainous terrain was expected and amazing to see. The small, mismatched, dilapidated buildings dotting this landscape were surprising and a little disappointing. Copious amounts of litter lined the roadway. We were no longer in affluent modern Europe. We were in a much poorer area of the world. This was going to take getting used to.

We crossed a dirty river that bisected a small dingy town and headed uphill. Soon, we turned onto a narrow private road lined with large trees and came upon a closed gate. A woman on the front porch of a small, tidy house on the other side waved to our driver, and the gate opened. The driver continued through the gate and up the road into the farm. We gasped in astonishment. The gate was like a portal that crossed us through to another world. This was a totally different Costa Rica.

The farm, or finca as it is referred to in Spanish, was a microcosm of affluence in an otherwise impoverished country. The setting was idyllic. It was a stark contrast to the world outside the gate. Every facet of the farm was juxtaposed to the life we saw driving here. On the finca, the houses were tidy and orderly. All of the landscape was neatly trimmed and manicured. There was not a speck of litter to be seen. This was the Costa Rica we had seen in travel brochures and television shows before arriving. But was it the real Costa Rica, I wondered?

For now, taking in the lush green tropical landscape was all we could handle. The driver pulled up in front of a charming single-story house wrapped by a huge porch. This was to be our new home for a while. It was far more than we expected. From the porch we had an amazing vista of the mountains and the valley below. Cattle grazed lazily on the grass in the front yard, and a myriad of colorful birds chirped and fluttered in the trees above us. This was definitely a little slice of paradise.

We unloaded the van and went inside. The house was colorfully decorated in traditional Costa Rican style with even more exotic plants on the inside that enjoyed the abundant natural light from the huge windows. The front room was open to the porch so that you felt like you were living outdoors. There were three bedrooms in the back, which the boys quickly claimed one each. Mish and I took the remaining one. Luckily, they let us have the one with the queen-sized bed. Two full bathrooms and an open kitchen and dining area completed the home. It would do nicely.

Shortly, the head farm hand, Oscar, came over and introduced himself. He spoke very little English, and our Spanish was not too extensive either. He took off his worn sun-bleached hat with one hand and extended the other one in the universal gesture of welcome. I took it and noted that it was a hand forged from many years of manual labor, strong and calloused. It matched his tanned face and stout figure. He was definitely a man who worked the earth for a living. His warm smile and exuberant handshake foretold that this was the beginning of a close friendship.

By now, we were used to unpacking and setting up a new home. The boys busied themselves with customizing their new rooms by carefully placing the treasured personal items they brought with them on shelves and nightstands. It was their way of having consistency in their nomadic lives. Each had items that were precious to them and created their little worlds wherever they went. Aaron had his collection of air and space memorabilia, and Elijah had his stuffed menagerie of animal friends. For them, these items, along with mom and dad, defined home.

Mish began unpacking our stuff and setting up shop. Since I was just in the way I decided to explore the farm a little. I stepped onto the expansive front porch and took in the breathtaking view. I was eager to see the farm, so I briskly walked down the steps and onto the thick green carpet of grass. I didn't get three steps when I heard someone yelling at me from behind. "¡Señor! Necesitas botas, no sandalias. Hay serpientes por todas partes. Es peligroso."

I turned to see Oscar quickly walking towards me, waving a hand, signaling me to stop. Even with my poor Spanish, I recognized two words: serpientes, which means snakes, and peligroso, which means dangerous. Two words that you don't want to go together, especially when they apply to you. I froze in my tracks.

Oscar came up to me, panting and excitedly pointing at my sandals. I loved walking in my Tevas, but apparently, Oscar felt differently.

"Sin sandalias. Hay muchas serpientes en la granja. Te mostrare," he repeated.

He beckoned me to follow him, so I did. We went to a small wooden shed across the drive from our house. Inside, he pointed to three steel oil barrels against the far wall. He went to the nearest one and pointed inside it.

"Serpientes," he said.

I cautiously looked down into the barrel. I jumped back when I immediately saw several very aggressive and very poisonous snakes slithering around. I knew enough from my prior studies of the indigenous wildlife of Costa Rica to identify them as vipers, one of several species of deadly snakes found throughout the region. They did not look happy to be detained in a can.

We learned, luckily right away, that the farm grew avocados, which attract mice and other small mammals, which attract the snakes. The snakes hang out in the trees to ambush their prey and sometimes mistake an unsuspecting hand reaching in to pick an avocado as an easy meal. Consequently, many farm workers get bit. This is how Oscar's father died. Oscar collects any snake he finds on the farm and turns it over to the national university, where it is milked to make antivenom. I guess this is his way of honoring his father and helping to prevent another snake fatality. Petrified, I quickly returned to our house to change shoes. Lesson learned.

Chapter 2 – Life on a Farm

"There are two spiritual dangers in not owning a farm. One is the danger of supposing that breakfast comes from the grocery, and the other that heat comes from the furnace." — Aldo Leopold, A Sand County Almanac

I've never lived on a farm. Of course, I've seen them and even been on some, but I haven't actually been part of the farming lifestyle. Mish enthusiastically gardens, and I see the hard work, sweat, and love that she pours into the craft. It is intense labor followed by optimistic patience. If you did it right and the agricultural fates were pleased, then you are rewarded with a bountiful harvest and the deep satisfaction of knowing that you created it. I think that is why tomatoes from your own garden always taste better than the ones from the grocery store.

I never really understood how connected farming makes you with your food, but I was learning every day living on the farm. Our farm grew two primary crops, avocados and coffee. I will put avocados on anything. Their creamy green omega-3-rich fruit goes well at breakfast, lunch, and dinner. I never paused, however, to consider where they came from other than the produce aisle.

Being a huge Starbucks aficionado, I relish all things coffee. Mish is certain I am their biggest customer, which is probably not too far from the truth. I have a venti non-fat, no-whip mocha every day, ok sometimes two. Just as with avocados, I voraciously consume coffee, but I don't really think about where it comes from. I was soon to learn much about both.

One Saturday morning, Oscar came around to our house and asked if we wanted to learn about avocados. By this time, we had worked out communicating by Spanglish and hand signals. We were all eager to be educated in avocado-ology, so we followed him over to one of the large open barn structures. Inside were long, shallow parallel troughs. Oscar beckoned us to stand alongside one. Shortly, a tractor came rumbling around the corner, pulling a trailer filled to the brim with freshly picked avocados.

The driver skillfully backed the trailer up to our trough. Oscar opened the back gate of the trailer, and hundreds of avocados rolled down past us. He picked up one and said, "Hass." We admired the dark green leathery orb and repeated, "Hass." "Es bueno," Oscar proclaimed. He picked up another smaller and rounder avocado and said, "Florida."

Obediently, we repeated, "Florida."

"Es ok, Hass is mejor," Oscar stated.

We understood that the Hass variety was preferred. He told us that these were the two most common avocado varieties grown in Costa Rica, but there were over 500 other varieties. Another lesson learned.

We were instructed to separate the avocado varieties and place each into separate large cardboard boxes. Additionally, we learned how to check for ripeness. The too-soft or too-brown ones got put into another box. I asked Oscar where those went. He replied, "Vacas." The cows in Costa Rica eat well.

You might think that doing pro bono farmwork in your spare time would be boring and tiring, but it was actually fun. The boys really got into it. They treated it like a game of who could spot the most or biggest Haas and who got the more rotten avocado. Brothers inevitably will find something to compete over. Aaron and Elijah definitely fought the avocado war. They would proudly proclaim victory when one would triumphantly hold up a large, shiny green orb. Moments later, the other would claim they had found an even bigger one. Ah, sibling rivalry.

Even this small one-time task was meaningful in an unexpected way. Not only did we learn something about avocados, but more importantly, we learned a little bit about our farm mates. Despite the language barrier, we got to really know them as people and not just faceless laborers in the fields.

They were very hardworking and adept at their job. They ran circles around us as they jovially conversed while instinctively sorting the fruit. It was a tedious task but one that needed to get done nonetheless. Instead of complaining or procrastinating, they simply did it. They made the job palatable by interacting with each other, similar to our overzealous boys but with less one-upmanship.

I've seen farmworkers back in the United States laboring in fields and orchards but never gave them too much thought, to be honest. I think I had the same general mentality as most people back home. This is the way things are, some people are born into a life of servitude, and others are not. If the less fortunate work hard, then they can overcome their lot in life and become successful like the rest of us. I would realize how wrong that thinking is. I was learning another lesson.

The afternoon blended into the evening. Mish and I could tell the boys were running out of energy. They were no longer as exuberant about sorting avocados or besting each other. It was time to head back to our house and get ready for bed. We said goodnight to our newly made friends and thanked our teacher, Oscar. It turned out to be an unexpected educational and fun time.

The next day, we got a tour of the farm. Oscar fired up his large blue tractor, and we climbed into the attached wagon and rumbled off into the avocado fields. Being in Costa Rica, nothing is flat, not even a farm. The trees were at a relatively steep angle to the ground as the land rose and fell with the mountainous terrain. The tractor, with us in the wagon, would have to precariously tilt sometimes as it navigated the farm. Oscar, accustomed to the area, seemed oblivious to our white-knuckle clinging to the wagon sides.

Despite our fear of toppling over, we greatly enjoyed the ride. The farm was very expansive. It covered several hillsides with avocado trees. It also covered more hills with coffee trees. We abruptly transitioned from one fruit to another. Yes, coffee is actually a fruit, too. Technically, it is not a tree either; it is a bush.

Oscar pointed things out as he drove and talked about the farm and its crops. We were learning a lot along our personal guided tour. This is why we really travel, to have authentic experiences and come away more worldly than before. We were immersing ourselves in the culture, not just seeing the country from inside a tourist bubble.

I asked Oscar if the farm, by chance, sold coffee beans to my favorite roaster, Starbucks. He said, unfortunately, they did not. Starbucks has very strict rules on who they will buy beans from. Growers must meet their guidelines on sustainability and environmental practices, he informed us. The farm was trying to come into compliance with them but was still not quite there yet. My hopes of scoring some fresh Starbucks coffee were dashed. At least the coffee in Costa Rica was superb despite not having the green mermaid symbol.

I noticed more of the long-eared cows meandering throughout the fields. They look a lot like Jar Jar Binks from Star Wars but much less irritating. I asked Oscar if the farm also raised them for export. He replied, "No, No, ellas mantienen a las serpientes lejos." Apparently, the snakes don't like the large bovines stomping around, so the cows keep them away. I remembered my previous lesson about snakes and put my hands back inside the wagon.

Once again, Oscar provided us with an education on farming. He seemed to take real pride in his work and the farm. As he drove, we talked over the rumbling of the tractor. I learned he was born and raised on this farm. His father was the prior farm manager, and when he died, Oscar took his place. The owner provided his family with free housing in a new home they built just for them. In one way, it seemed like an idyllic life; in another, it seemed horribly confining.

Oscar only had ever known the farm. He had never been out of the country. He had never even explored all of his own small country. These hills were his world. I wondered if he wished for more. Did he have childhood dreams of becoming something other than a farmer? I did not know him well enough yet to feel comfortable asking such personal questions, but I really wanted to know. I took it for granted that our boys could dream of becoming anything they wanted. I never thought that other people might have limitations on their dreams.

Oscar pulled up to our house, and we disembarked and thanked him again for the education. We were learning a lot about farm life and now added coffee growing to our expanding knowledge base. I would never sip my favorite beverage again without thinking about this time.

Several days later, we finally met the owner of the farm. A nicely dressed gentleman drove up to our house in a silver Land Rover and introduced himself.

"I am Francisco. My family owns this farm," he said in English with a thick Spanish accent.

He was a stark contrast to Oscar. While Oscar was tanned and weathered by years of outdoor work, Francisco obviously was accustomed to a more sedate indoor existence.

Either way, he was still very friendly and just as enthusiastic about showing off his farm. Most importantly, he wanted to show us his prized crop. He walked us across our house to three very large glass greenhouses. He needed very precisely controlled environmental conditions for his hobby, he explained as we walked up to them. We wondered what needed better conditions than Costa Rica naturally provided.

As we walked inside, we beheld his delicate plants, orchids. Apparently, Francisco was a very passionate orchidist. He stretched out his arms towards his flowers and proudly proclaimed, "These are my orchids!" He looked at us to see if we were dutifully impressed. We were. We did not know anything about orchids but genuinely admired their delicate beauty.

Francisco walked us around the greenhouse instructing us in the cultivation, displaying, and competing of all things orchids. Apparently, orchids are a very big deal in some circles, obviously ones that we did not socialize in. Now that we lived in Costa Rica, however, we would have to start.

Francisco would have stayed all day, and probably longer, lecturing on orchidology, but Aaron and Elijah were not as enamored with orchids and started to get restless, which is never a good sign in high-energy young boys. They have a way of getting themselves into trouble. They also gave us a fortuitous excuse to politely excuse ourselves. Francisco was a wealth of knowledge, but we were in orchid overload. We thanked him and headed back to our house with a standing invitation from Francisco to attend the exclusive Costa Rican Orchid Show.

The next week Francisco's wife, Maria-Melba, paid us a visit to invite us up for tea at the main house. We were flattered and graciously accepted. We had not been to their home yet and were anxious to see it.

We caught glimpses of it walking on the farm. It was a large Spanish style home large enough to be called a mansion that sat on the highest point on the farm. Mish was definitely eager to see the inside, now she would get her chance.

In between farm tours, I continued to teach at the small international school. My ankle was still in a restraining boot, so I used my knee scooter to get around. Since I couldn't drive, the school kindly provided me with a van service to pick Aaron, Elijah, and me up every morning and take us to school and back while Mish took taxis to go shopping. It worked but was not very convenient. We needed our own transportation, so I started to look at options. Luckily, in Costa Rica, any foreigner can legally drive in the country as long as they have a valid driver's license from their home country. Great, now all we needed was a vehicle.

It turned out that automobiles in Costa Rica are not cheap. Since they do not make their own, all cars are imported. In addition, gasoline is expensive here, too, for the same reason. Mish was hoping for something similar to the small, economical, and reliable Mercedes we had in Germany, but I had other ideas.

I had watched too many National Geographic documentaries as a kid I guess. I dreamed of exploring remote, exotic places. The vehicle that conquered those lands was the original Land Rover. I became enamored with them. In all of those shows, I saw intrepid explorers trekking across the Serengeti in their trusty aluminum-clad 4x4s. Those ubiquitous rovers went everywhere, from deserts to jungles to the Arctic. I really wanted one.

To be honest, I did not know anything about Land Rovers. Had I, I might have been persuaded to buy something, anything, else. They will truly go anywhere, but not fast or comfortably. They are essentially truck-like cabs mounted on farm tractor chassis with small, under-powered motors and finicky transmissions. A modern family sport-utility vehicle they are not. Since I was ignorant of Land Rovers' flaws, I fervently searched for one we could afford.

Unfortunately, we couldn't afford much. As I searched, my expectations became lower and lower. Finally, I found one in our price range. The seller agreed to bring it to the farm so we could see it. I asked Oscar if he would do me a favor and look it over and help negotiate a price. Thankfully, he agreed. He also loved Land Rovers so I figured he would be on my side in any deliberations with Mish.

I arranged a day and time for the Land Rover to come and anxiously waited outside for its arrival. Like a child on Christmas Eve, I impatiently waited for my present and kept a keen eye on the farm drive. That's when we heard the rumbling and saw the black smoke before the actual vehicle.

Slowly crawling up the dirt road came a bright red rover. It was billowing black exhaust and noticeably struggling. It came to a shaky halt in front of us and died. Oscar looked at it disapprovingly. Mish raised her eyebrows in disbelief. For me, it was love at first sight.

Against his better judgment, Oscar reluctantly helped me inspect the vehicle. He approached the rover with skepticism and muttered inaudibly in Spanish. All I could make out was, "No bueno." Undeterred, I approached the vehicle with boyish excitement. Here was a piece of my childhood fantasies come to life, just waiting for me to touch it.

The rover was a 1973 Series III, 88 type, which meant it had two doors. As a bonus, it had a removable soft top. It also had the original small four-cylinder diesel engine. This helped explain the black smoke and noise. It would need a serious tune-up, but other than that, I was sold. I turned to look at Mish, who was still in a little disbelief. Oscar and I made our cases. He focused on the rover's issues, and I focused on its possibilities. In the end, Mish surrendered to my judgement. I think she realized that by the bright pleading gleam in my eyes, it was a lost cause. I finally got my Land Rover!

Oscar thankfully agreed to help me fix her up. I think he, too, realized that my emotions overruled my common sense, and all he could do was try to keep me on the road and out of too much trouble. Thus began a close friendship founded once more over the common love of petrol-powered machines. Some things are just universal.

Saturday came quicker than expected, and it was time to go to tea. We were not sure what to wear, so we dressed nicely but not too formally. We hoped this compromise would be acceptable. Guys get off easy, clean pants and a pressed shirt, and we're done. Mish, on the other hand, spent a wee bit more time picking her attire. In the end, she chose a simple sundress. Aaron and Elijah obliged us and put on their nice clothes in exchange for their perpetually muddy and grass-stained ones. We made a very presentable family.

We clamored into the Land Rover, me in the right-side driver's seat, Mish on my left, and the boys in the open back. Mish slyly looked over at me and asked, "Will it start?" I just grunted in rebuttal and secretly hoped it would. Luckily, it turned over after a little hesitation and a puff of black smoke. I put it in gear, and off we chugged up the hill to the main house.

As we pulled up to the ornate entrance of the estate, I felt a little out of place and self-conscious. We weren't quite the Beverly Hillbillies but weren't not either. I timidly parked my old Rover next to Franciso's shiny new one. Mish couldn't resist asking, "A little Land Rover envy?" Ouch. "No," I replied. "I was just noting the differences between them. Mine is a classic," I defended. Ok, I was a little envious, but I would never admit that to her.

We disembarked and walked up to the massive front doors. Unintimidated, Mish rang the bell. Shortly, a door opened and we were admitted into the home by a sharply dressed man in a black suit. "A butler," I whispered to Mish as he escorted us deeper into the maze of hallways and rooms. She just shrugged. If she was impressed, she refused to show it.

The butler led us to a spacious room at the back of the home that looked out on a broad green lawn. There waiting for us were our hosts, Francisco and Maria-Melba. They greeted us warmly and motioned for us to have seats. Straight away, a uniformed maid offered us tea, which she poured from a silver pot into delicate porcelain cups. I sat at attention uncomfortably, sipping my tea. Mish looked perfectly relaxed.

Aaron and Elijah escaped the formal adult social affair. Francisco and Maria-Melba's son, Francisco Jr., came and rescued them. They went off with him to do more boy-appropriate affairs. Hopefully they would play nice and stay out of trouble. I reminded them to do just that as they quickly scampered off, thankful to be excused.

An elegantly dressed older lady came in, and Maria-Melba introduced her as her mother. She was obviously accustomed to being the center of all social events. She steered the conversation from the history of the farm to rescuing stray dogs to asking about us. All the time, the maid attentively filled our cups whenever they got empty.

They are very nice people. We profusely thanked them for letting us live on their farm and inviting us to tea. They sincerely wanted us to feel welcome and be comfortable. They inquired if we needed anything. Mish asked if they could do anything about the hot water problems we were having. Done. They would see to it right away. We were amazed and once more thankful for their hospitality. For some reason, we seem to fall into these amazing and surreal experiences. Serendipity, I suppose.

Our teatime came to an end with a tour of their magnificent home. It was a two-story square enclosing a large open-air courtyard. The design reminded us of the fine Mediterranean homes we had seen.

Everywhere were ornate fixtures and artwork that reflected a cultured and extravagant lifestyle. Apparently, farming was doing well.

The tour ended where we started at the main entrance. Once more, we thanked our hosts. They promised to have us back and expressed that they were happy to have us here. It turned out to be a wonderful time. We were making more friends we didn't expect.

As I drove the Land Rover, which thankfully started again, down the hill to our home I couldn't help thinking about life on the farm. The bottom of the hill with the farm workers was juxtaposed to the top of the hill with the farm owners. The irony that the lower class was literally lower on the hill compared to the upper class at the upper part was not lost on us. This would wear on my mind long after we left Costa Rica.

Chapter 3 – Pura Vida

"Pura vida" (Pure life) – Costa Rica's unofficial national slogan

"Pura vida." You hear it everywhere in Costa Rica. It is emblazoned on everything, too. It was even on a large billboard at the airport when we flew in. People will greet you with it and say goodbye with it. Out of politeness and wanting to assimilate as quickly as possible we adopted it right away but had no idea what it really meant.

Pura vida is much like the Hawaiian "aloha." The word is simple to translate, but the deeper meaning is much more complex and nuanced. Literally, the term translates to "pure life." In practice, however, it is all about enjoying life's little pleasures, slowing things down, and living life to the fullest. Easier said than done.

In our modern society, life gets complicated. We all know this and deal with it in our own ways. Some buy into the super-charged lifestyle and work themselves into the ground, keeping up in the notorious rat race. Others surrender to it, realizing they will never win the race, and give up by settling on mediocrity. Still, others try to buck the system and do anything and everything to fight it and rebel against society's norms. The problem with all three of these approaches is that you are still being influenced by someone else's fantasy. Pura vida means living your life completely free of other's ideals, pure.

Costa Rica is often regarded as one of the happiest countries on Earth. The mentality of pura vida is partly why. Ticos are largely unconcerned with the trends, fashions, politics, and happenings of the world outside of their borders. They famously do not even have a military. This does not mean they are ignorant of the world, just that they do not let it influence them. They do their own thing. Mish and I have striven for this most of our lives.

Like I said, this is much easier said than done. Everyone seems to be unable to help but offer their advice, judgement, and criticism. No matter how well intended, most of the time, it is not asked for or wanted. We are guilty of it, too, to be honest. It is the trap of modern society. Ticos somehow evaded the trap.

As we lived in Costa Rica and got to really know the locals we became aware of some stark contrasts between them and Europeans, and even Americans. In the United States, we live in advertising Hell. As I mentioned before, we are accustomed to the incessant bombardment of overt and subliminal marketing everywhere. We are born, live, and die, being told what to wear, eat, drive, live in, smell like, associate with, say, and even think. This is certainly not a pure life.

Europe does a much better job of limiting blatant commercialism but still imposes strict societal norms. We saw this in England for sure. In Germany, we learned that rules and regulations dictate every facet of daily life. They were certainly not pure lives either.

Here in Costa Rica, it seemed like they were largely content with just living day to day. I am not saying that their country is perfect or that other countries don't have their merits. For us, this new way of thinking was very different and, in some ways, very refreshing. We were willing to give it a try.

The only downer in our newfound life was rain. Obviously, we knew before coming here that Costa Rica is covered by "rain forests" and that they are called that for a reason. We even looked at rainfall averages in the country to compare to Washington, which also receives a fair amount of liquid sunshine. Seattle gets approximately forty inches of rain per year, while San Jose gets a whopping one hundred inches per year. We prepared accordingly, or so we thought.

One of the many running jokes back home is, you know, if you are from Seattle and half of your wardrobe is made of Gortex and the other half flannel. Fair enough. If you looked in my closet, you could guess where I was from. Also, only the tourists carry umbrellas in Seattle. True. I do not own one. I thought we were well prepared for a little rain.

The real difference between rain in Seattle and San Jose is not the total amount, it is the duration that it spreads over. In Seattle, we get our share sprinkled out over most of the year. In San Jose, however, you get it all at once. The rainy season in Costa Rica is from June to October, that is only five months. So, doing the math, Costa Rica gets more than twice the amount of rain in less than half the time. Whatever fraction or percentage difference that works out, it is a lot.

When it rains in Costa Rica, it really pours. I am talking about buckets upon buckets non-stop for days, no exaggeration. I never thought it could rain that much. How can the clouds hold that much water? Rainforest indeed!

It got so bad sometimes that the windshield wipers on my Land Rover were useless, and I had to pull over until I got a break in the deluge. Poor Aaron and Elijah usually got more than a little soaked riding to school in the back of the rover with its soft removable top, which had a tendency to leak. Now I know why there are huge canyons on either side of the roads. Everywhere, gushing rivers carved new waterways as they pushed through anything in their way. For the first few months, we stayed mainly homebound.

When the rain eased up a bit, we wanted to shake the cabin fever and get out. Since we had an all-terrain exploration vehicle, we were anxious to see more of Costa Rica, rain and mud or not. Oscar and I had been working on getting my Land Rover up and running smoothly, or at least as smoothly as it could get. It was ready, so we planned our first excursion to Mount Irazu, an 11,000-foot volcano just next door. It is the highest volcano in Costa Rica.

We could see the imposing mountain from the farm. We learned that you can actually drive all the way to the top where there is a huge caldera you can walk around and see into. I asked Oscar if it was active, and he said not now, but it had been recently. He saw the worried look on my face and added, "No problema, usted tiene un Land Rover!" I was not comforted. We were all very excited to see the volcano up close despite the possible danger and decided to go for it. Pura vida!

Saturday morning, we set out for our first adventure. The road up was steep and winding but paved, thankfully. It offered spectacular views as we ascended the mountain. Everywhere we looked was a lush green landscape topped with blue sky. We were amazed that even on the knees of a semi-active volcano, cattle grazed amid small farms. People will dare a lot to have their little piece of paradise, I guess.

The intrepid Land Rover was steadily, albeit slowly, chugging up the mountain. I was behind the wheel feeling rather National Geographic-ish, and Mish, our team photographer, was busy taking pictures for the upcoming documentary. Behind us, I heard the clop-clop of hooves on the pavement. Slowly overtaking us on our left came an old man riding a two-wheel ox-drawn cart. He smiled and tipped his large sombrero as he passed. Mish smiled broadly at me as she turned her camera on the man to capture the moment. After he pulled ahead and widened his lead, she couldn't help but burst out laughing. Refusing to be embarrassed, I patted the dashboard of my beloved Rover and kept driving.

"We'll get there," I assured her.

"Today or tomorrow?" she teased.

Eventually, we turned the last switch back and crested the top of the mountain, and descended into the caldera. I brought the rover to a stop in front of the small visitor center. It had valiantly conquered the mountain and earned a rest. I was very happy it made it. Had it not, I never would have lived it down with Mish.

The boys eagerly scrambled out of the back and looked in awe at the otherworldly landscape. The caldera was almost devoid of vegetation, giving it a moon-like appearance. At the bottom rested a completely still turquoise lake that perfectly reflected the clouds above.

The lake, Diego de la Haya, hid the ominous volcanic vent below its peaceful surface. The scene was as chilling as it was beautiful.

We went into the visitor center to learn about the volcano. The locals call it El Coloso because of the destruction it has caused in the past. As recently as 1963, it unleashed its fury onto the lands below. I hoped the rover could go down the mountain much faster than it went up in case the mountain started rumbling.

At the top, the temperature is much cooler than the tropical climate far below. It is one of the very few places in Costa Rica where it will get below freezing. Luckily, the visitor center also housed a small café where I got a hot mocha. Even on the top of an active volcano, I can get my drink!

Outside, the views are breathtaking. On a clear day like this, you can see both the Atlantic and Pacific Oceans. As I sipped my coffee, I noticed across the large valley another mountain billowing grey smoke. A little alarmed I asked a park attended about. She assured me it was safe. The mountain, Turriabla, periodically vented like this. We were awestruck and astounded that people actually live in the shadow of these menacing giants.

After taking a brief walk around, we clamored back into the Land Rover. This time we costed quickly back down the mountain with gravity on our side. I kept an eye out for the old man on the ox cart, hoping for a rematch. I'd show him wheels are better than hooves.

We arrived back at the farm without event. My rover had completed its first expedition. Oscar came out to greet us and asked how it went. We bombarded him with details and descriptions of our experience. I think he was pleased with how impressed we were. Volcanoes were probably something he took a little for granted because he has grown up around them, like us with the mountains and forests back home. You tend to lose some appreciation for familiar things, no matter how extraordinary they truly are.

We were all very hungry from trekking up a mountain and debating on what to eat. Mish had a wonderful idea. She offered to get some beer and steaks to grill outside and invited Oscar and his family over as a thank-you for all their help. I thought this could be a great time and readily agreed.

We invited Oscar on the spot. He seemed a little hesitant, so we wondered if we caught him off guard and if maybe he had other plans. I was worried that maybe we put him in an awkward situation. We told him if he was busy no problem, maybe another time. He said that he and his family would love to come and thanked us. All set, our second Costa Rica social event was booked!

Mish readied things at the house while I ran out to get some steaks to toss on the fire and cold beer to wash them down. I learned at the store that red meat is very expensive in Costa Rica, but since this was a special occasion, and we had told Oscar that was what was on the menu, I splurged. Normally, steak is not on the diet of most Ticos. I hoped Oscar and his family would like it.

I got back to the farm, ready to fire up the grill. That's when I realized I had forgotten charcoal. Embarrassed, I went next door to Oscar and asked if he had some I could borrow. Once again, Oscar to the rescue. He took me over to the back of the barn and showed me the large stash of charcoal he kept. He actually makes the stuff in huge earthen pits from cut-down trees on the farm. In Costa Rica if you can do it yourself, you do.

I was back on track. I thankfully took a bag of homemade charcoal and started a nice fire in the patio grill. As the flames greedily crackled and engulfed the coal, I noticed that the grill was made from welded parts of a tire rim and car fender. It was nice metalwork. I was impressed that Oscar seemed very handy indeed.

Mish came out to the patio and directed operations. She put the boys to work arranging furniture, carrying our supplies, and cleaning up. I did my part by monitoring the flames and staying out of the way. Shortly, Oscar and his family arrived.

Oscar introduced his wife, Olga, and his two young daughters, Maria and Sarah. I noticed he looked a little uncomfortable, dressed in a nice shirt without a hat for the first time. Olga looked much more at ease and smiled warmly. Luckily, she spoke very good English. She sheepishly handed Mish a homemade dessert of whip cream and fruit. Mish took it gladly and played hostess by ushering everyone to the patio. The party was getting underway.

The two families hit it off straight away. Before long we were eating and drinking as we chattered back and forth. Mish and I were genuinely interested in the farm, life in Costa Rica, and their perceptions of America. I think this surprised our guests. Olga was flattered that we took a sincere interest in their lives and wanted to get to know them better. We, in turn, were flattered that they cared about our opinions. It was an interesting and slightly bewildering dynamic. We traveled the world and took for granted meeting people of different cultures and exchanging information. I wondered what it would be like to grow up here.

The evening was going very well when we saw headlights coming up the long drive to the main gate. It was Francisco's Land Rover. Oscar looked up and inaudibly mumbled something in Spanish to Olga. He quietly got up and walked off the patio into the shadows behind the house. Perplexed, I asked Olga if everything was ok. She embarrassedly explained, "It is not good for Francisco to see him with us in this type of setting." Offended, I asked, "Why?" She looked even more embarrassed and lowered her eyes, "You are teachers and Francisco's guest on the farm. Oscar is his worker. We are a different status." Now I was really upset.

I was upset that Oscar felt he needed to hide from his employer. I was upset that someone thought they could dictate who we had over for dinner. I was upset that the night took a different turn. Mostly, I was upset that this type of caste system still existed in the world. We knew it did, but never had experienced it before. Now, it was real.

To be fair, the Cortez family is kind, generous, and welcoming. It is not their fault that they were born into wealth, no more than it is that

Oscar's family was born into lower income. On the one hand, they are a product of their culture. On the other hand, they don't seem to do anything about it. Maybe it is not my place to judge or suggest that their caste system should change. Everywhere we travel, we experience new and sometimes conflicting ideas. The incident this evening, however, caused me to consider these things. Was this really living pura vida?

Chapter 4 – Playing Tourist

"There are two worlds: the world of the tourist and the world of everyone else. Often they're side by side. But the tourist doesn't actually see how people live." – Paul Theroux

School was going fine. Teaching is teaching the world over. Some students are motivated, and others are not. Our job is the art of getting as much knowledge into all their young minds as possible, given the time and resources allotted. This school was no different. It is a relatively pleasant mix of expats and wealthy natives. It afforded us to live in Costa Rica, so it works.

On the weekends, we got out to see all that Costa Rica has to offer. It is a beautiful country. We made a long list of things we wanted to see and do and started to check it off. The next item on the list was the famous Manuel Antonio National Park.

Manuel Antonio is located on the Pacific Ocean side of the country. It is the smallest national park in Costa Rica but undoubtedly the most popular. Its popularity is partly due to its proximity to the airport and partly due to its native inhabitants, monkeys. I'm pretty sure Mish's motivation to go was the adorable little primates.

I was ready to take the Land Rover on another expedition. I asked Oscar if he would help me get it ready. Land Rovers need some tender love and care, along with some mechanical tinkering, before they are able to set off. We both enjoyed chatting about all sorts of things while we worked on my rover. The more we worked, the more we learned about each other. I guess this is what you might call a form of male bonding. I relished simple times like these.

Oscar and I got the Land Rover ready on time so off the family and I went in search of monkeys. The drive from the farm to San Jose is largely boring and, by now fairly well known by us, but after we left the city behind, the real Costa Rica emerged. The dense urban concrete jungle was replaced by a denser, verdant, wild one. The landscape was painted in a hundred hues of lush green. The rover rambled along as the magnificent scenery passed by. I looked up just in time to see parrots flying by. "Real wild parrots," I exclaimed! Mish's camera clicked away. We have seen them many times in zoos and pet stores, but here, the wild made them even more beautiful.

I looked for a place to make a rest stop since we all felt a little stiff from bouncing in the rover and needed to stretch and get some cold drinks. I noticed a large bridge where several cars and one tour bus were stopped. Before, it was a small store and café. It seemed like as good of a place as any, so I pulled the Rover over to the side of the road.

We climbed out of the Rover, stretching and moaning a little. I lovingly patted my mechanical baby while Mish frowned at me and rubbed her bum. "It's not exactly built for comfort, is it?" she jokingly complained. "Nope, but it gets the job done," I rebutted in defense of my Rover.

I was very curious about what all the people were doing, looking over the bridge railing and taking pictures of. I left Mish and the boys stretching and getting feeling back in their limbs and walked out to the middle of the bridge. I looked down and froze in fear and awe. Without looking up, I frantically waved at Mish to come over and see. The bridge had no shoulder, so she tightly held the boys' hands as she cautiously made her way across. When they reached me, they all looked down and let out gasps in unison.

Approximately thirty feet directly below us in the river were more than a dozen large crocodiles. These were not the small Florida alligator types. They were twenty-foot-plus prehistoric-looking monsters. Hungry monsters and not in cages, too! We watched in astonishment as a man threw whole frozen chickens over the side and into gaping jaws below. The beasts greedily caught and devoured the free meal. We watched the gruesome spectacle for a while, transfixed by the sheer power and size of these creatures. Mish reminded us, "These things swim in the wild here." Note, we were never swimming in anything other than a pool here.

Eventually, we diverted our eyes and got back in the Land Rover to continue our journey to the park. The drive just got more beautiful and dramatic as we went. Soon, the Pacific Ocean came into view. It might be one big ocean encircling the globe, but it looks different here than back home. The water is a brighter blue and the sun reflects more sparkling off it. The ocean in Washington is dark and cold. It is beautiful, too, but in a different way. This ocean looked warm and inviting. We couldn't wait to be splashing around in the waves.

We were anxious to get to our hotel but were getting hungry. Our perpetually ravenous boys were making grumbling sounds in the back. I assured them I would pull over at the next available spot. As I was keeping one eye out for a lunch place and the other eye on the magnificent scenery, I noticed a large airplane coming into view on the side of the road. Intrigued, I pulled in. The delay was not popular with the boys until they found out that it was a restaurant built inside the cavernous fuselage. Mish took them inside to get a table while I explored the outside of the plane. Food trumped an aviation lesson from Dad.

I recognized the plane as an old Fairchild C-123. They were very common cargo planes from the Vietnam era. Outside the plane I read its history on a large information sign posted by the nose. I was incredulous. This was one of the infamous "Air America" planes from the President Reagan administration.

I knew the story well because it all went down when I was in college. It was in all of the news and a subject of many conversations in classes. At the time, it was one of the biggest presidential scandals of all time, probably second only to Watergate.

If you don't remember the events, here is a brief history lesson. In the 1980s, President Ronald Reagan established a covert system to sell arms to Iran in exchange for the release of American hostages in Lebanon and to secretly raise money to fund the counter-revolutionary guerilla fighters, or "Contras," in Nicaragua. Coincidentally, the Contras were also battling the Cuban pro-Sandinista government of Fidel Castro. The arms broker for this wild and illegal scheme was U.S. Army Lieutenant Colonel Oliver North.

North, purportedly under Reagan's direction, used the CIA to buy a 30,000-acre ranch in northwest Costa Rica and built a landing strip as the base of operations. They raised a whopping $16 million to buy two planes, one of them right in front of me, and loads of weapons and ammunition.

The plan was simple. The two C-123s flew night missions from the airstrip in Costa Rica across the border into Nicaragua and airdropped the munitions into the Contras' hands. Astoundingly, this went on from 1981 to 1986. Everything was going well until the night of October 5, 1986. One of the planes was shot down over the jungle of Nicaragua. The pilot parachuted safely to the ground and into the hands of the revolutionaries, who were not happy with America's unwanted involvement in their revolution.

The incident exposed the whole bizarre operation and led to a congressional investigation called the Tower Commission, culminating in North taking the fall for Reagan. Subsequently, North and others were pardoned by Reagan's vice president, George Bush, when he took over the Oval Office in 1988. It was an embarrassment for the United States and soured U.S. and Central American relations for decades. Not even Hollywood could make this stuff up.

I went back inside the plane with a sense of awe. This was an amazing piece of history indeed. In 2000 some Costa Rican entrepreneur purchased the abandoned plane and shipped it here to be a restaurant and reminder.

I sat down with the family and told them what I had discovered about the plane we were in. Mish was as amazed as me. This was part of our relevant history. I had a hard time explaining a much watered-down version of the story to Aaron and Elijah. Hopefully, when they are older and fully understand the history, they will remember and appreciate this experience.

After lunch and a brief history lesson, we found our hotel and checked in. Mish found us an amazing place built on the steep slopes among the trees. It had a Swiss Family Robinson treehouse look. I parked the Land Rover and once again was secretly glad it made it all the way here without mishap. We climbed the steep steps to our room, got on our swimsuits, and headed to the beach.

Being a mom, Mish tried her best to lather the boys in sunscreen when we got out in the hot tropical sun. It was a lost cause. As soon as Aaron and Elijah saw the enticing water calling them, they were off running to dive in. They had never been in warm water, so this was a completely new experience. This was an ocean you could actually play in without getting hypothermia. They were in Heaven. They splashed and yelled at me to come in and play with them. I was in Heaven, too. Enjoying simple times like this with the family is what life is all about.

When we were sufficiently cooled off, we decided to take a walk through the park, by we, I mean Mish and me. Aaron and Elijah were very content to stay in the water and play until they grew gills. Mish, however, knew the secret word to get them out, "monkeys." Not much can trump playing on the beach, but cute fury critters can. Elijah especially was susceptible to this ploy. Animals were always at the top of his list of priorities. Within minutes, we set off on a jungle trek in search of wild animals.

Manuel Antonio has easy, short hikes through one of the most beautiful coastal areas in Costa Rica. As we walked, we saw toucans, sloths, parrots, and more, but no monkeys yet. Finally, we came upon a sign that said in both Spanish and English, "Caution, Monkeys." We eagerly proceeded. Elijah was jittering with anticipation.

Just past the sign sitting on the ground waiting for us was our quarry. Two small brown eyes intently peered at us from a round fury face as if sizing us up. It didn't move, but its eyes stayed focused on us as we slowly approached. When we got about ten feet from it, it extended a tiny human-like hand towards us.

Mish searched in her backpack and produced a granola bar. I pointed to another sign that clearly read, "Do not feed the animals." Mish just waved it off and knelt to offer a piece of the human treat to the little bugger. Without hesitation, it ambled forward and snatched the piece. It knew that these humans were illiterate and could be hustled for an easy meal.

The monkey backed up two paces to enjoy its snack. Almost instantly, its companions appeared from nowhere. We now were surrounded by the local gang. They had this routine down. Send one of them to do a reconnaissance on approaching humans. Securing food was the "all-clear signal" for the rest. I wondered if they took turns being point monkey or if they shoved the smallest one out in front. Either way, these were not dumb animals.

Mish and the boys did not mind being taken advantage of by a troop of small primate hustlers. They eagerly gave them pieces of our snacks, and the fury freeloaders just as eagerly took them. What a racket. I was glad a park ranger did not come by and chastise us for feeding the animals.

Once the snack wagon was empty, the monkeys lost interest in us and moved on to shake down other unwitting humans. Reluctantly, Mish and the boys said goodbye, and we continued our hike through the park in search of other wildlife. We saw many species of birds sporting an infinite array of brightly colored feathers. The biodiversity was amazing.

Eventually, we came out to the beach again. Hiking and feeding monkeys are tiring work, so we went in search of someplace to rest in the shade. We passed a man selling coconuts along the way. We stopped to watch as he held a coconut in one hand and, with the other, deftly cut off the top with a large machete. He then poked a straw into the opening and offered it to Elijah. Elijah eagerly took it and quickly sipped up the sweet juice inside. I thanked the man and gave him a few dollars. It seemed everyone had some kind of scheme to hustle tourists. I didn't mind, though. In the end, everyone was happy, and that's all that mattered.

We had a wonderful time at Manuel Antonio. We snorkeled in the clear water over coral reefs and saw a myriad of colorful fish, walked around the small town and admired local artisans' works, and sampled a variety of new foods. Even though this part of Costa Rica is heavily tourist trafficked, it was worth the visit. Sometimes, playing tourist is relaxing and enjoyable. It might not have been as authentic as our experiences back on the farm, but it was still another facet of the country we got to see.

Chapter 5 – Finding Balance

"Balance, peace, and joy are the fruit of a successful life. It starts with recognizing your talents and finding ways to serve others by using them." – Thomas Kinkade

Our mini-vacation to Manuel Antonio was over. Sometimes I wish we had the means to permanently stay on vacation. I wonder if not working for vacation would take the magic out of it. I also wonder if not working would cause me to lose purpose and motivation in life. I would like the opportunity to find out at least. Striking a balance between work and play is difficult. For now, I have to do the best I can.

I had to teach during the week. I still love teaching, luckily, so going to school was not too much of a chore. The boys, however, are a mixed bag.

Aaron most days likes going to school. He is a social creature and needs human interaction. He is also very studious and loves to learn. We rarely have to worry about his grades. We think he will be university-bound after high school to study some engineering or science discipline.

Elijah, on the other hand, so far sees school as an unnecessary and annoying interruption to his day. He goes willingly, thank God. His two favorite classes are recess and lunch. We have no idea what direction he will go in life. Right now, we are trying to encourage, support, and have patience with him, the last one being the most difficult.

Since the boys go to the same school where I teach, I can keep an eye on them. Being on campus gives me a unique opportunity to observe both of them. I try to give them space, but also can't help peeking in on them.

One day at recess, the principal of the elementary school came over to me as I stood outside sipping my coffee and enjoying the Costa Rican sun after a long, heavy rain. The smell of the wet tropical forest is refreshing and almost overpowering. I was enjoying the quiet time between classes when she matter-of-factly informed me, "I'm a little concerned about Elijah." "Why?" I responded as I snapped out of my trance by the unexpected intrusion.

"He doesn't seem to be adjusting to school or making friends," she explained.

I looked across the small quad area to the grass field beyond. Elijah was there, alone, lost in his own imaginary world. He was spinning around in the sun with his arms outstretched and his eyes closed with a big smile on his face. I watched him for a few minutes. I knew he was off in some fantastical place fighting dragons or riding a tiger. He didn't appear to be bothered that all the other kids were playing four-square and tetherball. He was content.

"I think he is fine. He just likes to do his own thing," I replied.

That evening, I talked to Mish about Elijah and the principal's concern. Her assessment was the same as mine, Elijah is extraordinarily independent. He is not antisocial or depressed. He will play with other kids and even make friends. He simply can find happiness and fulfillment on his own. I worry if this trait will be a strength or handicap later in life.

To keep some consistency and ensure the boys were not missing out on some things, we joined a scout troop. Amazingly, there was a good old Boy Scouts of America contingency in Costa Rica. It was on the other side of San Jose in an area called Escazu. I asked Oscar if he knew where it was, and he chuckled. He saw my confused look and explained, "Gringo land."

I know what "gringo" refers to, but still did not understand the reference. He further explained that Escazu is a small American enclave where many ex-pats live because the U.S. embassy is there. I asked if it was looked poorly on by native Costa Ricans. He shrugged and said, "It is very American-looking."

We were not exactly sure what "American looking" meant, but could imagine. We would shortly find out because the first troop meeting was coming up in a few days. In the meantime, we needed to get back into serious hiking shape. We easily fell into a rut of waking up, going to school, coming home, doing homework, eating, sleeping, and then repeating. Mish worked from home still teaching online so she could squeeze in a workout. The boys and I needed to catch up, especially me. I was paying the price for being out of commission with a broken ankle for four months. Now that I was back on two feet, I really needed to shed some weight. Therefore, the boys were obliged to participate in Dad's new fitness regime.

I mapped out a walking path that made a half-mile loop from our house, up the hill, along the field, through the banana trees, and back down to home. I pledged I, and by extension, Aaron and Elijah would complete at least four laps every night after dinner. I reasoned that in no time, we would be back, ready to tackle our first scout hike.

Getting moving again took more than I originally thought. My ankle was extremely stiff from months of immobility. I was also packing more than a few extra pounds. I was determined to get back to pre-accident shape and waistline, so I pushed myself forward. Looking in the mirror every night kept me motivated.

Aaron joined the school's cross-country team, so was in prime shape. He made easy work of running his laps. I'm pretty sure he didn't even break a sweat. He also sported a twig-like runner's physique. Every time he passed me on the loop made me more determined to work through the pain. I'd show him, maybe.

Elijah is our little tank. He chugged along the path lost in his own world. I could see him talking with his lips and hands to some invisible character as he walked, oblivious to all else around him. He never complained or tried to get out of our nightly walks. He simply knew what the goal was and kept going.

One night, a storm brewed in the mountains. I could see the dark clouds rolling in and smell the coming rain. A bright flash of lightning and a loud crash of thunder prompted me to quit my walk early. I went inside to take a shower. Aaron, of course, was already showered and quietly reading in his room. I got some water and looked around. Mish was working on her laptop. I then noticed something was amiss.

"Where's Elijah?" I asked.

"I don't know. I thought he was with you," she replied without looking up.

In a panic, I grabbed a flashlight and ran outside. I hoped Elijah had gone inside. Frantically, I called his name and waved the flashlight around, searching for him. The approaching storm made the twilight darker than normal and so hard to see. I scanned the farm and saw, silhouetted against the fading light, a small figure trudging up the hill. Relieved, I yelled at him, but he didn't hear me. I sprinted up the hill in pursuit. I reached him out of breath, part irritated he did not come in, part grateful he was ok. The second emotion won me over, and I gave him a big hug.

"Why didn't you come in?" I gently scolded.

"I needed to finish my laps," he said matter of fact.

I wanted to burst with pride and scold myself for not looking after him closer. The second emotion won again. I felt very ashamed and took his small hand.

"It's time to go inside," I told him. Parenting is the hardest thing I have ever done. It is an emotional rollercoaster.

Safe back inside Mish just looked at me. She didn't say anything, but her eyes clearly expressed what she was thinking. "I found him," I guiltily mumbled. Elijah shuffled off to get ready for bed, completely unphased by the incident. It could have ended badly. Thankfully, it did not. Note to self: Don't lose one of the boys. Another lesson learned.

We continued our nightly walks, albeit with Elijah and I side-by-side. Scout night came, and we set off in search of "Gringo land." It was extremely easy to recognize. We drove through the city of San Jose, with its potholed streets lined with rubbish and barred window storefronts. It is not a pretty or safe city, to be honest. We crossed a main street and suddenly were in a totally different world.

The streets became smooth and lined with beautifully manicured palm trees and flowering shrubs. Immediately, we recognized several name-brand chain stores and restaurants, like TGIF, Olive Garden, and Applebee's. Parked neatly in front of them were Mercedes, BMWs, Porsches, and even a Ferrari. What just happened, I thought? This looked more like Southern California than Costa Rica.

"I guess this is the place?" I remarked.

"This is definitely Americanized," Mish responded.

I began to worry that my trusty Land Rover looked woefully out of place. I spotted many new models brightly waxed among the other high-end automobiles. I doubted that most of these cars ever left this artificial world. Gringoland indeed.

We found the school that hosted Boys Scouts. It was a much larger and better-equipped international school than mine. I knew of it but decided I wanted a more authentic experience when I applied to places. Now that I saw where it was, I was glad I did. It was very nice and modern. However, it clearly catered to a very different clientele. Each to their own, I suppose.

I was very thankful that a scout troop existed in Costa Rica. I really wanted Aaron and Elijah to keep with the program no matter where we traveled. Not only do I think very highly of the program, but it also gives them continuity and the chance to make friends. Plus, I get to wear my snazzy scout leader uniform.

The meeting went well. It was a small troop of only a dozen scouts. The Scout Master, however, was very energetic and committed to creating a great experience for the boys. I offered to do my part. Mish always jumps in with ideas and support, too. It looked like this would be a good troop, so I was very excited.

Things seemed to be going well so far. My ankle was healed, we had our own transportation, the school year was off to a smooth start, we were making friends, and now Boy Scouts was back scheduled every Monday night. The only thing missing was fishing.

The boys and I love to fish. Ok, Elijah and I love to fish. Aaron obliges me. He likes being outside on the water with us, just not the fish part. I am grateful he makes the sacrifice willingly and without complaining whenever I grab our poles. I grew up fishing and have fond boyhood memories of it, and want to share the same experiences with our boys. They will both have memories of fishing with me for sure; I'm not sure how fond the memories will be for both boys, though. I'm only batting fifty percent on this father-son activity.

I went to our got-to Costa Rica expert, Oscar, and asked him if he knew of a decent fishing spot. Of course, he did. He let us in on a little local secret. There is a small pond nearby that is stocked with trout, he informed us. The owner keeps the place very nice with fishing supplies you can borrow and tables for cleaning the fish. You only pay for the fish you catch and keep. Score! Elijah and I were ready to go. Ever the little trooper, Aaron agreed to tag along.

One of the many quirks about Costa Rica is that it does not use addresses. When I asked Oscar for the specific address of the pond, he gave me some directions. I thought he misunderstood what I wanted and asked again. He repeated the directions again. Thinking that our language barrier was causing confusion, I held up my cell phone and pointed to the map application. He looked confused. I was at a loss. Oscar called for Olga to help interpret.

Olga knew what I wanted. She understood the American mail system well enough to know why I was perplexed. She explained that in Costa Rica, there are no street numbers or zip codes, unfortunately.

"How do you mail letters or packages then?" I asked.

"You write the closest directions on the label, and the postman figures it out," she said with a shrug.

How many parcels get lost in this country, I wondered? Apparently, our "address" on the farm literally translated to something close to "The farm next to the Christian school over the river in Tres Rios." If a delivery miraculously made it to the main gate, someone would figure out from there who on the farm it went to. Seriously?!

Olga explained to her husband what I was used to. Oscar nodded his head in understanding. As a consolation, he drew a crude map to the fishing spot and handed it to me. I thanked him and went off, scratching my head in disbelief. Oh well, we would have all day Saturday to find the fish. It would be like a treasure hunt complete with a pirate map, I guess.

Saturday came and we decided that it was a good day to go fishing. Supplied with the directions Oscar provided we set off once more in the Land Rover on another Costa Rican adventure. Along the way, we went by a large church. Oscar had mentioned it. He called it the Cathedral de Los Angeles. Technically, it is the Basílica de Nuestra Señora de los Ángeles. It is a Roman Catholic Basilica located in the city of Cartago and dedicated to the Virgen de los Pardos. The basilica was built in 1639 and was partially destroyed by an earthquake but rebuilt. We decided the fish would have to wait and stopped in to see it.

Granted, the basilica is not as grandiose as the cathedrals of Europe. However, it is, in its own right, very ornate and striking. The nave is built from wood, not stone like the ones we were used to, but is painted in brilliant gold with colorful accents so that it still inspires reverent awe. At the time of its construction, stained glass was very difficult to get in Central America, so clear glass was mainly used. This has the benefit of filling the cathedral with an abundance of natural white light that makes it feel very bright and open.

We walked around the cathedral and discovered some of its history. We also learned that it is the largest and most sacred of all churches in Costa Rica. Supposedly, the Virgin Mary was witnessed performing miracles on the site. There were many faithful followers placing flowers and small silver charms on one of the church walls in hopes their prayers would be answered. We paid our respects, too, and left.

We continued on in search of fish. The pond was not easy to find. It was hidden deep in the jungle of a large valley nearby. The dirt road into it was not well marked or maintained. To get to it required putting the rover in a four-wheel drive and fording a small shallow river. Yes! I got to use the rover for what it was intended!

The trek was definitely an adventure. I don't think Mish enjoyed it as much as the boys and I. They hung on in the back as the Rover bounced and crawled its way up the valley. Elijah let out a big "Whoo-hoo" when we splashed up a large wake as we crossed the river. Meanwhile, our stalwart canine, Albie, laid on the floorboards, seemingly unphased, as he was unwittingly dragged on another family outing.

We eventually reached the fishing spot. The Rover was muddy but none the worse for wear. Mish climbed out a little more worn. The boys and I quickly disembarked and shook off the bumpy ride. We were eager to fish.

The location was idyllic. The small pond was fed by a bubbling waterfall and surrounded by lush tropical vegetation. A thatch-covered bamboo cantina completed the postcard-like scene. We could clearly see numerous fish lazily swimming around in the clear water. This will do very nicely, I thought.

Mish took Albie on a much-needed walk while the boys and I went in search of fishing gear. A very nice old man came out of the hut to greet us. He didn't speak English but correctly assumed we were here to fish. He carried three short sticks wrapped with a fishing line. By miming, he instructed us how to fish Costa Rica style. He put some bait on the end of the hook on one line, unraveled a few yards, and swirled it in a vertical circle. When it reached sufficient momentum, he let the line go, and the hook with its offering shot out into the pond and landed with a splash in the middle of the water. The impact sent out ripples, disturbing the calm surface. Within a few minutes, the fish came to check out the commotion. Without warning, they struck the bait. The line went taut as a hungry fish tried to make off with his meal. The old man gave the line a jerk. The fish jumped in protest, only to be reeled in as the man wound the line around the stick. Shortly, he was dangling his prize from the line in triumph, a lovely fourteen-inch trout.

Elijah practically went giddy with excitement. He eagerly held out his hands for a stick, desperate to get a line in the water. The old man smiled and handed him one. Even Aaron was anxious to give this style of fishing a try. It was not flyfishing, but a fish is a fish. I took a stick, too.

Within moments, the three of us were hauling in sleek, wriggling fish. Mish came over and watched, amazed, as we quickly brought in dinner. Her three mighty hunters were providing a bountiful feast. We each stopped at three fish. They would make a tasty meal when cooked on the grill back home.

The old man motioned us over to the cleaning station. He unsheathed a long, sharp knife at his side and pointed to one of the fish Elijah held. Elijah gave it to him and curiously watched as the man easily slit the fish's belly from head to tail. He then reached in and scooped out the inner contents. He searched through the bloody tangle of organs until he found what he was looking for. He cut a small piece out and held it out for us to see. In his weathered palm was a still beating heart. Elijah, wide-eyed, leaned in for a closer inspection. Aaron was aghast. The man placed the heart in Elijah's hand, who turned to give his older brother a better look. That was it, Aaron turned white and stumbled back a step. Mish steadied him with a motherly hug and tried not to laugh. That's our boys, so similar and so different at the same time.

With the successful fishing expedition over, I felt that we were really settled into our new home. Once again, simple things like scouts and fishing help bring a sense of balance to our sometimes hectic lives. We really enjoy being together as a family. Enjoying experiences together instead of going off to do separate activities is extremely important to us. I am extremely grateful that Mish is a shutterbug and photographs everything to chronicle these times. I am sure that when we are much older, we will fondly look at the pictures and smile. Pura vida.

Chapter 6 – Orchids and Leaf Springs

"The difference between rich and poor is that the poor do everything with their own hands and the rich hire hands to do things." – Betty Smith

The road to the fishing spot was a little harder on my Land Rover than I thought. As we drove home from school one day I noticed that it was riding low on the back right tire and made a horrible grinding sound when I hit a pothole, which in Costa Rica is often. Elijah desperately held on tight in the back as the poor Rover limped back to the farm.

I was very happy when we finally reached the farm gate. I didn't need to wait to ask Oscar to look at the rover for me because he heard and saw it coming up to the house. He ambled over to us as I parked, and the boys thankfully climbed out. Elijah looked at Oscar and pointed to the leaning rover.

"It's broke really bad," he exclaimed and shuffled off inside.

Oscar looked at the Rover with a critical eye.

"What happened?" he inquired.

"I'm not sure," I answered. "I think I broke something in the suspension, maybe a shock."

Oscar graciously offered to take a look at it again. He pointed to his garage area across from our house and told me to drive the Rover over. I delicately coaxed the injured Rover into an open-air stall made of old wood beams and a corrugated metal roof. I stopped at the entrance too nervous to drive anymore forward. The garage consisted of a large earthen pit spanned by two suspicious-looking large wood beams. This was Oscar's solution to accessing the underside of a vehicle. Instead of a hydraulic lift to raise vehicles, which was too expensive, he dug a space to lower the mechanic instead. Problem solved.

Oscar saw my hesitation and nimbly walked out on one of the beams to guide me into place. He kept his eyes on my front tires and motioned with his hands left and right as I wiggled the Rover out onto the beams. It was a little unsettling since I couldn't see the beams and had a sense of driving on air. I reached Oscar, and he raised his hand palm out, directing me to stop. I opened my door to get out, only to realize I was six feet off the ground. I carefully maneuvered myself out of the Rover and around it on the narrow space left over until I reached the safety of the ground behind the vehicle.

Oscar and I climbed down rough stairs, cut into the dirt, and reached the bottom of the pit. Precariously sitting above us was three-thousand pounds of Land Rover. I looked nervously at the set-up, but Oscar seemed unconcerned, so I tried to relax and not think about being squashed like a trapped bug.

Immediately, we both saw the problem. The back right leaf spring on the Rover was clearly broken. Instead of riding on the suspension, the vehicle frame was riding on the rear axle. Even I, with limited mechanical knowledge, knew that this was not good. It was not an easy or quick fix, especially if I couldn't get the parts. Repair parts in Costa

Ria are an iffy at best proposition. I scolded myself for not being more careful.

I asked Oscar if he knew where to get a rear leaf spring for my rover. I hoped he had a secret contact with a local who ran an underground Land Rover parts operation, but no such luck. He was well aware that my luck of getting a replacement spring was about as good a chance as snowing here for Christmas. My heart sank. We were back without a vehicle.

Oscar intently studied the broken spring like an experienced doctor examining a patient with a difficult condition. After a bit, he gave his prognosis. We would need to remove, repair, and re-install the broken leaf spring with whatever we could find. I was skeptical. Oscar, however, was undeterred. He climbed out of the pit and walked behind the barn. I amenably followed, wondering what he had in mind.

Behind the barn was a plethora of mechanical parts from a variety of unknown machines. There was an old tractor with a missing engine, the frame of an unidentifiable car, different size exhaust pipes, stacks of used tires, piles of scrap metal, just to give a sample of the treasure stashed away. Oscar rummaged around, looking for something. Soon, he triumphantly produced a complete leaf-spring assembly taken from an old farm wagon.

"Will that fit my Rover?" I asked incredulously.

"No," Oscar replied, "but we can take it apart for a single leaf to replace your broken one."

I was amazed. This is problem-solving at its best. Oscar was a master of ingenuity. He identified the problem, formulated a solution, and made his plan work with the resources he had available. He did not let lack of materials or tools prevent him from completing the job. When he encountered obstacles, he skillfully maneuvered around them. I was dutifully impressed.

Since it was late on Friday afternoon, we agreed to reconvene on Saturday morning to perform surgery on my Rover. I got up early and met Oscar in his operating room. We instinctively agreed on him being the head surgeon and I, his assistant. It is easy being humble, especially when you know you are outclassed and have no idea what you are doing. I try to not let pride blind me. I know when I am in the presence of a master. He could direct the procedure while I hand him tools.

Oscar really is a very resourceful individual. He knows his way around all manner of machinery. Over his life, he has acquired an impressively large and diverse skill set. What amazes me more is that he is all self-taught. He never went to a formal school beyond sixteen years old, yet he is extremely knowledgeable on a wide range of topics. I truly believe he could fix anything.

Not only am I extremely grateful for him fixing my rover, but I also sincerely enjoy our time together. I learn a lot from his tutelage. He patiently explains what he is doing and why and tolerates my incessant questions. I hope he finds our interactions rewarding. I know I am not much of a help to him, but at least I know what end of a wrench to hand. Maybe my Ph.D. should stand for Part-time Helper Dude?

As I watched and learned, Oscar disassembled the back right suspension of my rover. This required lifting the rover's body by using another make-shift contraption of old wood beams and a rusty car jack. Once more, I was both impressed and nervous. It worked, but it looked seriously sketchy. There is no way it would pass safety inspections back home. I just hoped it would not come down on us rover and all.

Within twenty minutes, Oscar had the rover's suspension out and on a workbench in the barn. He pointed to four bolts and nuts holding the leaf spring assembly together and directed me to undo them. I actually got to do something! Excited to be useful, I grabbed a wrench and got busy while Oscar measured the broken leaf.

He found one the same size, or close enough, in the old tractor's leaf spring he salvaged from behind the barn yesterday. As I continued taking apart the Rover's leaf spring, Oscar simultaneously disassembled the tractor's. I felt a little embarrassed when he came over with the leaf from his while I was still taking mine apart. He waited patiently for me to finish.

"These nuts are very rusted," I explained.

"No problem. Take your time," Oscar casually replied. I was very thankful he did not point out how rusty his were.

With mine finally apart, we were able to continue with the transplant. The procedure was simple enough. We swapped a broken spring on the Rover for a comparable, non-broken one from the tractor. Once the transplant was successful, we re-installed the fixed leaf spring back into the rover. A thorough cleaning, inspection, and greasing of the underside and the operation was complete.

Thankfully, Oscar's homemade garage contraption lasted through the entire procedure. I was so ecstatic that the Rover didn't fall on us, and it was fixed too, I didn't even get offended when Oscar backed it off the beams and back onto solid ground. Why potentially mess up a good repair job by driving the Rover into the pit at the end?

Oscar and I took the Rover for a short test ride on the farm. This time, he let me drive. The Rover crawled up the dirt roads like a champ. The repair appeared to work. I pulled it into its normal parking spot in front of our home. I thanked Oscar profusely and offered him money for his hard work and the part, but he refused. I felt guilty. He just smiled and shook my hand. I was touched and once more humbled while he waved goodbye as he walked back to his home.

I looked at my watch. The day had gone by faster than I realized. I had just a couple of hours left to catch up on schoolwork and then get ready for our big night out. This evening was the annual Cost Rica Orchid Show that Francisco had promised. We were going as VIPs of one of the judges, Francisco himself.

Men can get ready for any social event in fifteen minutes, twenty tops. Women, however, take a wee bit longer. I shave, shower, put on a suit, maybe spray cologne, and run my fingers through my hair, done. I'm ready to roll. I should know by now that Mish has a few more steps. I'm a slow learner. I semi-patiently waited on the front porch for her. The cool night air felt refreshing after a hot day playing mechanic.

As the sun went down and the light faded, I could dimly make out the small fluttering wings of bats doing aerial acrobatics in the evening sky. Oscar had told us that these were "vampiros," or vampire bats. They actually drink the blood of warm creatures. Tonight, they were in search of the cows that graze in the field in front of our home. Using their infrared detection ability, they find the unsuspecting cow. Once located, they land on the cow and cling on with their small, clawed hands. They secrete an anesthetic in their saliva that numbs their bite so the cow doesn't feel it. While the cow dozes, the bat feeds. Luckily for the cow, the bats do not drink a lot and leave it unharmed and unaware. They don't even get turned into vampire bovines.

I asked Oscar if the bats had ever been documented feeding on humans. "Rarely, only a few times," he assured me. I was not assured. Note to self, make double sure our tents are closed tightly on scout camping trips. I'm not sure if I want to tell the boys about the bats. Aaron will hunker down inside with a scarf around his neck, and Elijah will stay out all night trying to catch one.

I was contemplating the bats when Mish came out on the porch to join me. She looked lovely, as usual.

"Ready?" I nonchalantly asked with raised eyebrows feigning irritation. I already knew the answer.

"Yes, you can't rush these things," she replied, smiling, giving her usual answer. She knew I was teasing her.

After years of marriage, we had adjusted to each other very well. We knew the routine. That didn't stop us from trying to bait the other one from time to time. It was sort of a private little game. These impromptu banter sessions somehow made our relationship seem more special. They are a quirky way we express our affection. No one else listening in would get it, which made it even more endearing. Relationships can be crazy like that.

Francisco's shiny silver Land Rover came down the hill from the large estate house. We were riding with him and Maria-Melba to the show.

"Wow, his Land Rover is really quiet and smooth," teased Mish. Shots fired.

"It's probably coasting down the hill, that's why," I scoffed. Volley returned. There's that playful banter again. I wasn't offended. I was actually glad we were riding in style, but I would never admit that to my wife.

We arrived at the orchid festival unbruised and non-disheveled. Francisco's rover was a tad more refined, I'll admit. He pulled it up to the main entrance, where a sharply dressed valet took it from there. This was a fund-raising pre-show before the public viewing by invitation only. We did not know what to expect. Francisco was a suave host, however. He smoothly navigated the four of us into the show and began introducing us to a myriad of people. We quickly lost track of who was who.

As Francisco guided us around, servers continually circled through the crowd, offering long, elegant flutes of champagne along with assorted fancy hors d'oeuvres. We had never seen anything like this. It was very sophisticated and formal, a veritable who's who of Costa Rican socialites. I felt a little self-conscious again. Mish looked at ease. She sipped her glass and listened intently as Francisco explained how to properly judge orchids. I just ate the little cracker snacks and pretended I understood.

Francisco suddenly stopped his orchid lesson.

"Oh good, he is here. There is someone I'd like you to meet," he said.

We obediently followed as he ushered us across the room to a small group of people standing a little apart from the crowd. A few somber-looking men in dark suits formed a tight ring around a man who looked around, smiling at the scene. Undeterred, Francisco walked straight up to the man in the center. His attendants didn't hinder Francisco's intrusion. The man recognized Francsico immediately and extended a warm handshake.

"Mr. Vice President, I am very honored you could attend tonight," Francisco said as he shook the man's hand.

The vice president of Costa Rice? I was more than a little astounded. Mish and I just looked at each other in disbelief.

"Sir, I would like to introduce you to my guests," Francisco continued as he motioned to us.

We bashfully stepped forward. The vice president firmly shook our hands in turn.

"It is very nice to meet you," he said. "What brings you to Costa Rica?" he asked.

I explained that I was a science teacher at a nearby school and Francisco had generously offered us a place on his farm while we were here.

The vice president seemed genuinely interested in us and expressed sincere gratitude that I was teaching students in his country. It was such a surreal experience to be talking to the second in charge of the country that I'm not sure exactly what I said, but I hope I didn't sound like an idiot.

Francisco probably knew the appropriate amount of time to engage the vice president and not to overstay our welcome. After a while, he thanked the man, and we moved on. I sensed a little swagger in his walk as we drifted back into the crowd. He knew we were impressed. Indeed, we were. How rich and connected is our host, I wondered?

Francisco seamlessly picked-up his orchid lesson where he left off. He explained what makes a winning orchid. I was shocked when he told me that some enthusiastic collectors would pay over ten thousand dollars for a single prize specimen. This definitely is a hobby for the wealthy. I could not comprehend paying that much for a flower. With my luck, I would buy one, and it would die right away. I guess if you have the money, it is all relative.

The evening ended with obligatory speeches from some orchid officials and, finally, the vice president. I really wanted to nudge the person next to me and say I knew the guy, but resisted the temptation. Sometimes, I know when to keep my warped sense of humor in check.

Francisco dropped us off back at our home on the farm. We thanked him and Maria-Melba for an amazing night. It really was a once-in-a-lifetime experience. We will never forget it.

I remarked to Francisco as I climbed out of his rover that we needed to go off-roading together sometime, my rover versus his. He just laughed.

"Maybe," he replied to my offer. "I need to have our driver take mine in to be tuned up first."

That night, as I sat on the front porch enjoying the quiet evening with a nightcap, I couldn't help but compare the two very different but very rewarding experiences I had today. Time with Oscar was sharply juxtaposed to time with Francisco. Each man intrigued me but in uniquely different ways.

Oscar, on the surface, appears to be a simple provincial farmhand. I am learning that there is much more to him than that. He is soft-spoken and thoughtful, almost stoic. He accepts his lot in life and makes the best of it. Being of humble means does not prevent him from learning, growing, and providing for his family. He finds rewards in the simple things in life, like family, friends, and a job well done. Whatever he dreams of for himself or his family, I have yet to discover. I do not think, however, that he is content to resign his four daughters to servitude on the farm like him.

Francisco, at first, comes across as a rich playboy. He exudes wealth and influence. I am coming to realize that he is playing the role born of him as best he can. He has always been rich and, in all probability, will always be rich. He knows nothing else. Deep down, however, he also enjoys simple pleasures, like growing orchids and driving his Land Rover. He wants the best for his son and daughter, too. He just has more resources to help them get a better start in life. What he wants from his life and children, I also haven't figured out.

Neither of these men's lives are my business. I do not pry or intrude. I am, by nature, an incessantly curious person, though. It is the researcher in me, I think. If I wasn't a science teacher, I probably would be a sociologist or anthropologist. Human nature and development fascinate me. Living on the farm in Costa Rica is turning out to be more fascinating and rewarding than I ever imagined.

Chapter 7 – Creepies and Crawlies

"There is nothing like the thrill of walking through the jungle looking for a tiger and knowing they could be watching you already." – Ashlan Gorse Cousteau

Everything in Costa Rica bites, stings, or eats you. Whoever said the jungle is a dangerous place wasn't kidding. By now, we had come to expect that a venomous creature of some kind might be lurking almost anywhere. We just never expected it in our home.

I was getting ready for school one morning when I happened to look in the bathroom mirror. To my horror, I noticed a very large and hairy spider hanging from the ceiling above and behind me. I quickly spun around to face my assailant. It was a huge tarantula. When I say huge, I mean I could clearly look into its many black eyes as it coldly stared me down.

I ducked out of the room and closed the door. I was not sure how to handle the situation. Then, I had a wicked idea.

"Hey, Mish," I called.

"What?" she replied from the bedroom.

"Come here for a second. I want to show you something," I slyly told her.

She emerged from the bedroom, still brushing her hair. I knew that this would get me in heaps of trouble, but I couldn't resist. The little

384

devil on my shoulder won over my angel's better judgement. Sometimes, the risk-to-reward ratio favors the reward.

I cautiously opened the bathroom door and told her to step in and look up. Obligingly, she did. Bad move on her part. She should know by now.

She saw the eight-legged beast and screamed. She jumped back out of the room, almost knocking me over. The terrified look in her eye told me I was in trouble.

"What the heck?" she angrily questioned.

"I just want to know what you want me to do with it," I defended myself.

"Get rid of it, now!" she demanded.

I knew I had once again pushed my luck, so I didn't argue and went to grab a broom. I came back to find Aaron and Elijah had come running to see what was going on. They stayed a smart distance away but remained transfixed on the spider, who had not moved from its place of ambush.

I summoned my courage and bravely re-entered the bathroom, ready for battle. I took a clean swipe at the creature and knocked it to the floor. It recovered with amazing speed and agility. It now faced me head-on. We squared off like two gladiators in the arena. I took a step toward it, and it reared up on its back legs, brandishing its fangs and hissing loudly. I was not expecting that. You must be kidding me, a spider with an attitude that hisses?

I dealt the first blow with an overhand swing from my broom onto the spider's head. The spider was not amused. Even though I dealt it a solid smack, it stood its ground. I leaned in for another swing and it actually advanced forward on me. I really wasn't expecting that. I jumped back. What the heck?! This thing was not playing around, it meant business.

I called for reinforcements. I told my family, who were crouched behind me watching the match, to get me something, anything, to catch the spider in. Mish hurried off and quickly came back with a small trash bin from the kitchen. I summoned my courage and moved in on the spider for the win. With one arm, I swept the broom as a decoy and, with the other, quickly put the bin over the spider. I had it trapped. Now what?

While I was figuring out how to get the spider out of the house, Mish got a piece of cardboard from somewhere. With it, she helped me slide it under the bin, thus trapping the beast. I kept a firm seal on the bin as I hurriedly took the bin and unwanted visitor outside.

I know how much Elijah loves all animals, but with spiders, he draws a clear line. Normally, he would beg me to release the pest back into the wild, like he did with the mice I caught in our basement back home. I asked him what he wanted me to do with the spider, just in case he wanted to grant a pardon.

"Kill it," he coldly replied. Done.

We did not want the spider encounter to deter us from seeing some of Costa Rica's other native inhabitants. I learned from a colleague at school that there was a nature preserve on the east side of the country that was well known for its biodiversity called La Selva. University researchers come from around the world to study the area. It has even been featured in National Geographic. This sounded like a wonderful place to learn more about the plants and animals here, so we set off once more in the trusty rover to explore a new place.

The drive to La Selva was on one of Costa Rica's newest and most modern built roads. It went up and over the mountains and down into the vast eastern plain towards the Atlantic Ocean. The smooth pavement made a nice ride for a change. The rover needed a little bit of TLC after the last expedition. I didn't want to fix another leaf spring anytime soon.

Along the way, we passed miles and miles of banana fields. Apparently, Dole owns huge tracts of land in the country to grow the delicious fruit, mainly for export. We noticed that the bunches of fruit were wrapped in blue plastic bags while hanging on the tree and wondered what they were for.

We learned from Oscar that original bananas are almost extinct. What we call bananas today and buy in our supermarkets are actually plantains. Native bananas were almost completely wiped out by the Panama fungus in the late 1800s. By the 1960s, the original banana, the Gros Michel, was replaced by a hardier fungus-resistant but less tasty cousin, the Cavendish, which we still eat today. Ironically, the banana imposter is the world's most popular fruit. It is grown in many areas of

Central America and the Caribbean and shipped to every corner of the planet. Costa Rica happens to be the fifth largest exporter at over one billion dollars annually.

Oscar, of course, has a secret grove of true banana trees behind his home on the farm. He let us in on this little secret. One afternoon, he brought over some small, thick, fleshy, banana-looking fruits. I asked what they were. He said these were real bananas as he peeled and handed one to me. Skeptical, I tried it. Wow! He was not fooling. They tasted amazing. It was like eating a concentrated banana-flavored treat. I had no idea this was what I had been missing all my banana-eating life. Unfortunately, this was the only place I could savor them. I would never look at bananas back home the same way.

We found the park very easily as there are signs for it along the way. We guessed it truly must be famous. The sign at the entrance read La Selva Biological Research Station. I drove the Rover through the open gate and into the station. Straight away, we were in awe. The banana fields had given way to a tropical paradise.

In the trees above us were dozens of large iguanas sunning themselves high up in the branches. I remembered a bit of information about them from a National Geographic documentary. Apparently, they have a bad habit of falling off the branches in their sleep. I made sure not to park my Land Rover under any trees. I did not want to come back and find a splattered iguana on my hood. Keeping the insects off was bad enough.

After making sure the Rover was safe from raining iguanas, we walked through the main entrance of the station to a small wooden building with a large sign that read, "All visitors stop here, please." The attendant inside informed us that since this was a research area, we were not permitted to walk around unsupervised. She called on her walkie-talkie for someone to come and escort us. Shortly, a young man wearing a large, brimmed straw hat came to take us on a tour. He politely ushered us out of the building and onto a paved walking trail. He informed us that we needed to stay on the path so not to disturb the delicate ecosystem of the station. The area was kept as close as possible to its original condition for study.

As he guided us along the path, he pointed out many interesting things and explained that researchers who came here were afforded a unique opportunity to study a pristine environment. It did indeed look like someplace out of a David Attenborough nature special. Other than the path, there was no sign of any human incursion.

The guide stopped suddenly and pointed to a small tree approximately three to four yards from the path. Cautiously, he stepped off the path and, with a long stick, lifted a large green leaf off the forest floor. Underneath, coiled around the base of the tree, was a thick brown and black snake with its head pointed straight at us. This was no run-of-the-mill serpent. It was the undisputed king of the jungle, a Fer-de-Lance.

The Fer-de-Lance, or terciopelo in Spanish, is a very large and extremely aggressive pit viper with a bad attitude. It is the largest viper at up to eight feet in length and has some of the biggest fangs of any snake, so it can deliver a potent dose of its highly lethal venom. One bite from this monster is usually fatal if not treated immediately. It is notorious throughout Central and South America for attacking anything that is unfortunate enough to come within its striking range.

Instinctively, I stepped back and put an arm out to keep Aaron and Elijah away. Mish gasped and asked if it was dangerous. Our guide reassured us that it was ok for now. The morning was cool, so the cold-blooded snake was partly paralyzed until the sun warmed it enough to become active. I wanted to be long gone before that time. He gently lowered the leaf back onto the snake and let it sleep some more.

The guide told us a story that last year a young girl was playing under a tree during recess at a local school. Out of nowhere, a Fer-de-lance dropped onto her from its ambush spot in the branches above. It miraculously did not bite her. Other than being traumatized, the girl was unharmed. I do not know if the snake realized too late before it pounced that the girl was not its usual prey, but thankfully, it must have once it landed on her. Great, in Costa Rica, you need to worry about careless iguanas and deadly snakes falling from the trees. I really wanted a suit of steel armor now.

We continued our tour, keeping as close to the center of the path as possible. We stopped to watch a long line of leafcutter ants hard at work. The diminutive Hercules' carried above their heads pieces of leaves much larger than their bodies, like green sails. Tirelessly, these tiny insects brought in their harvest to the nest while larger guard ants patrolled along the line, making sure the workers were safe. It was fascinating to watch them. We were amazed at how organized and methodical they were. They had a system, division of labor, and common goal that mirrored our human society in a way that was mesmerizing. We could have stayed longer, but our guide was on a time schedule.

Further along, our guide pointed out another, very different ant. Dubbed the bullet ant, this tiny, innocuous-looking insect packs a powerful punch. Its bite is so painful that it is likened to being shot, hence its nickname. Some victims have even gone into cardiac arrest from the severity of the pain. We were warned not to go near it. He did not need to tell us twice.

Once more, our guide pointed out another very common snake. Coiled on branches off the path and about eye level were a couple of eyelash vipers. They are so named because of the large spikey protrusions above their eyes. I would never have seen them due to their exquisite coloration that camouflages them perfectly in the trees. Not surprisingly, they are highly venomous. He quickly moved us on because they are also very territorial and are known to go on the offensive when you trespass. Great.

Before we saw them, we smelt them. As we walked there was a growing pungent smell of something like a combination of manure and body odor. When we emerged into a clearing of the forest, we saw the source of the stench. Laily grazing on the green grass was a group of peccaries. These pig-like creatures are also called skunk pigs, now we know why.

The peccaries were completely uninterested in us and continued their grazing as we walked past. If you could get past their particularly strong odor, they are adorable in a pig-like way. They are only two to four feet long with round hairy bodies supported by tiny, thin legs. They looked completely harmless and almost out of place. Finally, something that doesn't bite. I am guessing that they are towards the bottom of the food chain here.

Our tour ended where it started. We thanked our guide and walked back out the gate to the rover. Luckily, no iguana had kamikaze dove into it. I tried not to think of snakes slithering under the seat as we climbed in. We were learning a lot in a short time. Costa Rica truly is an unbelievably biodiverse country with amazing natural wonders to explore.

Chapter 8 – The Realities of a Third-World Country

"I wish I had known when I was in the White House what I know now about the Third World." – Jimmy Carter

We have been driving around the country for a few months now and have noticed a startling issue everywhere we go. Costa Rica has a huge trash problem. Along the roadways, on the riverbanks, and in the forests is a huge amount of litter. Sometimes, it is just a few carelessly discarded fast-food wrappers or soda bottles, and other times, it is small mountains of purposefully dumped garbage. Shocking to us is that no one seems to be doing anything about it. Here we are in a tropical paradise, but everyone seems content to spoil it. The exceptions to this mess are the strictly controlled tourist spots and the wealthy gated communities like our farm.

If you are just the usual summer tourist who stays in one of the carefully manicured all-inclusive resorts that cater to North Americans and Europeans, you would leave thinking Costa Rica is Heaven on Earth. Step out of the tourist areas, however, and you will experience a very different Costa Rica. After all the façade, it is a poorer country with all the problems that plague emerging nations, like lack of infrastructure, poor law enforcement, improper waste disposal practices, and even cultural norms.

Costa Rica has always had the reputation of being a "green country." I think it wants to be but doesn't know exactly how to live up to its hype. That is not to say that parts of it are not spectacular. As I mentioned, the parts where the money flows are amazing and live up to the postcard images. Other parts are an environmental disaster.

We went to a very exclusive gated community where wealthy foreigners can buy a vacation home on the beach. We are not interested in buying anything, but they had an open house, so we decided to pop in and be nosey. Mish is good at playing a prospective client, so the agent was more than happy to let us in and show us around.

The lush grounds were flawlessly maintained by a small army of gardeners. It looked like an award-winning botanical garden. Every blade of bright green grass was cut to precision. All of the bushes presented large, colorful flowers without a single drooping petal. The palm trees were trimmed sharply to the same height. The whole scene could not have been painted to more perfection.

We walked through the community, admiring the grounds and the cleverly designed buildings. The architect crafted the place to look like an old Spanish town. There were faux brick and stone facades with large wrought iron railings on the buildings to add to the effect. In addition to the impressive townhomes, the development company built a small shopping village in the center for the inhabitants' convenience. An expansive marina, championship golf course, and private beach nicely completed the resort.

Despite its impressive presentation, it fell flat with us. It had a very Disney-esque Pirates of the Caribbean feel. It looked cool at first, but you realized deep down it was fake, a fantasy. It was not the real Costa

Rica. The real Costa Rica was outside the carefully guarded gate. Ironically, the gate prevented Costa Rica from entering.

Mish and I talked about the stark differences between places like this, and our farm, and the rest of the country. We couldn't help being a little judgmental. I felt a little disdain for the type of people that would be duped into living here. They would never get to know authentic Costa Rican culture. They would see the country from the safe confines of an artificial bubble.

I also felt a little frustration for the Costa Rican natives. How could they let their beautiful country be polluted and spoiled? The foreign developers seemed to be taking better care of it. I wanted to chastise them for not being better stewards of the environment.

I talked through my conundrum with Mish. I worried I was being too harsh on both sides. The developers were not doing anything illegal. In their defense, they were bringing in much-needed money to the country. How much of that money actually reached Costa Rica banks and was not sent to foreign investors, I did not know. I suspected a fair amount was never spent in the country, though.

Costa Ricans, in their defense, lacked some basic services I take for granted in the wealthier nations. In America, for example, we have regular and reliable trash pickup services once a week. We have our garbage neatly taken away and properly disposed of for us. We have a cadre of other services that help keep our towns and cities clean. All of which are paid for through tax dollars from people who can afford it, thanks to well-paying jobs in a rich nation.

I continue to struggle with this dilemma, the dichotomy of the haves and have-nots. I do not pretend to have any answers. I have a stubborn sense of fairness that I desperately want to impose on the universe. As unrealistic as that is, it still permeates the core of my being. I become very frustrated when I see what I perceive as injustices and want to right the wrongs. Superman to the rescue. As Mish constantly reminds me, I am my own worst enemy.

As I was rambling on to Mish, we walked out to the private pristine beach. The white sand had been meticulously raked into neat parallel grooves along its entire length. Only the gentle waves of the turquoise water disturbed the gardener's work. I felt almost guilty when we let the boys run amok on it, but you can't keep kids away from the sand.

I noticed a river bisecting the beach a little way down the coast. Then, to my disgust, I realized that this was the same river that we crossed upstream outside the gated development. Back there, it was horribly polluted with used tires, diapers, tin cans, plastic bottles, and all manner of trash. Gross, I thought. That same water was flowing out to the beach.

I told the boys that they were not to go in the water. They gave me some very unhappy looks but obeyed. I did not want to have to get them tetanus shots today. I wondered how many of the owners in this community knew what chemicals and parasites may lurk in their water. Maybe this is a form of karma, I mused.

With our curiosity satisfied, we hopped back in the Land Rover and headed home. When we crossed the river again, I almost gagged in revulsion, thinking of swimming at that beach. Sometimes, ignorance truly is bliss.

We drove back into our little bubble on the farm. I was more conscious that the farm gate separated us from the rest of the country. Inside the gate, the farm was idyllic. We were extremely fortunate to live here. Oscar and his crew were amazing and very helpful, and our hosts, the Cortez family, were simply wonderful. Everyone did everything they could to make us feel wanted and comfortable.

Mish mentioned one day to Maria-Melba that the shower did not produce hot water. Promptly later that day, one of the farm workers came by to fix it. In the United States, we are accustomed to large energy-hogging hot water tanks that supply us with almost unlimited water for long, steamy hot showers. In Costa Rica, we were somewhat getting accustomed to small individual point-of-use electrical heaters attached to the faucets. These awkward-looking but energy-efficient devices only supply water where needed. They are not great because they only have enough time to heat up the water as it passes through the pipe. The faster the water moves, the less hot it gets. Therefore, you either get a warm, slow trickle or a cold deluge. This made quick morning showers brisk and refreshing.

Our unit had stopped working altogether. The boys and I can deal with cold showers, but Mish will have no part in that. She wants her showers as close to scolding hot as she can get without boiling herself alive. She was very grateful when the man came to fix it.

I'm pretty sure that the farm worker who did the repair job was not a certified electrician. I suspect this because I was the first to take a shower with the fixed heater. I should have realized by the liberal use of electrical tape that something was amiss. Ignoring that electricity and water usually don't mix, I hopped in and turned the knob anticipating a nice hot spray of water. As the water cascaded over my body, I immediately felt a strange tingling sensation. My skin began to itch all over. I reached to turn off the water and received a sharp spark from the metal faucet handle. I quickly jumped out of the shower. Very cautiously, I reached back in and turned off the water.

The little devil on my shoulder tried to convince me to not tell Mish and let her take a shower this evening. The little angel on the other shoulder knew better. After the spider incident, I learned my lesson not to surprise my wife with unpleasant encounters. I opted to tell her so she could get the repair man back out ASAP.

Mish called Maria-Melba and almost as soon as she hung up the phone, the want-to-be electrician and Oscar came over. Oscar apologized profusely. I told him it was no big deal and not to worry about it. After all, I lived, and I didn't try to electrocute my wife. Win-win.

He examined the repair job with dissatisfaction. I couldn't make out what he told the worker in Spanish, but it was obviously a rebuke. The man looked repentant as Oscar unwrapped all the electrical tape and exposed the bare wires. After careful examination, Oscar said he would have the whole unit replaced and sent the worker out to get a new one.

Once he left, Oscar and I looked at his botched repair and chuckled. We both knew that it was so obviously wrong that it was comical. The fact that I could have been killed was lost in the moment. Another of my nine lives spent.

With the shower fixed correctly, Mish had another small request. The back door of our house opened to a dirt path that was overgrown by dense bamboo. She wanted to know if the plant could be cut back and something put on the dirt to keep us from tracking mud inside. I worried that we might be overstaying our welcome, but Maria-Melba seemed more than happy to correct this, too. She truly is a very generous and kind person. Also, it is easy enough for her to call down to Oscar and have him assign it to one of his workers.

The next day, our electrician, now turned mason, showed up to work on this new project. I really hoped he was better at landscaping than wiring. I think he was eager to redeem himself because he set to work right away.

He first tamed the bamboo and other plants by cutting them back so that they no longer posed a barrier to the door and a potential ambush place for snakes. He then started to excavate the dirt path. Day by day, I watched his progress with interest. I thought he was just going to dig down a little to make a small bed for gravel or sand in front of the door and call it good. After a full week of digging, however, it was clear that he had a more ambitious plan.

Every day after school, when I came home, I would inspect his progress. In the end, he excavated a thirty-by-ten-foot area behind the house. By now, I was really intrigued. One day, I came home to find bags of concrete and stacks of stone blocks and tile at the construction site. I asked Mish if she knew what he intended, but she didn't know either. It became our daily entertainment home improvement show.

Occasionally, Oscar came over to monitor the worker. He made corrections and revisions to the work as necessary and then disappeared again to take care of his own tasks. Day by day, the master plan was revealed. In two weeks, the worker, who we now knew as Mario, had completed the job.

Mario single-handedly built a large, tiled patio off the back of our house. It was enclosed on two sides by the house and on a third side by a low-walled garden area for the neatly manicured bamboo. It made a beautiful courtyard where we could enjoy from the bedroom window. We were very impressed.

Maria-Melba came down one afternoon to inspect the project. She asked Mish if this was ok. It was far better than ok. We did not expect this much trouble from a simple request. I warned Mish not to ask for anything else because we might get the whole house remodeled. That did not deter her from looking around to see what else needed improvement, though. We were feeling pretty pampered at this point.

In Costa Rica you do not need a lot of money to be pampered. Mish was feeling overwhelmed cleaning the house, cooking, and doing laundry while working teaching full-time online. The boys and I did our parts but were gone all day. She mentioned her plight to Oscar one day in passing. He offered a solution. One of the workers who also lives on

400

the farm has a wife who is looking for work. Since they are trying to raise a family, they could use extra income. We have never had a maid or cook before, but the idea sounded tempting.

Mish went over to meet the woman and inquire if she was available and how much would she cost for her services. It turned out that the woman, Andrea, was eager to work. She and Mish worked out a schedule where she would come over once a day to do the dishes, clean the house, and wash the laundry. I was more than happy to give Mish some relief but worried about the cost.

"How much does she charge?" I asked Mish when I got home.

"We agreed on twenty dollars a week," she told me.

I was shocked at how little that was and guilty that was all Andrea got for compensation. In the United States, she would command a much higher price. I didn't want to take advantage of her. Mish read my mind, and before I could voice a concern, she explained that it was twice the going rate in Costa Rica, and Christina was very grateful for the money. I did not argue. If that is the deal they agreed on and both were happy, so be it. Mish now had her own maid.

Having Christina around did make life easier. She is a very nice young lady and does a great job. Her young son reminded me a lot of our own boys, full of energy. Every once in a while, he would accompany his mother on her rounds. We didn't mind. Aaron and Elijah had a new playmate. Even though Anthony is a few years younger, they all got along very well. I think Elijah liked not being the youngest for a change. He now got to be the big brother.

I was talking to Oscar one Saturday morning. Our weekend chats had become something of a routine. I hoped he didn't mind me coming around. I usually brought coffee and a litany of questions. He seemed to genuinely like the company and not just pretend being nice to his boss' guests.

At first, Oscar was a little shy and restrained around me. I was not quite sure if it was because I was a stranger, a foreigner, a VIP-ish guest, or of a different socio-economic status. It couldn't have been for my witty personality, could it? Once he got to know me or tolerate me, he opened up quite a bit. I was glad and flattered by his willingness to share himself. I learned a lot about the man and his country through our talks.

One of the things that I found remarkable was that Oscar literally had spent his entire life on the farm. His father was the previous farm manager, so Oscar was actually born on the farm. He grew up helping his dad and learning the job. He wanted to become a horse trainer or anything that would keep him close to the animals he loved. When his father died, however, that dream vanished and was replaced by the reality of needing a job and a place to live.

If his father was no longer the farm manager, then he and his mother and siblings were out. In what probably seemed like a great solution at the time, Don Cortez offered the position to the sixteen-year-old Oscar. Don Cortez got a new and already trained and familiar farm manager and Oscar and his family continued to live on the farm. Win-win for everyone except Oscar.

Whether or not Oscar has regrets for his decision, he has never told me. His duty and obligation to his family are paramount. He accepts his fate and makes the best of it. I greatly admire that in him. I think most people would not be as stoic.

Oscar did confide in me during one of our talks that he wanted more for his four daughters. He was a huge proponent of education and pushed them to excel in school. He knew their ticket off the farm lied in university. Luckily, Costa Rica has very low-cost college tuition for its high school graduates. It is not free, but maybe affordable on Oscar's salary. It is, however, very competitive, so his daughters needed to apply themselves. Oscar saw to that.

Out of curiosity, I asked Oscar if his employers provided any tuition assistance for workers' families. They do not, he informed me. My curiosity overcame my tact, and I asked what benefits they do provide. He didn't mind me asking and told me that they provide a retirement plan, a place to live, and vacation time. Since Costa Rica has free national healthcare, they did not need to pay for that. They also were very generous and gave Christmas and birthday gifts to him and his family. All in all, it was a good set-up, sort of.

The system is designed to keep the status quo. Costa Rica is primarily an agriculture-based economy. Agriculture requires land ownership. Since all the available land is already owned by wealthy families, there is no room for anyone else to move in. Therefore, the wealthy provide jobs for the non-wealthy. They treat their workers well enough to continue to work and be reasonably happy but not well enough to elevate themselves to a higher standard of living. Nice for the haves, but not so nice for the have-nots.

To be fair, this type of caste system is not unique to Costa Rica. It is seen the world over. The ability to own land is still key in many placed, even the United States. At least in the U.S. and other developed countries, non-tangible holdings, like stocks and investments, allow for upward mobility.

My intrusive judgmental side was starting to get a little triggered the more I learned about the inner workings of the farm and the country in general. I needed to back down and not let my inherent sense of right and wrong cloud my experience here. The Cortez' are very good people. They sincerely believe they are kind and generous employers who provide for their employees, which they do. I realize that this is not my country and not my place to judge it. I just really wish there was more equity in the world. The Oscars should have the right to a better life.

Chapter 9 – Going Home for Christmas

"I'll be home for Christmas. You can count on me." – Bing Crosby

Before we realized it, the school year was almost half over, which meant Christmas was just around the corner. We had not been home for the last couple of Christmas' and the thought of a tropical palm tree with lights and decorations didn't ring in the holiday spirit. So, we decided to go home for Christmas instead.

Most people try to get away from the cold and snow in December, but we wanted to go back to it. Maybe it is cliché, but there is something magical about a white Christmas. Fluffy white flakes drifting down outside, a warm, bright fire under a mantle decorated with garland and stockings, the smell of freshly baked cookies wafting through the house, the familiar sound of holiday carols, and a huge colorfully decorated tree in the living room are the hallmarks of a traditional Christmas. We love them all and couldn't wait to experience them again.

We all wrapped up the first semester of school and boarded another airplane. The flight from San Jose to Seattle is long. Mish read and slept, Aaron and Elijah stayed up the whole way to watch movies and drink free ginger ale, and I restlessly watched the flight tracker, counting down every mile and praying for every turbulence.

We landed safely again. Another uncomfortable flight in those cramped aluminum tubes survived. With all of our engineering prowess, you would think that someone could invent a better way to travel. I like trains. Why couldn't there be a train to Costa Rica?

After a long, slow-motion stampede off the airplane, a long line at customs, and a long wait at baggage, we were finally able to exit the airport. Immediately, we realized that we were no longer in the tropics. This was the Pacific Northwest in winter, cold and wet. We didn't have any proper gear with us, so we had to shiver at the curb as I hailed a taxi.

"Why couldn't the rental car place be at the airport?" I said irritably to no one in particular.

We had another long wait at the rental car place and a long drive home. Over fourteen hours of traveling we were finally back to where we started six months ago. I pulled the rental car into our driveway and looked at our house. It looked dark and gloomy in the rain. It was almost surreal to be back.

The house was freezing inside. We were all too tired and cold to do anything other than turn on the heat and get in our beds under the covers. In the morning, we could unpack and check on things. For now, I definitely needed some sleep.

The next day, Mish was up early unpacking and taking stock of what we needed. She was very eager to decorate for Christmas and already was getting out boxes of ornaments from the basement. She wanted to maximize our time here and wasn't wasting a day.

"Up and at 'em,'" she prodded me. "We need to get a tree!"

I know there is no arguing with Mish when it comes to certain things, Christmas decorating is one of them. She always has it meticulously planned out in her head. I just go with it. I love Christmas, but she really loves Christmas. This was the first time home for the holiday in three years, so she was in full Christmas spirit mode.

Before I showered and had coffee, she had half the decorations up. I sleepily sipped my cup and wisely stayed back, less she hung garland and candy canes on me.

The boys were harder to get up. Staying up the entire flight watching Marvel movies had caught up with them. When I poked them, they just grumbled and rolled over in their blanket cocoons. Elijah is particularly difficult to wake up. He will stubbornly stay in bed despite all efforts to rouse him. I had one secret tactic, however.

"We're going to get donuts," I whispered in his ear.

He opened an eye.

"What kind?" he asked.

"Chocolate," I teased.

He sat straight up in bed and rubbed his eyes.

"I want two," he demanded.

With that, he stumbled out of bed and started to get dressed.

I checked on Aaron, who was already out of bed and pulling clothes out of his closet. Aaron was less motivated by food but was also less stubborn than his younger brother. He knew that resistance was futile and would obediently follow along. He also knew he would get a donut out of it, too.

When everyone was properly dressed for the cold winter weather, we set off to find a tree and some donuts. Mish would have nothing to do with run-of-the-mill trees from a tree lot. Only a freshly cut tree from a tree farm would suffice. Luckily, to the boys, a donut was still a donut. Getting them their bribe was easy. Getting a live tree on the spot was a little harder.

I drove to a tree farm we'd gone to before. Thankfully, it was open. It was a little out of our way, but was worth the drive. They had several acres of a variety of trees of different species and heights, along with free hot cider and cookies. I drove my truck around so Mish could scout the area for the perfect specimen. Several other tree shoppers were doing the same thing. Apparently, we weren't the only ones doing last-minute decorating. The race was on!

We rarely had to worry about competing with other families for a tree, though. Mish knew the exact height of our vaulted living room ceiling and selected a tree that would reach it. Few people get a fifteen-foot tree, so we usually have a selection to choose from. Once Mish homes in on the tree, we are sent in to retrieve it.

The farm provided saws for people to cut the trees down. Cutting a fir tree entailed getting sap and needles all over you as you slowly cut away with a dull saw. It was tiring work. Since the ground was cold and wet, I did the sensible thing and sent Aaron in.

"I'm passing on the family holiday tradition," I told him as I handed him the saw.

He just gave me a dirty look and took the saw, resigning to his fate. Dutifully, he crawled under the wet tree and began cutting. Several minutes later, he emerged covered in green needles and panting. After a short break, he dove back under to finish the job. I heard the telltale cracking sound of a tree about to be felled. With a slight push, over it went, exposing Aaron.

"Good job!" I praised him.

With the fresh-cut tree in the bed of my truck, we headed home to begin the task of carefully dressing it in holiday splendor. Mish really, really loved this part. She put on Christmas carols, got something warm to drink, and lovingly placed our keepsake ornaments on the branches. Each one was tied to a cherished memory. None of them were generic store-bought baubles. Mish had collected them over the years from all the places we have visited. When the tree was done, it was a living history of our family. I think that was why she loved it and one of the many reasons I love her.

Christmas day came, and it was as special as we hoped. Being in our own home, with our own decorations and traditions, made it magical. We reconnected with some friends and our neighbors. They all wanted to hear about Costa Rica. Talking about it sort of made me feel like we were living dual lives, which I guess, in a way, we were. I really wanted to somehow reconcile our life in the United States with our one in Costa Rica. Although I knew it is not possible, I really wanted one big get-together with our friends and family from each country. This was one of the conundrums of being a nomadic international travelers.

The holiday break was amazing. It also went by too fast. It seemed no sooner than we put the tree up than we were taking it down. The time to head back to our other home was fast approaching. We were looking forward to seeing everyone on the farm and getting back to warmer weather, I will admit.

Mish and I agreed that we wanted to bring back gifts for our friends in Costa Rica. She got presents for Christina, Olga, and her daughters, and the Cortez family and I got ones for Oscar and the other farm workers. It was really fun shopping for them. We put a lot of thought into the gifts and hoped they would like them. I just hoped we could get them all through customs.

For Andrea, Olga, and Maria-Melba, Mish put together baskets of lavender lotions, soaps, bath oils, and other very feminine products to pamper themselves. They were all locally sourced. Sequim, a small quaint town nearby, is the lavender capital of the world and renowned for its lavender farms and festivals. The baskets were a way of sharing a small part of our home with them. I thought it was a nice gesture.

For the guys, I opted for more manly presents. I bought a battery-powered set of quality tools for Oscar. It came in a sturdy case that included a drill, reciprocating saw, circular saw, and flashlight. After all the help he has been, I thought he deserved something nice. I also got him and two of the other farm workers handy multitools. I blew my budget again, and outspent Mish, but figured it was Christmas after all.

In addition to the presents, I needed to get back some repair parts for my Land Rover that I could not get in Costa Rica. I found them online and had them shipped. Luckily, they arrived before we left. I looked at the pile of stuff we were staging for packing and realized that we were going to be way over our weight limit. Since there was nothing we could do about it, I just tossed some more stuff on top and resigned to pay the exorbitant airline fee.

At the airport, the baggage handler weighed our suitcases. As expected, they were considerably over the fifty-two-pound limit allowed for international travel. I always thought that was an oddly specific number and wondered how the airlines determined it. My cynical side thought it was probably five pounds lighter than the average suitcase weight.

At first, the handler was not going to allow the overage. Mish told her we didn't mind paying, but that wasn't the issue. She informed us it was a full flight and that baggage weight was being strictly monitored.

"Really, five extra pounds, and the plane won't be able to take off?" I muttered irritably under my breath.

I let Mish handle it. She was our trip planner and manager. Besides, she had a much cooler temperament than me with these types of things. After some back-and-forth negotiating, our bags were checked. Whatever Mish did, it apparently worked.

"Did you bribe her?" I asked.

"No, I just told her the situation that we were residents of Costa Rica and returning with gifts," she answered.

Okay, one of these days, I need to learn diplomacy, I guess, I thought.

At the boarding counter, we had another issue. The attendant took our tickets and said we couldn't board with them. Costa Rica has a strict policy that visitors need to have booked return flights to prove roundtrip intentions. Apparently, they have had problems with people coming to the country and never leaving. Obviously, this does not apply to residents, which we were.

Mish produced our passports, which have the official Costa Rica visa stickers proving we were indeed residents. The man looked at them a little suspiciously. I could understand his concern, after all, we did have the same visa stickers for England and Germany.

"You have residency in four countries?" he asked dubiously.

Mish explained that I was an international teacher and we had moved around with my job. The man called for his manager, who also inspected our passports and tickets. He concluded that we could not board.

I lost it. I was tired, cranky, and very annoyed. Usually, I try to avoid flying, but now I just wanted to get on the stupid airplane. I told the manager he was an idiot. Before Mish could interject, I launched into a tirade of reasons to support my opinion.

The manager did not appreciate my evaluation of his job performance and got a little heated, too. Through gritted teeth, he semi-politely told me that he had the authority to bar us from getting on the plane. Luckily, Mish stepped in.

I backed off and let her handle it. While she talked to the manager, I walked a few paces away to cool off. The manager made a call and explained to someone higher up the situation. He hung up and informed Mish that we were cleared to go. She smiled and thanked him politely. The man gave her back her documents and told Mish to have a nice flight. He just glared at me as he handed me my passport. Ok, so there is something to this diplomacy thing.

On a typical cold and wet Seattle morning, we finally took off bound for our other home. As the plane jetted south, we all assumed our usual positions. The only airline providing direct flights from Seattle to San Jose was Frontier. The boys liked them for two reasons: they painted the tails of their planes with different animals, and they had a gimmick of baking fresh cookies in the galley and giving you one as you board. I quietly munched on my cookie while the moose-themed plane bounced around the sky.

We landed in warm, sunny San Jose once more and picked up my Rover from long-term parking. I was very happy to see my trustworthy Red Rover and eagerly climbed in. Mish just frowned and reluctantly took her seat.

After driving around in our more modern and comfortable truck back in Washington, she didn't seem thrilled to ride in it. Undeterred by her lack of enthusiasm, I fired it up. Thankfully, it started right away. I looked at her and smiled as I put it in gear.

413

"It's a miracle," she teased.

Ignoring her, I pushed on the gas pedal, and we were off.

I chugged up the long driveway to the farm gate. One of the workers recognized us straight away and jovially waved. He pushed a button, and the gate silently opened so we could drive through to our little idyllic world of the farm. It felt good to be back. I pulled the rover up to our house, and everyone got out and began offloading bags. We were only gone two weeks, but it felt longer.

Switching homes takes a little time to re-adjust.

After unpacking, we were anxious to play Santa Claus and give out presents. We gathered up the ones for Oscar's family and went over to their house. Mish knocked on the door, and Olga came out smiling. She let out a big "Welcome back!" and hugged Mish tightly and did the cheek-kissing thing. I still have not got comfortable with "la bise," as it is called in French, but endure it anyway. After Mish, it was my turn. I was very moved to be missed this much. It is nice to have such friends, even if I must do air cheek kisses from time to time.

Olga invited us inside, where Oscar and the girls were waiting. It was a grand reunion with a whirlwind of hugs, handshakes, kisses, and cheers with all ten of us crammed into their small kitchen.

After everyone had greeted everyone else at least once, we sat down and got caught up on the happenings in each other's lives. Even though the break had only been two weeks, it now felt much longer. When we were in Washington, the time went by very quickly, but sitting in

Oscar's kitchen talking about it made the time seem slower. So much had transpired between us that we found ourselves talking into the night much longer than we had originally planned. Mish eventually broke the conversation.

"We brought you Christmas presents!" she exclaimed.

Oscar and Olga looked a little shocked. I don't think they anticipated that we would get them something. The girls jumped up, excited to get a second Christmas. Mish reached down into the large bag she had been guarding and produced the gifts and handed them out one by one.

I handed Oscar his present that had been sitting on my lap the whole time. The large, heavy box was very conspicuous, but I don't think he realized it was for him until I handed it over. He took it carefully and looked puzzled as he felt its hefty weight in his hands. I knew he would be surprised. I was anxious, however, to see if he liked it.

Once distributed, everyone began excitedly opening their gifts. One by one, we heard gasps of joy and rounds of thank you. We were very pleased that they liked them.

Oscar removed the wrapping from his and saw the contents. He stared at it for a few moments without a word. I wondered if he liked it. He finally looked up at me with what I thought was a little glimmer of water in his eyes.

"Thank you, Curtis," he said in the sincerest tone I had ever heard. I knew he would like it.

With the presents given, we headed back to our house. We could give out the rest of them tomorrow. Right now, it was time to get ready to climb into bed. We had been up traveling since early morning, and exhaustion was creeping in. As I slipped under the covers, I had this strange feeling that we had never really left.

Chapter 10 – Back in Costa Rica

"All trails seem to lead to waterfalls, misty crater lakes or jungle-fringed, deserted beaches. Explored by horseback, foot or kayak, Costa Rica is a tropical choose-your-own-adventure land." – Lonely Planet

I woke in the morning to a beautiful Costa Rica sunrise. We had left the cold and rain behind and now got to enjoy a tropical climate again. With the rainy season also behind us, the weather was perfect. The warm blue sky beckoned us to explore the country some more.

Before going on another excursion, I needed to check in at school and see what transpired over the holiday. I had ordered some science supplies and was anxious to see if they came in, so I swung by school a few days before the break ended and school began again. As expected, it was mostly deserted and quiet except for the administrative department finalizing schedules and custodians getting classrooms ready to receive students.

I was pleased to discover that my supplies had arrived and were already in my classroom. I went down to check on them. Everything seemed in order. The supplies were all there, and the room had been thoroughly scoured, with the floor polished to a high luster. The smell of cleaning chemicals lingered in the air. I looked around to double-check that my desk was in order, textbooks were stacked neatly for distribution, desks were aligned in perfect parallel rows, and boards were cleaned so they could be filled with information.

After all these years as a teacher, I still need to perform this ritual of inspecting my little ship like a good Navy captain before a long deployment. I was satisfied I would be ready for another term and closed the door behind me as I left.

That evening, during dinner, I started to feel ill. My stomach ached, and I felt nauseous. I assumed it was just a travel bug as my body re-adjusted to another place and went to lay down.

Within an hour, I became violently sick. I started vomiting with diarrhea and spiked a high fever. I rushed to the toilet. I sat there, expelling stuff from both ends of my body, shivering. I never felt this miserable.

Mish came in to check on me. I must have looked like a wreck. You know your spouse is committed to you when they can see you at your worst in the most pathetic and helpless position and still love you. She has changed many diapers and cleaned up a lot of bodily fluids before, but not from me. This was embarrassing. At the time, however, I didn't care. I was bad off.

After several bouts of my intestines trying their hardest to get rid of whatever bug invaded me, I was spent. My innards were not done, though. They kept spasming and convulsing, which began to really hurt. I mean, really hurt. Eventually, I collapsed on the bathroom floor in agony. My poor diaphragm was so taut I began having trouble breathing. All I could do was lay there in my own excrement and hope it would stop.

Mish tended to me but realized I needed medical help. Not knowing what else to do, she told Aaron to get Oscar. Aaron turned pale and shook his head.

"What's the matter?" his mother asked impatiently.

"The dogs," Aaron quietly replied.

Mish forgot that Oscar lets loose the hounds after sunset. They are not your ordinary farm guard dogs. They are spawns of Cerberus, we think. They patrol the farm from sunset to sunup. We were warned to stay inside when they were out. The leader of the canine gang is a particularly large and aggressive dog affectionately named Pinky. Aaron was justified in refusing to follow his mother's orders. He had no desire to be eaten.

Not knowing what else to do, Mish walked out onto the back porch and shouted for help. After waking up most of the farm, a window opened next door, and Olga's head popped out. She called over, asking what the matter was. Mish explained that I needed help and didn't know what to do.

Olga arrived right away. When he saw my condition, she phoned for an ambulance to take me to the hospital. In my foggy haze, I could recognize the word hospital. In a panic, I remembered from the U.S. State Department brief on Costa Rica that visitors to the country were urged to not use the local medical facilities unless it was a serious emergency. I thought this qualified.

I had no idea how long it would take for the ambulance to arrive. I also did not know if they would find the farm, given Costa Rica's unique way of giving addresses. All I could do was lay there shivering and convulsing while trying to breathe and hope the ambulance drivers knew the area. Thankfully, the EMTs came quickly and carried me away. I don't remember much of the ride to the hospital other than I bounced around on the stretcher and prayed for God to be merciful.

At the hospital, I was taken into the emergency room and straight away given an IV. I had become dangerously dehydrated. The doctors pumped me full of fluids and started medication. I just wanted it to end. I was relieved when Mish arrived to comfort me. Oscar had driven her to the hospital. I definitely owed him another Christmas gift.

By the time the first IV bag was emptied into me, I started to feel better. The convulsions had stopped, and my fever had gone down. A doctor came in to check on me. He spoke decent English and explained that I had contracted a form of cholera. He had prescribed a standard course of treatment and thought I would be able to go home in the morning. I was relieved. I thanked him over and over. So, the Costa Rica hospital wasn't that bad after all. I just wish I hadn't found that out this way.

As I was laying there recuperating, another patient with the same symptoms came in on a stretcher. It was my school director. She also had become ill and was rushed to the hospital. I looked at her and felt pity. I could sympathize with how awful she felt. Misery loved company, I guess, so we were in the same boat.

My recovery took longer than I originally anticipated. I needed to stay on medication for two weeks. I couldn't keep down anything but tried my best to stop throwing up. I felt weak and tired all the time. I probably wasn't the most pleasant person to be around.

Eventually, after a few weeks, I felt mostly back to normal. My best guess is that I contracted the bug from the school's water. It used to get its supply from an open tank perched on a platform in the back of the school. From being idle over the Christmas break, it stagnated and bred the germs. Since the director and I were the first to get to school and drink the water, we got sick, so much for being the eager ones. At least they caught it because of us and sanitized the tank so no one else would get sick. That would have been really catastrophic if all the students went to the hospital. I don't think we could handle it.

I really needed to get out of the house after being stuck inside recovering. Mish did some research and found an interesting place high in the mountains above San Jose called La Paz. It was just what the doctor ordered, fresh air and exercise.

Once more we set off in my Land Rover on an adventure. The drive to La Paz is beautiful. The road winds up into the mountains, past more farms and ranches. The rover chugged along at its steady, slow pace. Luckily, no ox carts passed us this time. However, a red sports car came speeding up onto my tail. He obviously wanted to pass, but the country road was too narrow and had no place for me to turn off. He just had to wait.

421

The driver of the car impatiently stayed on my tail. If he thought nudging me from behind would get me to speed up, he didn't know anything about old diesel Land Rovers. I was cruising at flank speed. Eventually, we came to a place where the road widened for a bit, and he used the opportunity to race past me. I gladly watched him fade into the distance and went back to my slow but steady, relaxed pace.

We continued our trek into the mountains. The air got cooler and moister as we headed into the famous cloud forest area of Costa Rica. The vegetation got denser, and the hills got steeper the further up we went. We rounded a turn and, to our amazement, saw that a massive landslide had fallen down the mountain. A stretch of road about a quarter mile long was covered in mud and rock debris. At the edge of the slide, a line of cars was stopped, unable to get across.

I carefully surveyed the scene and realized that my Rover could make it across. I gleefully put it in four-wheel drive and told everyone to hang on. As I drove the Rover past the stuck cars, including the red sports car, I just smiled and waved. Here was my Rover's moment to shine. I intrepidly maneuvered it up onto the slide and began to trek across. With its big knobby tires and high suspension, the Rover easily navigated the muddy terrain. Aaron and Elijah joyfully clapped as we rolled down the further side. Mish just hung on and looked straight ahead.

"How did you like that?" I boastfully asked.

I didn't wait for an answer. I took the Rover out of four-wheel drive mode and continued to our destination, feeling pretty smug.

La Paz is amazing! It is a zoo, botanical garden, nature hike, resort, and restaurant all rolled into one. It is built on a river with several magnificent waterfalls cascading down the mountains through the lush jungle. It is as perfect a postcard of Costa Rica as you can get. When I pulled into the parking lot, I barely stopped the Rover before Mish and the boys hurriedly got out.

We had to start with the zoo section first because Elijah homed in on it and impatiently led us that way immediately after we entered. He kept waving back to us to hurry up as he charged forward on the lookout for animals. We quickly found them. Elijah let out a loud gasp, and his brown eyes went wide when he saw not one but two massive jaguars. Luckily, we met them from behind thick glass and not in the wild. They are truly ferocious-looking. As the one gracefully walked along a branch in its enclosure, we could see the powerful muscles rippling through its body. Its' mottled yellow and black coat had a slight sheen as if it had just been brushed. They are absolutely beautiful animals.

The jaguar just stared at us with its beautiful green cat eyes. Seemingly unimpressed with mere humans in its domain, it lazily yawned and prominently displayed two large white teeth. It knew it was the most badass thing around.

I read on the sign that it has the most powerful bite of any of the large cats. I pointed out to Elijah that with those teeth and that jaw, the jaguar could easily crush any of his bones and eat him whole. He didn't care, he would have gone in with it if allowed anyway.

We moved on and saw a menagerie of other animals, all native to Costa Rica. There were a variety of monkeys. These, unlike their wild relatives, had to stick to their diets and could not accept human handouts. There also were more bird species than I could count. Their combined feathers represented every color imaginable. Mish was mesmerized by the adorable, slow-moving sloths. Their round faces appear to always be smiling. She couldn't get enough of them.

I stopped to get a close look at the vampire bats. I have seen them many times in the evenings on the farm flying around, but not up close, so this was my chance. I noted that they are even smaller than I thought. I closely studied them with a morbid fascination. I could see their small needle-like teeth menacingly extending from their upper jaws. Their pug noses and beady eyes gave them a sinister look. I thought of them sucking my blood while I slept and shivered. We would definitely keep the tents closed tightly at night on scout camping trips.

The crown jewel of the zoo, at least for Elijah, was the reptile house. Reluctantly, we followed him inside. Our brave little adventurer was completely unafraid of any animal except spiders. He walked right up to the glass enclosures and had no fear of being nose-to-nose with some of the deadliest serpents on the planet. He eyed them with awe as they slithered or laid there. Their lidless unblinking eyes make them appear that they are always watching you. Despite my conscious logical self knowing that there was thick glass safely separating us, my unconscious survival self instinctively kept a respectful distance from the enclosers. In the back of my mind, I fearfully thought, what if there

424

suddenly was an earthquake and all the glass shattered? Another shiver went down my spine.

Elijah excitedly called me over. He pointed to a large brown snake coiled in the back of its enclosure. It was the infamous fer-de-lance. I stared in shock. It was huge. Its head was the size of a grapefruit, and its body was as thick as a motorcycle tire. I estimated it was at least eight feet in length. Here was a monster of terrifying proportions. I remembered our encounter with one in La Sleva. Now, I was extremely glad that one was asleep. I would never want to run into one of these in the wild.

Elijah was infatuated by this snake. I think he had a kind of reverence for its deadliness and status as the top snake of the jungle. So much was his admiration for it that come Pinewood Derby time he asked if we could build a fer-de-lance car. I had no idea how, but he was determined anyway. With Oscar's help, of course, we carved his block of wood to sort of resemble something that looked like a snake and painted it to match. Elijah made sure to add bright green eyes and large white fangs to complete the look. He was ecstatic with the way it turned out and couldn't wait to race it. Elijah tends to stand out from other kids at times.

We pulled Elijah out of the reptile house so we could see other parts of the park. We walked along the winding trails to the waterfalls. We could hear their loud roar and feel their cool mists before we could see them. The dampness magnified the strong, musky smell of the jungle. We also have large waterfalls in Washington, but they are fed from glaciers high up in the mountains, and so are freezing cold. These felt wonderfully refreshing in the hot sun.

Walking around the park was breathtaking. Everywhere we looked, we saw exotic plants and animals. After a while, we all started to get hungry and made our way to the restaurant. Being jungle explorers is hard work. Elijah had the map and once more led the way.

The restaurant was a large bamboo thatch-covered building made to look like an indigenous tribal home. It was the perfect setting for lunch. We ate and relaxed under large leaf-shaped ceiling fans that cooled us off in the heat. I looked around impressed at the whole park. It might be a little touristy, I thought, but the family had a great time. This would be a fond memory we would have for the rest of our lives, which I was very thankful for.

Chapter 11 – A Different Outlook

"Together with a culture of work, there must be a culture of leisure as gratification. To put it another way: people who work must take the time to relax, to be with their families, to enjoy themselves, read, listen to music, play a sport." – Pope Francis

Winter was fading, and spring was on the horizon. The only way you can tell the passing of the year in Costa Rica is by the rain. The country only has two seasons, the rainy one and the non-rainy one. We were now in the second one, and spring was upon us.

We definitely had a routine going. After being in the country for over six months, we were familiar with the area, the laws, and most of the cultural norms, or so we thought.

In the United States, Christmas trumps Easter in holiday grandeur. We were in a very Catholic country, however. For many faithful, Easter is the most important Christian observance. Christmas was Jesus's birthday, but Easter was his resurrection. His rising from the grave is the whole foundation of the New Testament in the Bible. Catholics take this season very seriously.

For us, Easter is a time when the Easter Bunny delivers baskets filled with sticky marshmallows peeps, a rainbow of jellybeans, and chocolate rabbits, you eat the ears off first. We also participate in the ritual coloring and hiding of Easter eggs for children to compete in finding them. Why we do these bizarre things, I don't really know. They are long practiced traditions we pass down from generation to generation that help connect us. The actual event is not as important as the sharing of memories, I think.

Like trying to explain our Halloween in England, explaining our Easter in Costa Rica was difficult. Once again, we assumed that everyone practiced American holiday traditions. Egg hiding was not something done here, we found out, though. Mish decided to change that.

She went next door to ask Olga and Andrea if they would like to have their children come over and color eggs. They were a little aware of the American penchant for dyeing perfectly good white eggs but were curious to learn more. They said they would love to, so Mish got to work organizing the first Easter egg coloring party on the farm.

Eggs are easy to get when you live on a farm. The dye is another problem. We are used to the grocery store kits that come with colored pellets you drop into bowls of hot vinegar water to dip the eggs in with the included wire thingy. Mish improvised and found some substitute food coloring from the store that would work. She made up bowls of dye and boiled lots of eggs.

The day before Easter, all of the children on the farm came over to experience Easter egg coloring American style. Mish didn't have to give many instructions. They very quickly got the idea and soon were having a great time dying eggs in every color combination imaginable. They didn't care that their fingers were dyed as well. The young Van Goghs were expressing their artistic sides.

When every last egg had been dyed to perfection, Mish collected them. She told the children that tonight, the Easter Bunny would hide them and they would have to find them in the morning. I whispered to Mish that she should hide them inside and not outside with the snakes. She readily agreed and revised her original plan. You have to adjust to your surroundings sometimes, especially if snakes are involved.

The next day, the kids returned early. The Easter Bunny must come to the Catholic houses first so they can make Easter Sunday morning mass. Mish, aka the Easter Bunny, had hidden the eggs the night before and arranged small baskets for each child. When they were all present and anxiously waiting, she gave the go signal.

The eight kids, including our two, were like small whirlwinds spinning around the house. Each one was determined to find the most eggs. The older kids were more methodical in their search as they went from room to room, looking for eggs. The younger ones, on the other hand, had no apparent plan and just dizzily raced around in a frantic hope to spot an egg. Mish cheated a little and gave them some covert pointing and hints. One poor kid in such a frenzy, with his eyes darting in every direction, couldn't see the bright pink egg in the green plant right in front of him. Mish mercifully pointed straight at the egg. After a few seconds of complete confusion, he finally zeroed in on it, snatched it up triumphantly, and then scurried off to find some more. A little clueless but highly motivated. We couldn't help laughing at such boundless energy and enthusiasm.

The kids made short work of finding all the eggs. Mish passed out their chocolate-filled baskets as rewards. Spin the kids up, give them lots of sugar, and send them to sit still and quiet through a long church service, I loved this plan. The parents thanked Mish over and over. I wondered if they would be as thankful in an hour or so. Chuckling to myself at the image of kids lathered in chocolate climbing over church pews, I went to make coffee.

Sunday mornings are normally very quiet on the farm. On Easter Sunday, it is especially quiet. Everyone is either asleep or at church. Not much is open in town either, so you are forced to relax, which sometimes I need. I sat down on the front porch with my coffee and just admired the view. I was contemplating the choices that brought us here when my tranquility was broken by Mish calling from the kitchen.

"Remember, my parents will be here next week."

Time had gone by so fast that I forgot they were coming right after Easter. We had not seen them since England when they visited us there. They didn't come when we lived in Germany, so it has been almost two years since our last get-together. I know Mish was very excited to see her folks and share our life here with them. I, however, always have mixed feelings about their visits.

I love Philip and Nancy both, but they can be challenging at times. They are both retired and can travel whenever they want. Instead of waiting for one of our breaks, they always pick a time when we are still in school. When they arrive, our lives are supposed to stop and host them instead. We have tried to tactfully address this issue with them, but

430

it hasn't made a difference. They always have some reason for their inconvenient visits. Being her parents, Mish doesn't put her foot down. I, as the dutiful son-in-law, begrudgingly go with it.

"Wonderful," I replied to her half truthfully.

I went back to looking at the view. I heard a slight whimper and looked down. Albie was sprawled out on the deck, sunning himself. Every so often, he would twitch and softly bark in his sleep. I wondered what he dreamed about. He shouldn't have nightmares because he lived a life of leisure and security. He must be the most well-traveled dog in the world. Whatever he was dreaming, he was really deep into. He moved his legs slightly like he was trotting along somewhere. Whoever said, "It's a dog's life," obviously never had a dog.

The week went by fast and soon it was time to pick Mish's parents up at the airport. Mish had warned them ahead of time that my Land Rover might be a tad cramped and uncomfortable for them. They opted to rent a boring generic car instead of riding in style. If they didn't want an authentic Costa Rica experience in my cool adventure vehicle, that was fine by me.

Mish got to drive the rental because her father surprisingly wanted to ride shotgun with me, and her mother sensibly wouldn't drive here. I was more than happy to show off my cherished red baby and told dad to hop in and hold on. Mish had not driven in Costa Rica yet, so she was a little nervous. I told her to just follow me.

"That will be easy. I just follow the black smoke, right?" she teased.

"Ha ha," I replied. I was a little offended. After all, my Rover didn't smoke that bad.

We convoyed to the farm and pulled up in front of our house. Her dad slowly climbed out of the Rover with only a few grunts and moans.

"That's a real nice vehicle," he lied.

"We had air-conditioning," Mish added, just to rub it in.

I think dad liked the adventurous image of the Land Rover but not the implementation. I still don't mind compromising some small comforts for the nostalgic feeling when I drive it. I'll admit, it can be a little hard on the back and rear end. Despite its flaws, I still very much enjoy driving around in it, even without air-conditioning. It's the sacrifice I make to look like a National Geographic explorer.

I did my son-in-law's job and handled the luggage while Mish took her parents inside for a tour. I told Aaron it was his turn to be a good grandson and handed him a bag. He rolled his eyes and waddled up the steps carrying it. Elijah had already ducked inside. For such a young little boy, he had already figured out when to disappear to avoid work.

That evening, we had a big party with Mish's parents, Oscar and his family, and Andrea and her family. Mish wanted her parents to meet everyone so they could put faces to the names she told them about. We all crowded onto the front patio and merrily chatted back and forth over drinks while I cooked on the grill.

I felt bad not inviting the Cortez family, too, but knew it would have been awkward. I learned from the last party that the two asunder worlds of farm worker and farm owner didn't mix. We would invite them to a separate event later. Their loss, it was a great party.

Soon, we were all talking like old friends who hadn't seen each other in a while and had to catch up. I think the farm families were a little surprised and embarrassed that Mish's parents knew a lot about them. They had become such a major part of our lives that Mish shared our experiences with them with mom and dad and vice versa. It seemed natural and fulfilling to have such an extended circle of relationships.

After everyone finally said goodnight and shuffled off back to their homes, we settled in for the night. Mish's parents were exhausted from traveling and wanted to get a good night's sleep because tomorrow, we were going to play tourists. They wanted to see as much of Costa Rica as possible in the week they were here. Mish thought that starting local would be a good way to introduce them to our life here, so she suggested we go to the secret fishing spot first. I readily agreed.

We got up early to another beautiful tropical sunrise. After a hearty breakfast on the front porch, we headed out. By we, I mean one parent with Aaron, Elijah, and I. There was no way the rental car would be able to get to the fishing spot, and there was equally no way that at least one of Mish's parents would ride in the back of the Rover. Therefore, we split up. Since Philip loves to fish, he opted to go with me. Nancy badly wanted to see the Cortez's big house on the hill, so she and Mish went up there for tea instead. In the end, the boys got to play in the mud and water outside while the girls got to sit prim and proper comfortably inside. We boys think we got the better deal.

Aaron and Elijah were excited to school Grandpa fishing in Costa Rica. The nice old man met us once again with sticks and lines. Elijah eagerly took his and immediately cast out his bait. Philip followed his lead and cast his out, too. In no time they both were reeling in fish that violently splashed around as they fought back. I'm not sure who was more excited, Elijah or Philip. Aaron even got in on the action, too and caught one. Meanwhile, I took pictures for Mish, who would be upset if she missed the action.

We departed with a haul of fresh fish and headed back to the farm. Over lunch, we compared our days. As I suspected, fishing sounded more fun than chit-chatting over tea. To each their own.

At least we brought back a tasty dinner.

The talk turned to questions about how things were going, both here and back home. Mish wanted to know how the rest of her family was doing and what her parents had been up to. It seemed like everything was the same old routine. Her sister was working at the hospital, and her nieces and nephews were working or going to school. Her parents were enjoying retirement by working on their house and traveling.

All was well.

In turn, Mish's parents wanted to know what else we had been up to and our future plans. We really didn't have any. Aaron was starting high school next year, so we wanted to be in one place for four years. Traveling the world with Mom and Dad when you are little and carefree is awesome. Moving around when you are getting serious about academics and sports becomes difficult, especially if you are eyeing some elite universities. Throwing in friendships and dating and the thought of moving schools is outright terrifying for a teenager.

We knew this and wanted to make the best decision for both boys. The problem is we just didn't know what that decision looked like. We could stay here. It was, in many ways, an idyllic situation, but to be honest, I was not impressed by the school. It was not challenging enough and did not offer much to help Aaron get to where he wanted to go. We could go to another country. I did have job offers on a few different continents. Going someplace unknown, however, was a crapshoot. We would have no idea what we would be getting into. We could go back home. That was sounding more and more like the best option. We still had time and were mulling over things.

Somewhere in the conversation I casually mentioned that I wanted to stay teaching no matter where we went.

"You'll never make a decent living being a teacher," Nancy scoffed.

At first, I was stunned by her rude remark. Then, my blood pressure started to climb higher and higher. I have always looked at education as a noble calling, selfless service to others and society. True, it is not the best-paying career, but we were doing fine. We strongly believe that there are far more important things in life than money. I want my legacy to be about how I made the world a little better place and not how much material stuff I accumulated. I know my mother-in-law, and I did not see eye-to-eye on this.

435

Mish saw me fuming, and before I could explode, she intervened.

"We're happy with our lives," she said. "Curtis is almost done with his doctorate program, too," she added.

"You're a professional student," Nancy proclaimed, trying to thinly disguise the barb with a chuckle.

I'm pretty thick-skinned and can take a lot of stuff thrown at me, but when it is done in front of my sons, a line has been crossed. Here she was in our house, eating the food I cooked, insulting me. After all these years of being a faithful husband and good provider for my family, as well as a decorated veteran and highly respected teacher, my net worth comes down to my bank account. I could feel the anger about to erupt in me.

Mish squeezed my hand and gave me a look I knew meant to please let it go. I looked back at her and saw the understanding in her beautiful brown eyes. I know she truly loves me and respects me as a partner and colleague. We chose our life together and have no regrets. Her touch reminded me that she was the only approval I needed. I let the anger evaporate. I took the higher ground and suffered the indignation. After all, I only deal with her judgmental comments every year or two.

Whether it is because of the age gap, the generation differences, our upbringings, or some combination, I don't think I will ever know. The bottom line is that they and I do not see the world the same. I was never going to get them to see my viewpoint, so I didn't try. Amazingly, Mish shares my values and beliefs. I don't know how that worked out, but it did.

To be fair, Philip and Nancy are good people, and from what Mish tells me were good parents, too. We just place importance on different things. Nancy highly values material possessions, status symbols, and money. I equally value personal relationships with family and friends, my contributions to society, and the legacy I will or will not leave someday.

I know that the old saying, "You can't take it with you," is accurate. The only part of me that will endure is the memories I leave in the minds of the people I knew when I die. I get one chance at making them good ones, so I try to go through life thoughtfully and purposefully. As their father, I hope Aaron and Elijah will do the same.

We finished dinner and headed to bed early again. Tomorrow was another day of sightseeing. Luckily, I had to go to school. The boys also had to go to school, but since grandma and grandpa were here, they got a get-out-of-jail card so they could go with them. I didn't approve of them missing school, but lost the battle.

Once more, I bit my lip. In a perverse sense, Mish got lucky that my parents are no longer around. She does not know what it is like to deal with in-laws.

In the morning, I chugged off to school in my Rover alone while the rest of the family took the rental car to tour Costa Rica. When we rendezvoused later that evening, we caught up on each other's day.

Mine was fairly usual, teaching kids about chemistry and physics. Their day was much more fun, going to the beach and feeding monkeys again. C'est la vie.

The rest of the week went by fast. Before we knew it, we were saying our goodbyes. I followed Mish to the airport. They dropped off the rental car and then headed to their gate. Mish gave her parents one last hug and kiss and left them to board their flight while I waited at the curb in the Rover. She came out, wiping some tears from her cheek. I know she really loves them. Despite their differences, they are still her family.

We drove back to the farm quietly.

"Thank you for being so understanding," she said, breaking the silence.

"Yeh, well, it's a small price to pay to get you," I told her.

She leaned over and gave me a kiss on the cheek.

All is well in the world, I thought.

Chapter 12 – Decisions, Decisions

"The most difficult thing is the decision to act, the rest is merely tenacity. The fears are paper tigers. You can do anything you decide to do. You can act to change and control your life; and the procedure, the process is its own reward." – Amelia Earhart

We still didn't know where we would end up next school year, but just in case, we wanted to see as much of Costa Rica as we could squeeze in this year. Even though it is a relatively small country, it still offers a lot to experience. The one place we hadn't been yet was the Atlantic Ocean side. Since we were about to go on spring break, this seemed like a good time to go.

Mish found a quaint small hotel in Cahuita, a small coastal town close to the Panamanian border. It is about a three-hour drive by car or five-hour one by Land Rover. Since we were never in a hurry on vacation, the extra couple of hours just meant more time to enjoy the scenery.

We loaded up the Rover and everyone took their positions, Mishele riding shotgun navigating, Aaron and Elijah in the back jump seats holding on, and Albie on the floor sleeping. That dog has been on so many airplane flights, boat trips, and car rides that I think he could sleep in a rowboat at sea during a hurricane. Occasionally, I could hear him snoring over the Rover's engine.

We set off early in the morning so we could stop along the way if we wanted to. Since we had not been to the east side of the country before, we did not know what we might find. For us, that is the only way to travel. Pick a final destination, but be open for unexpected detours. Sometimes, the detours were the best part of our trip.

The Atlantic Ocean side of Costa Rica is not as developed as the Pacific side. Most of the big resorts and tourist attractions are up and down the west coast. Plus, the airport and capital are on the west side of the central mountains making it much more accessible. It is more rugged and mountainous with dense jungle, so it is very spectacular and picturesque.

The east side of the country flattens out to a large plane down to the ocean with less forest. It is not as scenic, but the water is clearer and calmer, making for better snorkeling and diving. It would be a different part of the country we were anxious to explore.

We chugged up and over the mountain passes to Turrialba. It is famous for being the second-largest volcano in the country and having world-class white-water rafting.

Luckily, the volcano was asleep and let us pass by. It has erupted in recent years, forcing the evacuation of the city and the closure of the highway. Volcanic eruptions are just another day in paradise. You learn to put up with these pesky nuisances when you live in Costa Rica.

We had been to Turrialba before. One of Aaron's school friends invited him to his birthday party here. The reason it was here was that they were all going tubing on the river. I remember crossing a very sketchy and narrow suspension bridge over the river with my Rover to get to the party. The bridge was so narrow that I could not even open my door. I nervously inched the Rover across it as the bridge creaked and groaned under the weight. I finally breathed when I reached the far side.

We were not stopping to go tubing this time. We were all hungry and needed to find a bathroom instead. We found a nice outdoor café on the main road and pulled in. I was famished. The boys eyed the menu hungrily, too.

While we ate, one of Costa Rica's sudden torrential rainstorms poured buckets of rain down on us. We quickly scrambled to get under cover before we were thoroughly soaked. Just something else you get used to in the tropics.

After eating and drying off, we got back on the road to continue our trek to the Atlantic Ocean. We reached the port city of Limon and finally saw the turquoise water and white beaches of the coast. Technically, eastern Costa Rica is not on the ocean; it is on the Caribbean Sea. Straight across the water are the Cayman Islands and Jamaica.

Right away, we noticed the difference. This was more of a beach vibe than the West Coast, with long, flat beaches bordered by tall palm trees.

We turned south and headed down the coast. Along the way, I decided to take a detour. There was an exit off the road that led straight to the beach. I couldn't resist.

Spontaneously, I turned left and headed to the sand. This is heaven. I was driving my rover on a deserted beach in Costa Rica! The boys were leaning out the sides to feel the breeze and enjoy the ride, even Mish seemed to finally appreciate my rover for a change. I got a little daring and ventured out into the surf just enough to get the tires wet. This is what Land Rovers were meant for.

I don't know if it is legal to drive on the beach in Costa Rica. I didn't care. I was having too much fun. Every once in a while, you need to break the rules. This was a rare opportunity for me to do something rebellious.

I had my fun and turned off the beach. I figured I had pushed my luck enough. I didn't want to get stuck or, worse yet, run over a sea turtle. I got back on the paved road feeling ecstatic. I could check that off my long bucket list.

We eventually pulled into our hotel in Cahuita. The town is very small, but the perfect size for what we wanted. The first order of business was to hit the beach again, without the Rover this time.

While I was coming out to get something from my Rover, a couple of other tourists were standing next to it taking pictures. I approached them curiously.

"Is this your Land Rover?" one of them asked.

"Yes, it is," I answered proudly.

"Totally awesome ride, dude!" he exclaimed.

Ok, that was one of the highlights of this trip. Someone else recognized how incredible my Rover is. I beamed with pride as I went back to tell Mish.

We all changed into bathing suits and were on the beach in no time. To be honest, the beaches on the East Coast are better than the ones on the West Coast.

The backdrop is not as beautiful, however. That was fine with us, we were looking the other way out to sea at the magnificent blue water. The boys couldn't get enough of it. They splashed around and built sandcastles all day.

I brought some snorkeling gear so we could explore under the water, too. Elijah is not too keen on breathing through a tube, but Aaron is. He and I ventured out onto a small reef and saw some cool fish and corals. That evening, we went back out to see the aquatic nightlife, too.

We only stayed two nights and headed back. It was a short trip but very rewarding. On the road, we saw something we missed on the way down, an animal refuge. This was not just any animal refuge; it was the Costa Rica National Sloth Sanctuary. The world's first sloth-only facility for injured, orphaned, and abandoned sloths. How did we miss it before?

We really wanted to stop in. Unfortunately, we had to get back home because school was starting tomorrow. With disappointment in everyone's face, we passed it by. Mish made a note that we would have to come back and stop next time.

Regrettably, I continued driving, wondering if and when we would be here again. Taking detours and not putting things off for another time is still the best way to live, I think.

Spring break was over and we needed to get through the final sprint to the end of the school year. Decision time was upon us. The school needed to know if I was staying or going. Staying was easy. All I needed to do was sign my contract and keep doing what I was doing. Going was harder. I would need to find a suitable job somewhere else. Sometimes, life is easier when you don't have options. I could use some kind of sign from a higher power at times like this. Actually, what I really need is a huge neon arrow pointing me in the right direction.

Since I either didn't get a sign yet or I missed it, we continued to agonize over the decision. We asked the boys for their input. Elijah loved the farm and was content to stay. Aaron was leaning towards going home. So, they were a split decision. Mish taught online and was able and willing to travel anywhere but was open to going home, too. Great, another noncommittal vote. I did not want the decision to come down to me. I definitely did not want to go back to my old life. That was why I embarked on this journey to begin with. Help.

In the end, it came down to what we thought was best for the boys. Aaron needed the best high school we could put him in and stay there for four years. On his heels, Elijah would be in the same situation next.

The logical choice was to move back to their original home so they would have the stability they would need to set them up for their futures. After they graduated, Mish and I could always head back out if we wanted. We finally reached a decision; we would go back to Washington.

Chapter 13 – Knocking out the to-do List

"Do not dwell in the past, do not dream of the future, concentrate the mind on the present moment." – Buddha

For good or bad, we were returning to Washington. Now that the decision was made, I felt a huge weight lifted off my shoulders. For me, deciding on a plan is the hard part. Implementing the plan is just sorting out the details and doing it. So, we got busy preparing for another international move, our last one.

We were still over a month out from leaving. I wanted to experience as much of Costa Rica as we could in the time remaining. We have had such a great time here. I didn't want to reminisce about our experiences yet, nor did I want to obsess about what lay ahead. For now, I wanted to enjoy the time left and be present in the moment.

One evening over dinner, we talked about what we hadn't done yet. The list was long. Some of the things were simply impossible to fit in. We concentrated on the ones that were possible and prioritized them. At the top of the list was doing some very touristy type of stuff.

After all, we couldn't leave Costa Rica without ziplining through the jungle canopy, riding horses on the beach, or seeing an active volcano. People back home would be disappointed if we hadn't.

Mish planned our last excursion in the country while I readied the Land Rover for another trip. By now, Oscar and I had worked on almost every part of my Rover. It wasn't perfect, but we had brought it back from the grave, and was in far better condition than when I bought it. I didn't know what I was going to do with it. Leaving it here would break my heart, but I had no idea how to get it back to Washington.

I decided to take an extra-long weekend from school along with the boys for our trip. I know pulling them from school at the end of the year is not the best idea, but I reasoned this was a special circumstance and made an exception. This was probably the last time we would be in Costa Rica, at least for the foreseeable future. I wanted them to remember our time here.

We headed northwest to the small town of La Fortuna. It is the epicenter of the tourist area of Costa Rica. From there you can hike the Monte Verde Cloud Forest, climb Arenal Volcano, soak in the Chachagua hot springs, tour a cacao plantation, splash under the La Fortuna waterfall, and many more amazing activities. We were going to try to hit them all.

The drive is only about three hours, or five by Land Rover again, and very scenic. We gauged how far we were from how close the volcano looked as we drove. Arenal is almost a perfect cone shaped volcano that looks like something straight out of a Jurassic Park movie set, even though we had learned Spielberg snubbed the location. His loss, the mountain is incredibly prehistoric looking.

It is the youngest of all the many volcanoes in Costa Rica. After being dormant for over four hundred years, it suddenly and violently erupted in 1968 and has been spewing hot lava and ash ever since. We really wanted to see it up close. Sometimes you have to live dangerously.

We found our hotel first off and checked in. It was a very small room but would do as a base camp of operations. We didn't plan on spending any time there other than to shower and sleep. We were here to experience the wild part of Costa Rica.

We dropped off the luggage and poor Albie and headed back out for our first activity, ziplining. Everyone was very excited to go flying through the trees on a thin steel cable and flimsy harness, except me. I prefer to keep my feet close to the ground. I could have skipped it, to be honest, but I was dared into it. My loving family wasn't about to let me get away with not going. I would never live it down, so under duress, I went along on the crazy adventure.

The ziplining was falsely advertised. The brochure should have clearly stated "ziplinings," plural. I was prepared for a one-zip trip, not six zips. The company wanted to make sure you got your money's worth, I guess. I would have been fine as a one-hit wonder. Now, I had to muster up the courage five additional times.

We sat through the five-minute safety briefing, signed our lives away on the release forms, and squeezed into our gear. Actually, Mish signed the boys' forms. If something went wrong, they could blame her. We then hiked up to the first zipline platform.

The first line was supposed to be the shorter and lower introductory trip. It didn't look that short or low to me. I stared over the edge to the river below and then out across the ravine to the other platform on the far side. Who thought that this would be a great idea? Seriously, strapping your kids onto a single wire and hurling them out into thin air a few hundred feet above the ground is legal? Did anyone consult CPS on this?

Our intrepid airman, Aaron, eagerly volunteered to go first. He bravely stood on the platform as the guide clipped him in. With a gentle push he was off soaring across the river. We could see his big smile the whole way. No fear.

Mish went next. Aaron got her daredevil genes from mom, definitely not me. She eagerly climbed on the platform, too, and allowed the guide to clip her in and shove her off. She went flying after her son. Her loud "whoo-hoo" echoed through the canyon.

Elijah was next. He looked at me, a little uncertain. I reassured him it was safe. Great, I was lying to my son when I was more scared than he was. He hesitantly stepped up and was clipped in, too. I worried that he might back out.

Secretly, a part of me hoped he would so I would have an excuse not to go. No such luck. Before Elijah could think about it, the guide pushed him off, and away he went.

Lastly, it was my turn. I stepped up, clipped in, and jumped off without waiting for the guide before I could talk myself out of it. I felt the harness tightly hug me in some uncomfortable parts of my body and the wind in my face. I looked down and gulped. The view was amazing from this high up. Just as I was kind of enjoying the ride, I landed on the other side. The whole flight lasted a mere ten seconds.

With all four of us and the guide safely on the other side, we hiked to the next and longer zipline. We repeated the sequence. The only difference was that this time, Elijah was thrilled to go again. Once he experienced flying, he was hooked. I was a little more confident, also. However, I could have stopped there and been good.

Each zipline was a different experience. One went over a gushing waterfall, another right through the canopy among the trees, and another paralleled a river. The longest one was left for last. The final flight went for almost a full minute. It was almost long enough to take a nap on.

We hiked in a circle and ended up back at the base camp. As we took off our harnesses and helmets, we excitedly talked about our experience. I couldn't wait to see the pictures that Mish had somehow managed to take as she hung on and sped across the lines. We all agreed that we needed to do it again sometime.

We went back to the hotel to rest and check on Albie. Tomorrow was going to be another exciting day. Unfortunately, it entailed more high-altitude activities.

We got up early and, after breakfast headed out to the hanging bridges park. This time, instead of zipping over chasms on a wire we would be walking over them on thin suspension bridges with see-through bottoms. Why do so many activities in this country involve heights, I wondered.

The bridges were also very worthwhile. They give you a rare opportunity to immerse yourself in the forest canopy and see what few people get to. The forest changes with elevation. On the cool ground, it is dark and damp. As you progress higher, it becomes brighter and warmer. The plants and animals change accordingly. We could see this stratification of the jungle from the bridges. It was like watching a whole nature documentary live. I knew the boys were learning more here than in school.

As we walked from bridge to bridge, we were so intently focused on the scenery that we weren't paying attention to where we walked. That is when Aaron stepped on a snake.

As soon as the sole of his shoe touched the slithering serpent, his instincts told him something was wrong. He looked down just in time to see the snake. The snake darted into the bushes, and poor Aaron shot into the air. I'm not sure who was more surprised, him or the snake. We didn't get a good enough look at it to be able to identify it. Luckily, the snake was probably so scared that it didn't think to bite. As Mish consoled Aaron, I stopped Elijah from going after the snake.

We left the hanging bridge park and moved on to our next activity, horseback riding. Finally, something that doesn't involve heights. Mish and I had ridden before and so were somewhat familiar with horses.

This, however, was the boys' first time. It was Aaron's turn to have some trepidation. He looked up at the horse which towered over him and hesitated, not sure what to do. Meanwhile, Elijah was scrambling to get up his horse's harness. The guide came over and lifted him into the saddle, and gave him the reins. He looked so small on his big horse that it was almost comical. He didn't care. He was already kicking his heels and telling the horse to giddy up.

Mish and I climbed onto our horses. We were all set. A real cowboy probably would scoff at our little steeds. These horses are bred and trained specifically to carry novice tourists around on well-worn trails. Consequently, they are very gentle and obedient. All they needed was a little nudge, and off they trotted in a single file through the forest. I bet that they have made this same trek dozens of times. They were fine with us, we are not seasoned rough-riders by any stretch of the imagination.

The horses took us to a small native village where indigenous people still live and practice their traditional way of life. Some villagers came out and greeted us as we rode up. They treated us to an authentic tribal celebration over a wonderful lunch of local dishes. Afterwards, they demonstrated traditional native crafts, like wood carving and weaving. It was another amazing learning experience. Mish purchased a beautiful and intricately carved mask depicting a native person surrounded by indigenous animals in bright colors.

We said goodbye and thank you to our hosts and rode our horses back to their coral. Along the way, we started to feel a little too comfortable with our steeds and coaxed them to a quick jog. Elijah went bouncing past me on his saddle a little faster than he should. Our guide quickly caught up to him and grabbed his reins to slow him down. The boy is going to give me grey hair.

Exhausted from another wonderful and full day, we headed back to the hotel. Albie was still there, patiently waiting for us. He wagged his little nub of a tail and jumped up to greet us. The dog must have supreme confidence that when we drop him off in some strange place, we will always come back for him. We would never leave him. He is a member of our family after all, just a furrier one.

We could only spend three days in the area because we needed to get back to school and finalize our departure plans. Even though it was a little touristy, the trip was extremely worth it. Not everything needs to be an authentic cultural experience. Every once in a while, it is ok to just do something because it is fun. We will remember this trip just as fondly as all the other ones.

Chapter 14 – Saying our Goodbyes

"How lucky I am to have something that makes saying goodbye so hard." – A.A. Milne (Winnie-the-Pooh)"

We always know before we arrive in each country that it is only temporary. We never planned on permanently ex-patriating to another country. That doesn't make leaving any easier.

Closing out another school year is easy. I have done it now fifteen times. I needed to give my final exams, wrap up grading, straighten my room, and turn in keys.

All of that I could do in short order, but saying goodbye to everyone would take much longer. I had made friends at the school, some Costa Rican, some American, and some from other countries. We promised to stay in touch and maybe meet up somewhere sometime. We now had friends from all over the globe. I don't know how we will be able to keep track of them all.

We told the Cortez's we were leaving and thanked them for their amazing hospitality. They were genuinely sad to see us go. They made living in the country an unexpected and incredible experience. We never imagined we would be living in this beautiful house on this wonderful farm and making all these dear friends when we got here a year ago. Without them, I think our time here would not have been as memorable.

Saying goodbye to Oscar and Olga, and the rest of the farm family was even harder. They had expected us to be here longer but understood.

We promised to have one last patio barbeque before we left, which everyone readily agreed to.

The hardest part for me was what was I going to do with my cherished Land Rover. I had come to love it more than when I first bought it. Oscar and I had put a lot of work into it and formed a friendship because of it. The family has had many adventures in it, and it has become an iconic part of our life in Costa Rica. Leaving it seemed almost like leaving a close friend behind.

We had one last Boy Scout camping trip we had been getting ready for and were excited about. Mish had been an integral part in planning it. It was to be the highlight of the year. Once that was over, we would have to say goodbye to our fellow scouts, too.

Boy Scouts like to have themes for our jamborees, so we decided on honoring the indigenous people of Costa Rica. Ancient Aztec and Mayan civilizations were further north, and Incan civilization was further south, so modern Costa Rica isn't aligned with any great pre-Columbian culture. Central America, in general, was, and still is somewhat today, a fringe area caught between two great powers. We flipped a coin to see which way we would go, heads north or tails south. It was tails, so Aztec theme it would be.

We reserved a large open camp area in the mountains as our site. Beforehand, we made traditional Aztec masks and decorations. Mish even researched and made authentic Aztec meals, or as close as possible. She decided that killing a wild boar or tapir probably was going too far, cow would make an acceptable substitute.

I learned how to play a ritualistic Aztec game called Tlachtli so I could teach it to the scouts, and they could play it. The ball game was extremely important in the Aztec world. It is kind of a mixture of basketball, rugby, and brawling.

The rules are simple. Basically, two teams of twelve try to get a small, hard rubber ball through stone hoops on either side of a large grass court. The ball cannot ever touch the ground, players may not use their hands, and the ball must, at all costs, stay in motion. Aside from that, all was fair game.

Not surprisingly, players got seriously injured and even killed in the game, which could last days. If a rule was broken, human sacrifices were often made to appease the gods for the infraction. I had to tone it down a little bit for the scouts.

We also made blowguns from PVC pipe and bows and arrows from carved tree limbs for the scouts to compete with. For three days, the boys had a high energy and wonderful time running around pretending to be Aztecs.

During the closing ceremony, we gave out awards and promotions. In scouting, it's all about the patches. Everyone went home with some mementos to remember the event. It was the perfect way to end the scout's year.

Now that Boy Scouts and school were over for another year, we were left with the final task of packing our stuff and saying final goodbyes. I looked into the logistics of shipping my Land Rover back to the United States. Driving was way out of the question. I did consider it briefly. The trip would take me at least a few weeks, providing no breakdowns. Plus, I would have to go through some pretty dangerous areas. I would be driving alone because Mish made it very clear that she would fly.

Shipping the Rover involved driving it to Limon on the East Coast to put it on a cargo ship that only left once a week bound for Miami. In Florida, I would need to personally pick it up and get it to Washington somehow.

In addition, I would need to pay to have it inspected and licensed in the U.S., along with paying the tax. In the end, it was not practically feasible. Remorsefully, I put it up for sale.

It seems silly, I know, but I wanted it to go to a good home. I worried some young hooligan would buy it and not appreciate it and take it out and trash it off roading.

Luckily, a team of researchers from the university came to look at it. They needed a hardy vehicle that was capable of trapesing through the jungle so they could study monkeys. They were on a tight budget, however, and worried if they could afford anything.

Ecstatic that my beloved Rover would become a real exploration vehicle, I offered them a discount. They were extremely grateful and graciously accepted the offer. I handed them the keys, knowing it was going to a worthy cause. I almost shed a tear as I watched them drive it out the farm gate.

With my Rover sold, all that was left was to get to the airport in time to make our flight. That evening, we had our last party on the patio with all the farm families there to say farewell. It was both a joyous and sad occasion. We talked about the times we had together, the experiences we shared, and our plans for the future.

Of all three places we have lived on our international adventure, Costa Rica was going to be the hardest to leave. Not because of the country but because of the people we met here. England has wonderful traditions and history we enjoyed. Germany has magnificent scenery and castles we explored. Although Costa Rica is a tropical paradise with exotic animals and plants, the farm is something special that nowhere else has. It will be a cherished memory.

The next morning, our final morning, we waited outside our house for the taxi. Oscar and Olga were there to give us one last hug and goodbye. As we were exchanging farewells, the taxi pulled up to the gate and waited for it to open. We knew this was it.

The taxi drove in and stopped next to us. The driver helped load our luggage, and we got in. Without anything left to do or say, I told the driver to take us to the airport, please. He obliged and put the car in gear. I sat back in the passenger seat and blankly looked out the window as we drove off the farm for the last time. In the back seat, Mish was wiping tears from her eyes.

Our plane departed on schedule. The boys, as usual ordered ginger ale from the stewardess and put on headsets to watch movies all flight. Albie was probably asleep somewhere in the luggage compartment, dreaming of something I would never know. Mish and I just sat back and held hands as we reminisced about Costa Rica and the rest of our travels abroad.

We do not know where we will end up. No one knows what the future holds. As my best friend, Chuck, often reminds me, "If you want to make God laugh, tell him your plans for the future."

I used to think I was more in control of my fate. Now, however, I realize I cannot control everything or even anything. It makes life scary but also exciting.

I do know that my family will always be my priority. No matter where we go or what happens, we will always be there for each other. That makes getting through this crazy, unknown thing called life much easier.

Epilogue

We have been back in the United States for several years now. It has taken me longer than I expected to finish writing our journey. Life has a habit of getting in the way.

Aaron graduated from the United States Naval Academy and is currently back traveling the world. This time, however, he is going by a haze grey steel ship. He is seeing places we have not yet traveled to, like Japan. He grew up largely living out of a suitcase. The only difference now is he traded it for a seabag. For him, being a global traveler is just who he is.

Elijah graduated from the California Poly Technical University and is currently teaching while working on a master's degree. He dreams of working overseas somewhere to continue exploring the world. He, too gets itchy feet after a while and wants to experience someplace new.

The idea of moving to a strange country is not intimidating at all to him. He grew up adapting to a semi-nomadic life.

All in all, we think that traveling the world for a few years did not negatively impact our children's education. In fact, in many cases, it enhanced it.

For example, Aaron's math ability was so advanced that when the high school in Washington tested him for placement, the counselor was astonished that he scored high enough for at least Algebra II as a freshman.

Consequently, he took AP Calculus as a junior and aced the AP exam. He was accepted into several elite universities and chose the prestigious Naval Academy.

Elijah liked to show off at his school in Washington and lecture the class and teacher on different art styles and periods. Apparently, he was paying attention during those museum tours at the Louvre. He also took and passed many AP exams and was accepted into major universities.

They have done very well. We are extremely proud of both of them. Mish and I emphatically agree that giving them the world growing up made them better in every way than if we stayed solely in Washington. The only downside is that they have no apprehension of flying the nest and leaving. The world is theirs.

We also agree that we are a tighter and more supportive family unit because of our traveling. We had only each other to rely on wherever we went. That closeness also is why we know that no matter where we all end up, we will always stay a family.

Mish went back into the classroom and continued teaching. She loves being in person with the students instead of online. Engaging in face-to-face conversation with them is much more rewarding than talking to names on black boxes over a teleconference. Her passion for teaching is just as strong as when she started.

As for me, I tried to go back to being a college director. I pretty much picked up where I left off before we went on this crazy adventure.

I had come full circle. I found that the world had not changed, but I definitely had. There was no going back.

Another school hired me, and I gave it my best shot, but my heart wasn't into it. After being there for only a couple of years, I remembered why I left that life for traveling. I resigned and went back into the classroom. I am, first and foremost, a teacher, I suppose.

My experiences have broadened and strengthened my skills as an educator. I have learned about other educational systems and seen different ways of developing young minds. I am trying my best to implement some of those best practices at my current school. To be honest, it is not easy. Change comes slow and hard in my profession.

I do have several takeaways from our journey. Firstly, go for it. Whatever "it" is, just do it. For us, it was living abroad. There was a myriad of reasons, some very valid, for not moving to England. In the end, they all were exposed as excuses to cover up the fear of acting on our desire. From an early age, we were very well trained to dutifully live someone else's fantasy. Stay in school, work hard, get a good job, retire, and then expire, was how we were told to live our lives. Sometime during our very short time on Earth, we hope to find moments to relax and enjoy ourselves. Maybe, if we are lucky, we will get to enjoy our elder years.

Venturing outside that paradigm was always forbidden territory. Says who? To blatantly borrow a copyrighted slogan, "Just do it."

Secondly, family is your most important asset, period. When the chips are down, when you need help, when you want to share a magical moment, when you just need a hug, your family is there. No matter where we went, we went as a family. Through good, bad, and outright chaotic times, we held strong together. I would not want to travel the world any other way.

Thirdly, no one country is the best or has everything perfect, not even the United States. Everywhere we lived had pros and cons. Some of the pros for one person might not matter to another, and some of the cons might not bother someone else. Everyone has their preferences. Mostly, our satisfaction living in a place came down to what we could tolerate versus how much we loved it.

For example, in England we loved the quaint countryside, long history, and friendly social pubs but didn't enjoy the over-burdensome government bureaucracy or British stuffiness. In Germany, we loved the breathtaking scenery, idyllic castles, and superb infrastructure but hated unyielding strict laws and policies and exorbitantly high taxes.

In Costa Rica, we loved the warm people, incredible tropical environment, and amazing farms but were very frustrated with extremely poor infrastructure and outdated caste social system.

In the United States, we love the 24/7 conveniences, great infrastructure, almost unlimited freedoms, and familiar culture but do not like the unacceptable violence, shameless corporate marketing, generic cookie-cutter towns, and growing vapid divisiveness in our politics. You must pick what you can live with and cannot live without.

Fourth, and maybe most importantly, we learned that people are people the world over. Everyone on the planet, regardless of nationality, religion, gender, sexual orientation, socio-economic status, and education, is all trying to get through life as best as possible. We have far more in common than most people realize. We are born into a situation we have no say in. So, we must play the cards as they are dealt. Some get lucky, while many others do not. In the end, we are all mortal, and so will all die. Death is the great equalizer. The only meaningful thing any of us will leave behind is the memories we have made in the hearts and minds of the people we touched along the way.

During our glorious summer vacations, one of the perks of being a teacher, we still travel the world for weeks at a time. Sometimes, we venture to a new location and other times, we revisit old stomping grounds. So far, we have added Scotland and Iceland to our travel log, with South Africa, New Zealand, and Peru on the itinerary. Wherever we go, we always stay in small B&Bs so we can get as authentic an experience as possible and meet the locals.

During our travels we continue to meet many people from a wide variety of diverse backgrounds. We will always remember them, and they will hopefully remember us. In some small way, this is our legacy.

Living abroad has changed us. I cannot recommend highly enough to get out and experience the world. There is an incredible, life-changing adventure waiting for you.

www.ingramcontent.com/pod-product-compliance
Lightning Source LLC
Chambersburg PA
CBHW030816090426
42737CB00009B/753